MW01153567

# LEARNING THROUGH CITIZEN SCIENCE

*Enhancing Opportunities by Design*

Committee on Designing Citizen Science to Support Science Learning

Rajul Pandya and Kenne Ann Dibner, *Editors*

Board on Science Education

Division of Behavioral and Social Sciences and Education

A Consensus Study Report of

*The National Academies of*
SCIENCES · ENGINEERING · MEDICINE

THE NATIONAL ACADEMIES PRESS
*Washington, DC*
**www.nap.edu**

THE NATIONAL ACADEMIES PRESS 500 Fifth Street, NW Washington, DC 20001

This activity was supported by contracts between the National Academy of Sciences and the Gordon and Betty Moore Foundation (#10002925), Howard Hughes Medical Institute (#10003301), and Simons Foundation (#10003402). Any opinions, findings, conclusions, or recommendations expressed in this publication do not necessarily reflect the views of any organization or agency that provided support for the project.

International Standard Book Number-13:  978-0-309-47916-5
International Standard Book Number-10:  0-309-47916-9
Library of Congress Control Number:  2018965026
Digital Object Identifier: https://doi.org/10.17226/25183

Additional copies of this publication are available for sale from the National Academies Press, 500 Fifth Street, NW, Keck 360, Washington, DC 20001; (800) 624-6242 or (202) 334-3313; http://www.nap.edu.

Suggested citation: National Academies of Sciences, Engineering, and Medicine. (2018). *Learning Through Citizen Science: Enhancing Opportunities by Design.* Washington, DC: The National Academies Press. doi: https://doi.org/10.17226/25183.

*The National Academies of*
# SCIENCES · ENGINEERING · MEDICINE

The **National Academy of Sciences** was established in 1863 by an Act of Congress, signed by President Lincoln, as a private, nongovernmental institution to advise the nation on issues related to science and technology. Members are elected by their peers for outstanding contributions to research. Dr. Marcia McNutt is president.

The **National Academy of Engineering** was established in 1964 under the charter of the National Academy of Sciences to bring the practices of engineering to advising the nation. Members are elected by their peers for extraordinary contributions to engineering. Dr. C. D. Mote, Jr., is president.

The **National Academy of Medicine** (formerly the Institute of Medicine) was established in 1970 under the charter of the National Academy of Sciences to advise the nation on medical and health issues. Members are elected by their peers for distinguished contributions to medicine and health. Dr. Victor J. Dzau is president.

The three Academies work together as the **National Academies of Sciences, Engineering, and Medicine** to provide independent, objective analysis and advice to the nation and conduct other activities to solve complex problems and inform public policy decisions. The National Academies also encourage education and research, recognize outstanding contributions to knowledge, and increase public understanding in matters of science, engineering, and medicine.

Learn more about the National Academies of Sciences, Engineering, and Medicine at **www.nationalacademies.org**.

*The National Academies of*
## SCIENCES · ENGINEERING · MEDICINE

**Consensus Study Reports** published by the National Academies of Sciences, Engineering, and Medicine document the evidence-based consensus on the study's statement of task by an authoring committee of experts. Reports typically include findings, conclusions, and recommendations based on information gathered by the committee and the committee's deliberations. Each report has been subjected to a rigorous and independent peer-review process and it represents the position of the National Academies on the statement of task.

**Proceedings** published by the National Academies of Sciences, Engineering, and Medicine chronicle the presentations and discussions at a workshop, symposium, or other event convened by the National Academies. The statements and opinions contained in proceedings are those of the participants and are not endorsed by other participants, the planning committee, or the National Academies.

For information about other products and activities of the National Academies, please visit www.nationalacademies.org/about/whatwedo.

# Preface

It is a daunting to be asked to chair a committee for the National Academies of Sciences, Engineering, and Medicine. You are around the table with a room full of exceptionally smart people, at least one with a Nobel Prize, and taking your place inside an institution that stretches back to Abraham Lincoln. You must leverage all the voices and intellect in the room while also recognizing the voices and histories that are not in the room. Working with the committee, you strive to answer concisely a narrowly scoped charge while simultaneously unpacking the larger issues implicit in that charge. As chair, you aim for a consensus that is not overly obvious by exploring the boundaries of agreement and even flirting with disagreement, because that is where the meaningful parts of consensus lies. In the final product, your report, you aim to say something new without getting too far ahead of the evidence; something that is small enough to be precise, but big enough to inspire.

Thankfully, you have the processes of the National Academies and the people on the committee to guide you. The process is designed to keep you focused on the topic and restrained by available evidence: Our committee joked that we were not able to use the word "is" without a citation. There were times in our process that this demand for evidence was frustrating: Sometimes we wanted to make a point about the way we would like things to be, engage in a speculative line of reasoning, or take an idea about education in citizen science and tease out its broader implications. In each case, though, an insistence on evidence and scope (often with some gentle or not-so-gentle guidance from the National Academies staff) brought us back to our task.

The committee, especially in its willingness to respectfully pursue and reach consensus, also helped illuminate the way. Evidence might be the raw material of this report, but it was the committee members who built the report from those raw materials. They collected, evaluated, and synthesized the evidence. They served as the (citizen) scientists who collected the evidence, the story-tellers who wove that evidence into coherent narratives, and the arbitrators who evaluated the evidence to produce findings and recommendations. They were good scientists because they were experts in their fields and listened carefully to our many invited guests; they were good story-tellers because they could pull from and synthesize evidence across a range of disciplines and experiences; and they were good arbitrators because, to the person, they cared more about producing the best answer than they did about proving themselves right.

One of the findings of the report is that the positive social interactions that are part of strong citizen science projects reinforce and create opportunities for learning. This was evident in our committee as well: We had fun together and we got to know one another, and those positive experiences helped us wrestle with necessary and productive disagreement. Learning, it turns out, involves not only new knowledge but also the integration of new and old knowledge and this process sometimes involves deconstructing some of that old knowledge. That part can be painful, especially in academic circles where knowledge is the currency of the realm, and the fact that we had fun together and trusted one another enabled necessary deconstruction. Excellent meals together helped as well.

The committee itself, along with National Academies staff, also represented one of the other findings of the report: people learn more and perform better in environments that welcome and integrate a diversity of experiences and perspectives. They were also, fittingly for a report on education, excellent teachers and learners. I learned as much about the science and practice of teaching and learning from watching them work together as I did from the evidence cited in the report. I am grateful to have had the opportunity to work with everyone on the committee and the staff at the National Academies, and richer for having done so.

At the end of the day, a National Academies report is an integrative summary of what is known about a single topic: These reports are expansive, complete, and up to date about what is known, and reflective of what is possible. Our report, like all National Academies reports, is not meant to move the field forward as much as it is meant to provide a solid waypoint from which the field can move forward. We believe it is an important document. We aim to provide a common reference of strongly supported understandings that can be a driver for further innovation and creativity and for iteration and refinement by citizen science researchers, designers, educators, and participants. I hope, though I suspect it is impossible, that you can learn as much from this report, have as much fun thinking about its big ideas, and find as many new ways of doing things, as I did in working with the committee and staff at the National Academies to produce the report.

Finally, some of the most exciting ideas discussed by our committee never made it to the final report. Although these ideas are not up to the standards of the report and go well beyond the scope of our charge, they are compelling. For me, the emergent line of reasoning goes like this: Effective citizen science projects create a kind of negotiated space where scientists and nonscientists can work well together. That means the most effective citizen science projects create a space where all people are considered intellectual partners and contributors. In this way, they offer a vehicle to challenge historic, and unproductive, divisions between those who are part of science and those who are not. They become places to expand participation in science not only by inviting people to do science, but also by inviting communities to use science in service of their goals and priorities. Citizen science poses questions about who participates in science, what it means to participate in science, who gets to decide what scientific questions to investigate, and even what kind of knowledge and practice count as science.

Raj Pandya
*Chair*, Committee on Designing Citizen
Science to Support Science Learning

# Acknowledgments

In the spirit of the social nature of much of citizen science, this report is the outgrowth of the tremendous work of many devoted individuals. We have learned quite a bit by having had the space, time, and resources to be proximal to one another's expertise, and we believe that this report benefits from the rare opportunity to synthesize many voices into one—an opportunity uniquely afforded through the processes of the National Academies of Sciences, Engineering, and Medicine. The Committee on Designing Citizen Science to Support Science Learning owes a debt of gratitude to a number of people for their support throughout this project.

First, we wish to extend a thank you to this project's sponsors: Janet Coffey from the Gordon and Betty Moore Foundation, Dennis Liu and Bridget Conneely from the Howard Hughes Medical Institute, and Greg Boustead and Jill Blackford from the Simons Foundation. At the first meeting, our sponsors were immensely helpful in establishing a tone for our investigations, and we are profoundly grateful for their support.

Over the course of the study, we heard from many individuals who were able to shed light on different aspects of citizen science and science learning. At our first meeting, citizen science champions Rick Bonney from the Cornell Lab of Ornithology and Sarah Kirn from the Gulf of Maine Research Institute offered framing perspectives on the potential of citizen science, and Leona Schauble from Vanderbilt University and Leslie Herrenkohl from the University of Washington provided insight into the landscape of science learning.

At our second meeting, the committee hosted a public meeting for extended consideration of specific issues related to citizen science and science learning. Cindy Hmelo-Silver from Indiana University and Joe Polman from the University of Colorado Boulder offered insight into the science learning literature. Heidi Ballard from the University of California, Davis, provided the keynote address with an overview on the potential of citizen science to support science learning, specifically the development of science identity. Bill Zoellick from the Schoodic Institute, Ruth Kermish-Allen from Maine Mathematics and Science Alliance, and Rebecca Jordan from Rutgers University conducted a panel on frameworks for designing learning opportunities in citizen science. Rob Dunn from North Carolina State University, Andrea Wiggins from the University of Nebraska Omaha, Jennifer Fee from the Cornell Lab of Ornithology, and Linda Peterson from Fairfax County Public Schools, conducted a panel on citizen science in K–12 classrooms; Gwen Ottinger from Drexel University, Michael Mascarenhas from the University of California, Berkeley, and Muki Haklay from University College London offered insight into citizen science and community learning outcomes. Karen Peterman from Karen Peterman Consulting and Cat Stylinski from the University of Maryland conducted a panel on assessing learning in citizen science, and Laura Trouille from Zooniverse and the Adler Planetarium, Kathryn "Kit" Matthew from the Institute of Museum and Library Sciences, and Sue Allen from Maine Mathematics and Science Alliance closed the event with a panel on citizen science in informal settings.

As part of its attempt to learn about ongoing citizen science projects in the field, the committee held an expo event for outside exhibitors to present their projects and sign up potential participants. The committee wishes to sincerely thank the following individuals and citizen science projects for taking the time to describe their work: Arielle Conti from Tree Inventory at Casey Trees; Mary Clare Hano from Smoke Sense; Caroline Juang from Landslide Reporter; Mark Kuchner from Backyard Worlds; Nadine Levick from Automated External Defibrillator Geolocation; Sophia Liu from Citizen Science During Disasters, Liz MacDonald from Aurorasaurus, Steven Silverberg from Disk Detective, and Katrina Theisz from the National Institute of Health's citizen science efforts,

This Consensus Study Report was reviewed in draft form by individuals chosen for their diverse perspectives and technical expertise. The purpose of this independent review is to provide candid and critical comments that will assist the National Academies in making each published report as sound as possible and to ensure that it meets the institutional standards for quality, objectivity, evidence, and responsiveness to the study charge. The review comments and draft manuscript remain confidential to protect the integrity of the deliberative process.

We thank the following individuals for their review of this report: Angela Calabrese Barton, Department of Teacher Education, Michigan State University; Steven B. Case, Center for STEM Learning, University of

Kansas; Dianne Chong, Assembly, Factory & Support Technology (retired), Boeing Research and Technology; Caren B. Cooper, Forestry and Environmental Resources, North Carolina State University; Mary Ford, Education Programs, National Geographic Society; Leigh Peake, Education, Gulf of Maine Research Institute, Portland, Maine; Joseph L. Polman, School of Education, University of Colorado Boulder; Leona Schauble, Department of Teaching and Learning, Vanderbilt University; Jeremy W. Thorner, Department of Molecular and Cell Biology, University of California, Berkeley; and William Zoellick, Education Research, Schoodic Institute at Acadia National Park, Winter Park, Maine.

Although the reviewers listed above provided many constructive comments and suggestions, they were not asked to endorse the conclusions or recommendations of this report nor did they see the final draft before its release. The review of this report was overseen by Philip Bell, College of Education, University of Washington, and Eugenie C. Scott (retired), National Center for Science Education. They were responsible for making certain that an independent examination of this report was carried out in accordance with the standards of the National Academies and that all review comments were carefully considered. Responsibility for the final content rests entirely with the authoring committee and the National Academies.

The committee wishes to extend its gratitude to the staff of the Division of Behavioral and Social Sciences and Education (DBASSE), in particular to Heidi Schweingruber, director of the Board on Science Education, who has provided ongoing wisdom and guidance as we navigated challenging intellectual and procedural terrain. To Anne Simonis, who joined our team *en media res* and who helped with critical drafting and editing processes. To Leticia Garcilazo Green, whose expert and efficient administrative leadership enabled smooth meetings and production, and Jessica Covington, who also entered a chaotic process and masterfully assisted in many of our administrative needs. Kirsten Sampson Snyder of the DBASSE staff deftly guided us through the National Academies review process, and Laura Yoder provided invaluable editorial assistance. Yvonne Wise of the DBASSE staff oversaw the production of the report.

Finally, the committee wishes to thank Raj Pandya, study chair, for his devoted, responsive, and impassioned leadership of this study. It has been both a pleasure and an honor to work closely with Raj, and this report is truly the better for his commitment.

Kenne Ann Dibner, *Study Director*
Committee on Designing Citizen Science to
Support Science Learning

# Contents

# List of Boxes, Tables, and Figure

## BOXES

## TABLES

## FIGURE

# Summary

In the past 20 years, citizen science has blossomed as a way to engage a broad range of individuals in doing science. Citizen science projects focus on, but are not limited to, nonscientists (i.e., people who are not professionally trained in disciplines relevant to a specific project) participating in the processes of scientific research, with the intended goal of advancing and using scientific knowledge. A rich range of projects extend this focus in myriad directions, and the boundaries of citizen science as a field are not clearly delineated. Citizen science involves a growing community of professional practitioners, participants, and stakeholders, and a thriving collection of projects. While citizen science is often recognized for its potential to engage the public in science, it is also uniquely positioned to support and extend participants' learning in science.

Contemporary understandings of science learning continue to advance. Indeed, modern theories of learning recognize that science learning is complex and multifaceted. Learning is affected by factors that are individual, social, cultural, and institutional, and learning occurs in virtually any context and at every age. Current understandings of science learning also suggest that science learning extends well beyond content knowledge in a domain to include understanding of the nature and methods of science.

Citizen science and research on science learning are mutually beneficial. Citizen science has much to learn from modern understandings of science learning and in order to support science learning through citizen science, it is critical that invested parties consider science learning in all its complexity. At the same time, citizen science offers a new venue in which to examine science learning, and seems especially well-suited to examining the way learning is social and culturally mediated, and how learning can intersect with equity, diversity, and power.

In response to a request from the Gordon and Betty Moore Foundation, the Howard Hughes Medical Institute, and the Simons Foundation, the National Academies of Sciences, Engineering, and Medicine established an ad hoc committee to study science learning and citizen science. The 12-member expert Committee on Designing Citizen Science to Support Science Learning included individuals with expertise in citizen science programming, research and evaluation of citizen science projects, the learning sciences, K–12 science education, informal science education, and afterschool or extended school science programming. The committee was asked to address the following statement of task:

> An ad hoc committee of experts will be appointed to conduct a study on how citizen science projects can be designed to better support science learning. The committee will identify and describe existing citizen science projects that seek to support science learning, consider research on science learning in both formal and informal settings, and develop a set of evidence-based principles to guide the design of citizen science projects that have science learning as a goal. The committee's final report will discuss the potential of citizen science to support science learning, identify promising practices and programs that exemplify the promising practices, and lay out a research agenda that can fill gaps in the current understanding of how citizen science can support science learning and enhance science education.

## CHARACTERIZING CITIZEN SCIENCE

The term "citizen science" can be applied to a wide variety of projects that share the core feature of nonscientists engaging in doing science. The committee identified eight common characteristics of citizen science projects. Citizen science projects actively engage participants, specifically engage participants with data, use systematic approaches to produce reliable knowledge, meet widely recognized standards of scientific integrity and use practices common in science, engage participants who are (primarily) not project-relevant scientists, seek to use the knowledge gained to contribute to science and/or community priorities, generally confer some benefit to the participant for participating, and involve the communication of results.

There are significant variations, however, in how citizen science projects support these common characteristics: how the participants engage, who organizes the projects, what the projects' goals are, who the participants are, and how results are reported. Participation might be one time or repeated, projects might be online or in person, projects might be longitudinal (i.e., for monitoring) or experimental, projects might prioritize community impact or advancing the field of science, and projects may be targeted to students or adults in formal and informal settings. Because this rich variation is part of what contributes to the suite of learning opportunities in citizen science, the committee elected to consider all these variations rather than develop or apply a restrictive definition. Recognizing the way in which citizen science projects are constructed, who it is that participates in these projects, the activities of those participants, and their different levels of engagement is critical for understanding the learning that occurs in citizen science and how to design for that learning.

## UNDERSTANDING SCIENCE LEARNING

In everyday use and in professional research and educational contexts, the word "learning" is used to capture a multiplicity of processes and outcomes. In recent decades both educational practice and research on learning have moved beyond a simple view of learning as an individual acquiring a fixed body of declarative facts and procedural knowledge to the recognition that learning is embedded in social interactions and involves complex reasoning and reflection. Understanding the nature of different varieties of learning, the processes that support them, and the ways in which they are expressed requires considering factors at multiple levels and scales— individual and social, situational and cultural, and through time. Science learning inherits all of the complexity of learning, and applies them to understanding how people interact with the methods, processes, norms, and epistemologies of science.

Modern understandings of science learning consider a range of learning outcomes that includes developing interest and identity as well as understanding scientific knowledge and engaging in the practices of science. The committee did not assign relative value to potential learning outcomes; however, we found evidence that some outcomes are harder to achieve and require more intentional support than others. Context also influences learning outcomes. When using citizen science in K–12 environments, curriculum can constrain the choice of learning outcomes, but the sustained engagement and built-in support scaffolds in K–12 contexts may be especially suited to supporting harder-to-achieve learning outcomes.

Citizen science has the potential to support science learning in unique ways. The properties of citizen science that make it particularly useful for science learning include the opportunity to participate in authentic scientific endeavors, the way in which citizen science is conducted in real-world contexts, and the way in which citizen science engages participants with real data. Additionally, the fact that citizen science often is motivated by interest- or concern-driven participation, is a social or communal activity, and offers opportunity for longer-term participation also provides opportunities for learning. Finally, the social and technological infrastructures of citizen science also enable learning opportunities. Viewing these characteristics in concert with one another, the committee used theories of science learning to investigate how citizen science can be designed to bring about specific science learning outcomes even though there are relatively few studies of learning specifically focused on citizen science.

Theories of learning make it clear that educational context and intent influence the kinds of learning outcomes that are achievable. We identify three broad contexts for learning in citizen science: (1) citizen science projects designed specifically for learning, (2) citizen science projects that are adapted in order to support learning, and (3) borrowing citizen science practices to support learning. Some contexts make it easier to achieve certain learning outcomes. For example, learning outcomes related to an identity as someone who contributes to science are easier to achieve in projects that are designed or adapted for learning, but harder to achieve when the data collection practices are borrowed from citizen science without contributing the collected data to some larger purpose. Further, whether particular learning outcomes are achieved also depends on the larger sociocultural context of a given project. The larger sociocultural context shapes participants' motivations for participating, their previous experience with science, the knowledge they bring to the project and how they respond to participating—all of which contributes to what participants learn through engaging in the project.

There is evidence that citizen science, leveraged effectively, can contribute to community science literacy. A term somewhat new to academic conversations about science literacy—community science literacy—is the capacity of a community to apply, do, and even guide science in ways that advance community priorities. It is a shared capacity, and it depends on and relates to the science learning of individuals as well as the connections, networks and agency that are distributed throughout the community (National Academies of Sciences, Engineering, and Medicine, 2016). Citizen science includes projects that grow out of a community's desire to address an inequity or advance a priority. When communities can work alongside scientists to advance their priorities, enhanced community science literacy is one possible outcome.

## DESIGNING FOR LEARNING

In considering how to design citizen science to support science learning, the committee arrived at three simple but powerful principles.

First, if designers are not intentional about learning (either in design or by investigating the learning in a project) than there is very little that can be said with confidence about participant learning in a given project.

Second, if one is intentional in design, there are proven practices that can help participants take advantage of the unique opportunities for learning associated with citizen science. Including stakeholders—anyone who might have a role to play in the project, such as project leads, scientists, people implementing the project and supporting participation and participants in the design process ensures that the processes and activities of the project—will be more attuned to learners' motivations and interests and better able to engage their skills and experiences.

Third, leaders and developers of citizen science projects interested in supporting science learning need to allow for iteration of the design. Rather than produce a full-fledged product based on a one-time interaction with stakeholders, it is more effective to produce a first cut or prototype and then engage with stakeholders in multiple cycles of feedback and refinement. This kind of process can help weed out ineffective design features.

In addition to these three overarching design strategies, the committee was also able to use research on design and practice to offer a number of guidelines that can be used in individual projects. Additional guidelines the committee suggests are

1. Know the Audience
2. Adopt an Asset-Based Perspective
3. Intentionally Design for Diversity
4. Engage Stakeholders in Design
5. Capitalize on Unique Learning Opportunities Associated with Citizen Science
6. Support Multiple Kinds of Participant Engagement
7. Encourage Social Interaction
8. Build Learning Supports into the Project
9. Evaluate and Refine

Some of these guidelines are easy to address, some are challenging, and all require consideration of not only the guideline itself but also the intersection of the guideline with the specific context and the participants. Project designers face choices about what people will learn, and must invest in the program design to support that learning. These choices require balancing values that sometimes compete, and sometimes are complementary. For example, if a project designer's highest priority is the collection of high-quality data, then it is reasonable to adopt a project design that emphasizes learning outcomes related to collecting, analyzing, and working with data. It is less reasonable (though not impossible) to expect that that same project would necessarily also offer substantive opportunity to reflect on the nature of scientific knowledge. On the other hand, if a project designer is hoping that participation will result in community action, than it makes sense to offer opportunities for participants to reflect about the nature of scientific knowledge and its relationship to culture. In summary, designers need to make choices about desired learning outcomes, and use those choices to design appropriate learning activities.

The committee hopes that the sum total of citizen science will offer a range of learning opportunities and outcomes and urges the entire community of people engaged in citizen science to be mindful of the portfolio of projects—always with an eye toward who may be left out or underserved by what already exists.

## ADDRESSING EQUITY THROUGH INTENTIONAL DESIGN

Citizen science project designers must grapple with issues of equity, diversity, power, and inclusion. They face these issues even if they do not set out to address diversity in their project and even when they are not consciously aware that these factors are at play in their project. This can be daunting: project designers necessarily have to make choices about how to use resources to best achieve multiple desired outcomes, and designing for broader participation can feel overwhelming. But where science learning is an expressed goal of participation, addressing these issues is essential: there is clear and ample evidence that diverse, equitable and inclusive program design advances learning for all participants. And, because participant learning outcomes support other project outcomes, this work can actually make it easier to achieve other project goals. Further, there is compelling evidence that not responsibly addressing issues of power and privilege can exacerbate learning inequities.

One of the most effective things project designers can do to attend to diversity is to question embedded and pernicious assumptions about who is capable of participation and what that participation can yield. This is especially true when thinking about members of communities that have been overlooked or marginalized by science, where these kinds of assumptions are more common, less questioned, and especially damaging to individual learning outcomes. Citizen science designers can make a special effort to welcome and respect the epistemologies, beliefs, practices, and skills that all people bring into citizen science. Collaborative design with participants from underrepresented groups (such as people of color, people of lower socioeconomic status, rural communities, women, etc.) helps to challenge limiting assumptions and create programming where all participants can learn.

## CONCLUSIONS

One of the goals of this report is to share the committee's synthesis of what is known about how practitioners can support science learning through participation in citizen science. As part of that work, several major conclusions emerged as this study's central findings.

CONCLUSION 1: Citizen science projects investigate a range of phenomena using scientific practices across varied social, cultural, and geographical contexts and activities. Citizen science allows people with diverse motivations and intentions to participate in science.

CONCLUSION 2: Because citizen science broadens the scope of who can contribute to science, it can be a pathway for introducing new processes, observations, data, and epistemologies to science.

CONCLUSION 3: There is limited systematic, cumulative information about who participates in citizen science. Community and youth projects are underrepresented in the available data suggesting that existing data are biased toward white middle- and upper-class populations.

CONCLUSION 4: Participants' learning through citizen science has benefits not only for participants and scientists but also for communities and science.

CONCLUSION 5: There is evidence that citizen science projects can contribute to specific learning outcomes in particular contexts and for some learners.

CONCLUSION 6: Citizen science supports learning outcomes related to scientific practices, content, identity, agency, data, and reasoning. Whether these outcomes are realized depends on the provision of learning supports and on intentional design.

> CONCLUSION 6a: Citizen science can be readily mobilized to help participants learn scientific practices and content directly related to the specific activities in the project.
> CONCLUSION 6b: With careful planning, intentional design, and learning supports, citizen science can
>
> * amplify participants' identity/ies as individuals who contribute to science and support their self-efficacy in science;

- provide an opportunity for participants to learn about data, data analysis, and interpretation of data; and
- provide a venue for participants to learn about the nature of science and scientific reasoning.

CONCLUSION 7: Science learning outcomes are strongly related to the motivations, interests, and identities of learners. Citizen science projects that welcome and respond to participants' motivations and interests are more likely to maximize participant learning.

CONCLUSION 8: Research on learning science in other contexts provides insight into some fundamental principles that can advance science learning through citizen science. These principles include the following:

- Prior knowledge and experience shape what and how participants learn.
- When participants' prior knowledge and experience are treated respectfully in the learning process, learning is advanced.
- Motivation, interest, and identity play a central role in learning, create learning opportunities, and are learning outcomes themselves.
- Most science learning outcomes will only be achieved with structured supports. These supports can come from specific tasks, tools, and facilitation.

CONCLUSION 9: Being aware of issues of power, privilege, and inequality, and explicitly addressing them in citizen science projects can help enable learning for all participants.

CONCLUSION 10: Community participation in citizen science activities can support the development of community science literacy.

CONCLUSION 11: Citizen science can create opportunities for communities, especially communities who have been marginalized, neglected, or even exploited by scientists, to collaborate with scientists and the science community.

CONCLUSION 12: Specific learning goals can be achieved with intentional design. Without intentional design, it can be hard to anticipate what learning outcomes will be achieved.

CONCLUSION 13: Research on program design shows that designing with input from stakeholders and building iteratively is an effective strategy for supporting learning. This is true for designing for science learning from citizen science.

CONCLUSION 14: Formal learning environments have more structured and intentional learning outcomes. Citizen science can provide useful activities for formal learning environments; however, educators may need to incorporate additional supports to achieve more challenging learning outcomes.

## RECOMMENDATIONS AND RESEARCH AGENDA

The committee was asked to develop a set of evidence-based principles to guide the design of citizen science projects. In reviewing research and practice, the committee discovered general principles that are relevant across citizen science and should be applied to the design and implementation of all projects. These principles derive from research and best practices in science education more generally: We present these overarching principles as recommendations. They are offered to all designers of citizen science projects, with the understanding that designers include a wide and representative range of stakeholders and that effective design extends well into implementation.

RECOMMENDATION 1: Given the potential of citizen science to engage traditionally underrepresented and underserved individuals and communities, the committee recommends that designers, researchers, participants, and other stakeholders in citizen science carefully consider and address issues of equity and power throughout all phases of project design and implementation.

RECOMMENDATION 2: In order to maximize learning outcomes through participation in citizen science, the committee recommends that citizen science projects leverage partnerships among scientists, education researchers, and other individuals with expertise in education and designing for learning.

RECOMMENDATION 3: In order to advance learning, project designers and practitioners should intentionally design for learning by defining intended learning outcomes, identifying a participant audience, integrating learning outcomes into project goals, and using evidence-based strategies to reach those outcomes.

RECOMMENDATION 4: In designing or adapting projects to support learning, designers should use proven practices of design, including iteration and stakeholder engagement in design.

As an emerging field, citizen science has opportunities to grow, to contribute to what we know about how people learn science, and to broaden participation in science. Not only will future research inform the design of citizen science projects but also design-based research in particular may be particularly well-suited to study the varied contexts of learning in citizen science. The next several recommendations explore how to maximize that potential. They are recommendations for building the field of citizen science.

The committee was also asked to lay out a research agenda that can fill gaps in the current understanding of how citizen science can support science learning and enhance science education, and those recommendations are outlined below.

RECOMMENDATION 5: The committee recommends that the educational research community perform regular analyses of the available evidence on learning in citizen science in order to identify and disseminate effective strategies.

RECOMMENDATION 6: The committee recommends that relevant researchers perform longitudinal studies of participation and changes in individuals' and communities' scientific knowledge, skills, attitudes, and behaviors, both within individual projects and across projects.

RECOMMENDATION 7: The committee recommends the citizen science community collaborate to develop shared tools and platforms that they can share to support science learning across a large number of citizen science projects.

## REFERENCE

National Academies of Sciences, Engineering, and Medicine. (2016). *Science Literacy: Concepts, Contexts, and Consequences*. Washington, DC: The National Academies Press.

# 1

# Introduction

Humans are an inquisitive species. From the beginning, humans develop knowledge by engaging in inquiry: in learning about the world, young children observe their surroundings, ask questions, and communicate about what they see with others. While Western society will turn some of those young explorers into professional scientists, the vast majority of individuals will be left to engage with science—both the institution and the content—from outside the gates of "professional" science.

In the past 20 years, the phenomenon of citizen science has emerged as one way to engage individuals of all ages and occupations in the doing of science. When asked about their experiences in citizen science, enthusiastic participants often celebrate that engagement. In conducting the study that would lead to this report, the National Academies of Sciences, Engineering, and Medicine's Committee on Designing Citizen Science to Support Science Learning heard from a number of experts whose experiences offer vivid insight into the potential of citizen science to bring all kinds of people into the community and practice of science. The stories these experts shared point to the diversity of opportunities available through citizen science. The committee heard the story of a middle school student whose experience working in a lab transformed her description of herself, from "klutz" to "expert in DNA extraction and science contributor." Similarly, the committee heard the story of a young man who was prevented from dropping out of high school when his participation in citizen science showed him, and helped him show others, that he was smart and could succeed. The committee also encountered the story of a woman, living in a senior center, who turned to citizen science to continue a lifelong tradition of volunteering. She found a deepened sense of purpose from knowing researchers depended on her data. The committee also learned about the West-Oakland Indicators Project, a community group in Oakland, California, that self-organizes to collect and analyze air quality data and uses those data to address industrial trucking around schools to reduce local children's exposure to air pollution.

These kinds of stories are also clues about the potential of citizen science to support learning. They point to skills gained, social connection, and community capacity. This report seeks to follow those clues toward answers to underlying questions about how citizen science can contribute to science learning. What kinds of learning can citizen science advance? What is it about citizen science that contributes to science learning? How would someone design citizen science to maximize learning? What can be learned from citizen science that can influence science learning in other contexts? What kinds of additional research would help educators and practitioners of citizen science in their ongoing work?

## CHARGE TO THE COMMITTEE

In response to requests from the Gordon and Betty Moore Foundation, the Howard Hughes Medical Institute, and the Simons Foundation, the National Academies of Sciences, Engineering, and Medicine through its Board on Science Education convened a committee to undertake a study of science learning and citizen science (see Box 1-1). The 12-member expert Committee on Designing Citizen Science to Support Science Learning

---

**BOX 1-1**
**Statement of Task**

Designing Citizen Science to Support Science Learning

An ad hoc committee of experts will be appointed to conduct a study on how citizen science projects can be designed to better support science learning. The committee will identify and describe existing citizen science projects that seek to support science learning, consider research on science learning in both formal and informal settings, and develop a set of evidence-based principles to guide the design of citizen science projects that have science learning as a goal. The committee's final report will discuss the potential of citizen science to support science learning, identify promising practices and programs that exemplify the promising practices, and lay out a research agenda that can fill gaps in the current understanding of how citizen science can support science learning and enhance science education.

included individuals with expertise in citizen science programming, research and evaluation of citizen science projects, the learning sciences, K–12 science education, informal science education, and afterschool or extended school science programming.

## INTERPRETING THE CHARGE

In interpreting the charge, the committee members asked themselves a series of questions. First, we embarked on a definitional exercise intended to help us calibrate our understanding of citizen science. We then attempted to arrive at consensus on our understanding of science learning, before turning to an investigation of what kinds of citizen science experiences support learning. Finally, we turned our attention to addressing the charge's most pressing question: How can citizen science be designed or leveraged to support science learning? The following sections offer insight into how the committee entered into this investigatory process.

### What Is Citizen Science?

To help orient this report, the committee arrived at an inclusive description of citizen science, rather than a specific, narrow definition. Citizen science projects are those that typically involve nonscientists (i.e., people who are not professionally trained in project-relevant disciplines) in the processes, methods, and standards of research, with the intended goal of advancing scientific knowledge or application. The committee found it useful to think about this description as it relates to specific examples. A project in which community members collect stream data using well-established protocols to monitor stream health fits this description of citizen science, but the same project where only professional water quality technicians collect the data would not. A project where students collect water quality data solely for their own edification does not fit the committee's description of citizen science. That is not to say that a purely educational project cannot share in the strategies and practices that have been developed for and proven effective in citizen science, but the committee notes the use of those practices in service of a larger goal—community action or scientific knowledge—as a defining feature of citizen science. As another example, a project where people play a video game (however much that game is dealing with real scientific problems like protein folding) is not citizen science unless the players know they are dealing with real scientific challenges, have some understanding of those challenges and the relevant science, and know that their individual results are useful.

There are several important elements contained in this description of citizen science. One is the active and continual engagement of nonscientists.

Even a project that is defined in close consultation with community members ceases to be citizen science when the community members cease to be involved—for example, if the research was all carried out by professional scientists. People who are the subjects of the research are not participating as citizen scientists, nor are people who are unaware that they are participating in a citizen science project. Another important element in the description of citizen science is the notion of communicating and using the results of the project, especially within the scientific community. Finally, projects must adhere to the standards of scientific integrity to be described as citizen science, and projects in which data are ignored or cherry-picked to advance an agenda do not fit this description.

What all this points to is that the practice of citizen science is not a clearly delineated well-bounded space with well-defined and well-accepted exclusion and inclusion criteria, which is consistent with a young field with diverse antecedents. The field is still relatively new and has not yet been fully codified. Citizen science, as it exists today, is a confluence of several different evolutionary pathways; the committee discusses these pathways in depth in Chapter 2 of this report. As a result, citizen science projects are designed and implemented with different motivations, theoretical frameworks, and content areas. Given these different considerations, the committee believes that citizen science is better suited to classification by description.

As a note, the committee uses the term citizen science because that is the term most commonly used within the scientific and science education communities to describe these activities. We recognize that the term "citizen," particularly in the United States, connects to a contentious immigration debate about who is eligible to participate in civic life, including science and education. While other terms can be used to describe citizen science, such as community science, public participation in scientific research, participatory action research, and community-based participatory research, none of them is as complete or widely used as citizen science. The committee uses citizen science despite its associated tensions.

## What Is Science Learning?

The committee interpreted science learning broadly, and elected to consider a range of learning outcomes. The committee found it helpful to think in terms of the learning strands identified in *Learning Science in Informal Environments* (National Research Council, 2009), which we discuss in Chapter 3 of this report. In addition to the learning outcomes typically presented in a discussion of science learning (such as the ability to generate or use concepts or the ability to participate in scientific activities) the committee purposefully includes the development of interest, motivation, and identity as a critical component of science learning.

The committee also acknowledges that learning outcomes—both in the context of citizen science and in general—depend on not only the educational context but also larger sociocultural contexts. This framing suggests that these sociocultural factors are part of the inputs, sometimes implicit, in any citizen science project. This includes, of course, the things people come into the project with: What a person learns is influenced by prior knowledge, motivations for participating, and previous experience with science, to name just a few. Our analysis of learning outcomes led us to consider the different ways people enter into citizen science projects, the different experiences they bring into and have as part of citizen science projects, and the way both of those things may influence learning outcomes.

## Who Is Learning?

Early on in this work, the committee realized that in order to effectively address the study charge as laid out, it was important to delineate not only what kind of science learning could occur through citizen science, but also who it is that learns through citizen science. After extensive deliberation, the committee agreed that although professional scientist practitioners of citizen science stand to learn a lot by conducting citizen science, the focus of this study is the science learning of citizen science participants. In the event that professional scientists are participating in citizen science as members of the public (and not in service of their own scientific goals), this study is concerned with that learning as well. Finally, we use the term "project designer" to indicate the entities involved in the structuring of a citizen science experience, including professional scientists and other relevant community stakeholders. The term "participant" is intended to encompass individuals and communities who engage in some aspect/s of a citizen science project or activity. Also along these same lines, we use the word "project" in reference to those citizen science experiences that are planned and constructed in service of specific citizen science goals, whereas citizen science "activities" refer to the various kinds of things one might do or engage with while participating in citizen science.

## How Can Learning Occur Through Citizen Science?

Though science learning can certainly happen as an unintended byproduct of participation in citizen science, the committee elected to focus its attention on the kinds of citizen science experiences where achieving science learning outcomes is an expressed goal of participation. Though "by-product of participation" learning outcomes are valuable, the committee was charged to "develop a set of evidence-based principles to guide the design of citizen science projects." As a result, the committee decided to focus its investigation on projects where participation leads to specific, intended learning outcomes as opposed to projects where learning was not explicitly identified as a goal for participation. This distinction helped the committee understand how projects planned for learning goals.

In its investigation, the committee identified three ways that citizen science supports intentional learning outcomes:

1. *Citizen science designed for learning.* These are projects that are intentionally designed to support science learning from the outset (often alongside other goals). In this example, scientists, science educators, and perhaps even community leaders, work together to design a project, from the beginning, with learning goals in mind and explicitly consider how learning goals and outcomes complement other project goals, like accurate data collection.

2. *Citizen science adapted or repurposed for learning.* These are citizen science projects that were originally designed without explicit learning goals and have been later used to promote learning. Often, this involves people who were not part of the original design who add additional learning supports to a citizen science project. For example, a Girl Scout troupe that participates in a citizen science project through Scistarter[1] and takes advantage of the supplementary materials prepared to help reflect on what the girls learned through participating and what it meant.

3. *Citizen science practices used for learning.* In this case, practices or elements of citizen science are used to promote learning, but some essential feature of citizen science is missing—often the link to some purpose beyond learning. For example, borrowing a GLOBE protocol for use in a classroom monitoring of a local stream, without sharing that data back into the wider GLOBE community or using it in local decisions.

Parsing these types of science learning experiences allowed the committee to be specific about both why and how science learning is likely to occur from citizen science activities—a task that is a necessary prerequisite to identifying project design considerations.

---

[1]SciStarter is a Web platform for individuals looking to "find, join, and contribute to science." For more information, see http://www.scistarter.com [October 2018].

## FRAMING CONSIDERATIONS

In addition to the challenging work of interpreting the committee charge, the committee also needed to have several other important conversations that would frame our later analyses. In this section, we explain which issues surfaced as particularly important and compelling in order to set up our later analytic discussions.

### What Counts as Evidence for Learning?

In interpreting this part of the charge, the committee agreed that the potential to achieve learning outcomes is not the same as achieving learning outcomes. Instead, we sought to focus on the evidence available to identify both potential and documented learning outcomes in citizen science. In order to sort through the plethora of claims about the potential of citizen science to support learning, the committee needed to agree on certain standards of evidence that could be relied on to support our argumentation. A very strong kind of evidence for learning comes from dedicated studies of learning outcomes in the context of citizen science but, not surprisingly for a field that has emerged relatively recently, focused investigations of learning outcomes in citizen science are rare. While the few available investigations are compelling, they do not provide enough evidence to make definitive statements about learning from citizen science. The committee found it more helpful to delve into the large body of research on learning science and map this robust literature to the landscape of citizen science. The bulk of this report, therefore, describes what research on science learning and teaching, including theories of learning, offers to the design of citizen science, or to using practices of citizen science to support learning outcomes. Similarly, literature on volunteerism was useful for understanding some of the aspects of science learning related to identity motivation and persistence in citizen science. For developing guidance on the design of citizen science projects to support learning outcomes, the committee delved deeply into literature on design, with a particular focus on design theory applied to designing for learning. Finally, the committee found the experience of citizen science practitioners, as reported in person, nonacademic writing, or conference presentations, to be invaluable pointers toward potential learning outcomes that could be investigated more thoroughly using peer-reviewed sources.

### Attending to Issues of Equity

The committee entered into this work with a commitment to exploring how people of all backgrounds can learn through citizen science, and that meant exploring the intersection of diversity, equity, and inclusion, and learning in citizen science (see Box 1-2). While recognizing that we have not reached parity in terms of all people's opportunities to learn, contribute to, and benefit from science, the committee is inspired by progress in the fields of science, education, and science education. Because citizen science is built around interaction between scientist and nonscientists, it offers an opportunity to welcome beliefs, epistemologies, and ideas that historically have not been as included in science. As we discuss in Chapter 7, however, this opportunity will only be realized if diversity, equity, and inclusion are part of the goals in the design and implementation of citizen science. Further, the committee notes well-established scholarship showing that failing to consider these aspects in the design of educational systems can lead to the perpetuation of inequity (Banks, 1997).

---

**BOX 1-2**
**What Are Equity, Diversity, and Inclusion?**

Equity, diversity, and inclusion are distinct but interrelated concepts. In order to effectively meet the learning demands of citizen science participants, people who participate in project design and implementation need to attend to all three concepts effectively.

Equity signals a distribution of opportunities and resources that enables all participants the opportunity to engage successfully. Attending to equity suggests an emphasis on constructing learning experiences so that all learners have can successfully pursue an optimal learning pathway that recognizes and values their experiences, cultures, and identities. Doing this requires an awareness of how systemic forces can affect the opportunities available to, or disrupt outcomes for, an individual. In acknowledging the different experiences that individuals bring to any situation, providing equitable opportunities suggests that not every experience will always be equal.

Diversity focuses on the differences among individuals, including demographic differences such as sex, race, ethnicity, sexual orientation, socioeconomic status, ability, languages, and country of origin, among others. Attending to diversity requires an emphasis on access to opportunities to participate, and representation in participation. Diversity is an asset that contributes to participant learning and development.

Inclusion refers to the processes through which learners are made to feel welcome and are treated as motivated participants and contributors. Attending to inclusion requires an emphasis on intentional engagement with diversity to support participant learning. Inclusive practices mean that project participants use differences as assets to enhance learning for all and advance science.

SOURCE: Adapted from National Academies of Sciences, Engineering, and Medicine (2017), Association of American Colleges and Universities (2015), and Malcom-Piqueux and Bensimon (2017).

No discussion of science learning is complete without careful attention to the needs and opportunities, barriers and access points, and assets and challenges for learners with different backgrounds, experiences, contexts, and histories. Further, the committee agreed unanimously that discussions of learning must consider who is learning, what they are learning, who is deciding on learning goals and outcomes, and how those goals are reached. Addressing these questions meant that the committee needed to wrestle with issues of privilege, acknowledge historic patterns of discrimination, grapple with current structural inequities, and explore biases.

Citizen science, like science, is practiced in an imperfect world. Unless they actively try to combat society's pervasive inequities, citizen science project designers are necessarily influenced by the world around them. For instance, if a project requires use of specific research protocols in order to participate but does not ensure that participants can read, understand, and work with the protocol, the project is likely to engage people with the education and experience necessary to complete the work. Narrowing the field of who can participate in this way has the potential to obstruct a project's educational goals and, ultimately, deepen existing inequities. People who design, implement, and participate in citizen science must therefore grapple with issues of equity, diversity, power, and inclusion. They face these issues even if they do not set out to address diversity in their project and even when they are not consciously aware that these factors are at play in their project. This can be daunting: Project designers necessarily have to make choices about how to use resources to best achieve multiple desired outcomes, and designing for broader participation can feel overwhelming. But where science learning is an expressed goal of participation, the committee believes that addressing these issues is essential.

## Advancing Science and Advancing Learning

The goals of citizen science often include a mix of goals around advancing science and goals around serving participants. Participant-oriented goals at the scale of the individual include advancing learning and motivation. At the scale of the project, scientific goals include accumulating high-quality information that can then be used in decision making—whether those decisions describe a scientific discovery or innovation, or a resource management, environmental health, or even human health outcome. Are these goals and scales compatible? Stated another way, can a citizen science project that promotes learning also advance science?

The committee suggests that science learning goals and scientific project goals are not only compatible but also mutually reinforcing. Evidence suggests that attention to participant learning can increase the quality of data and analysis in citizen science. First, however, it is critical to overcome unfounded biases against citizen science data (see Box 1-3).

If it is accepted that citizen science is a valuable tool for expanding and deepening scientific inquiry, then attending to the learning outcomes of participants should be an important consideration for project designers. This, in itself, is one way that advancing learning and advancing science are compatible: More science learning by participants has the potential to improve their contribution to the project and potentially enhance the chance of the discovery and scientific advancement in the project. Citizen science has the ability to spark new science questions or launch new investigations, and balancing participant learning goals with the scientific goals of the project provides an additional venue for interactions that can bring participants' ideas to the surface.

## ABOUT THIS REPORT

The committee made a number of methodological and analytic decisions in order to conduct the investigations necessary to complete this report. In this section, we detail our approach to addressing the study charge, as well as this report's intended audiences. We conclude with a description of the organization of this report.

### Addressing the Charge

The committee held four in-person meetings and one telephone meeting over the course of the study. The first meeting was largely information gathering at which we heard from a variety of stakeholders, including our project sponsors: Janet Coffey from the Gordon and Betty Moore Foundation, Bridget Conneely and Dennis Liu from the Howard Hughes Medical Institute, and Greg Boustead from the Simons Foundation. Rick Bonney from the Cornell Lab of Ornithology and Sarah Kirn from the Gulf of Maine Research Institute offered framing perspectives on the potential of citizen science, and Leona Schauble from Vanderbilt University and Leslie Herrenkohl from the University of Washington provided insight into the landscape of science learning.

The second public meeting took place over 3 days, and allowed the committee to delve into specific issues. Cindy Hmelo-Silver from Indiana University and Joe Polman from the University of Colorado Boulder kicked off the event, offering a deeper dive into the science learning literature. Heidi Ballard from the University of California, Davis, provided the keynote address with an overview on the potential of citizen science to support science learning. On day 2, Bill Zoellick from the Schoodic Institute, Ruth Kermish-Allen from Maine Mathematics and Science Alliance, and Rebecca

**BOX 1-3**
**Why Is Citizen Science Valuable for Science?**

Accepting citizen science into the scientific "toolbox" has deepened and extended science in the following ways:

Field-based projects can **ground-truth more remote data collection techniques** (e.g., satellite remote sensing) with geo-referenced, time-stamped data that may increase the accuracy of the more comprehensive sampling. For instance, the Community Collaborative Rain, Hail and Snow (CoCoRHaS) project, which focuses on daily recordings of precipitation type and amount, has been used to increase the detail of extreme weather events beyond radar capabilities, and is now regularly incorporated into weather forecasting nationwide (see https://www.cocorahs.org/ [May 2018]).

Broad-scale, regular monitoring projects can **detect rare events** that conventional scientific sampling miss such as range extensions (Zuckerberg, 2010). Another is early warning for invasive species. The Crab Team project, a citizen science project in Puget Sound, Washington, has been able to detect invasive green crabs (*Carcinus maenas*) through extensive citizen-based trapping, at levels undetectable by state and federal agencies, simply because of the increase in trapping effort afforded by the 225 participants (Washington Sea Grant, 2018, see https://wsg.washington.edu/v22017datasummary/ [May 2018]).

Projects with broad geographic extent, high spatial resolution, and decades of reliable data collection provide some of the **highest quality information on the impacts of a wider range of natural and anthropogenic forces available today** (Theobald et al., 2015). For example, Parmesan and colleagues (1999) used citizen science data from butterfly monitoring projects across Europe to document a northward shift in population centers associated with warming temperatures. Cooper, Shirk, and Zuckerberg (2014) found that citizen science projects are often the base of climate impact studies, as these projects are the only long-term datasets available.

Where citizen science uses crowdsourcing, **unique ideas, findings, and/or solutions** can emerge out of large collectives of participants. Examples of this phenomenon include the Foldit protein structure innovation (Foldit, 2018) and the Green Peas project (Green Peas, 2018).

Finally, the committee underscores that citizen science is, itself, part of a rich and productive tradition of expanding the tools and processes that are available to support scientific inquiry. Like any tool, it can be used well, used poorly, or misused. As an emerging tool, we are still learning its limits and most appropriate uses. Viewed in this way, it can be approached in the same manner in which the scientific community approached the development of any tool, such as numerical modeling technique or action research.

Jordan from Rutgers University did a panel on frameworks for designing learning opportunities in citizen science. Rob Dunn from North Carolina State University; Andrea Wiggins from the University of Nebraska Omaha; Jennifer Fee from the Cornell Lab of Ornithology; and Linda Peterson from Fairfax County Public Schools, conducted a panel on citizen science in K–12 classrooms. Gwen Ottinger from Drexel University; Michael Mascarenhas from the University of California, Berkeley; and Muki Haklay from University College London offered insight into citizen science and community learning outcomes. Karen Peterman from Karen Peterman Consulting and Cat Stylinski from the University of Maryland conducted a panel on assessing learning in citizen science, and Laura Trouille from Zooniverse and the Adler Planetarium, Kathryn "Kit" Matthew from the Institute of Museum and Library Sciences, and Sue Allen from Maine Mathematics and Science Alliance closed the event with a panel on citizen science in informal settings.

In addition to the public meeting, the committee held a listening session as part of the meeting of the Citizen Science Association's 2017 Meeting, as described in Box 1-4.

---

**BOX 1-4**
**Listening Session at Citizen Science Association Meeting**

As part of their research for the report, the committee hosted a listening session at the Citizen Science Association Meeting on May 19, 2017, in St. Paul, Minnesota. Practitioners of citizen science—people who lead and manage citizen science programs, do research on citizen science, and offer tools to enable citizen science—made up the majority of the meeting's 400 attendees. Committee members heard from approximately 40 meeting attendees in a 90-minute session.

Comments clustered around four main themes: (1) citizen science's potential to advance a broad range of learning strands; (2) its importance and place in formal K–12 education; (3) the need to support people, including teachers, who facilitate others' engagement in citizen science; and (4) the potential for citizen science to advance equity and inclusion in science. Participants also discussed how citizen science might be uniquely able to advance certain aspects of science learning or address certain concepts, particularly data literacy and uncertainty. Attendees also highlighted that citizen science offers opportunities for multi-generational learning, self-directed learning, and multiple touch-points through time, and urged the committee to consider how these factors enhance learning outcomes from citizen science. Attendees also reminded us that many citizen science participants, especially outside of school, are not participating with educational goals as their primary driver.

These comments were discussed at the committee's second meeting and then integrated into our evolving work plan, and ultimately became several of the report's most critical framing considerations.

After the public meetings, the committee met in closed session to review and debate evidence and develop consensus around conclusions and recommendations. The committee reviewed multiple evidence bases to develop their arguments around how citizen science might address science learning and how those opportunities could be designed to maximize specific learning outcomes.

Several fields of scholarship were considered throughout this work. The committee considered literatures from science education and the learning sciences, as well as the science of program design and design theory. Citizen science literature, while still a nascent field, offered invaluable insight into the specific issues one must consider when planning for citizen science programming. A growing body of research on learning in the context of citizen science helped us understand which learning outcomes were proximal to citizen science participation and which kinds of learning outcomes required more supports. As discussed above, the committee spent much of its time investigating the application of scholarship from the learning sciences and design theory to the practical work of citizen science in order to delineate the specific possibilities for learning that participation in citizen science might embody.

The committee also commissioned three papers to support its work. Heidi Ballard from the University of California, Davis, provided a paper that expanded on her keynote address from our public meeting on citizen science and science identity. Bill Sandoval from the University of California, Los Angeles, wrote a paper on design-based research in education and its potential in citizen science. Christopher Hoadley from New York University provided a paper on supporting science learning through intentional design strategy. These papers enabled the committee to address the entirety of the statement of task.

### Report Audiences

The committee discussed at length the breadth of audiences who might find this report useful. As a result, we have attempted to write throughout to meet the needs of multiple constituent groups. We want this report to be useful to as many citizen science stakeholders as possible. The following groups are just some of the audiences we hope will find value in our investigation:

- Educators, scientists, instructional designers, citizen science practitioners, who want to design and implement new citizen science projects in ways that maximize learning for project participants.

- Educators and community leaders who want to leverage existing citizen science projects to advance science learning in their communities, classrooms, museums, or programs.
- Citizen science project leaders who want to understand more about learning in order to provide better supports for participants in their existing programs.
- Researchers who want to understand the boundaries of what we know about citizen science and science learning and help push on those boundaries.
- Funders and policy makers who want to understand the promise of citizen science in order to support programs, policies, and projects that advance that promise through proven practices.
- Policy makers and curriculum designers who want to know how citizen science can be leveraged to support science learning.
- Researchers who want to advance our understanding of how citizen science contributes to science learning and what the practice of citizen science can reveal about science learning more generally.

### Organization of the Report

This report is organized into seven chapters, with four appendixes. Chapter 2 describes citizen science, detailing what differentiates participation in citizen science activity from other science experiences and mapping the landscape of experiences. Chapter 3 provides an overview of why citizen science is an appropriate and effective context for science learning. Chapter 4 provides a deeper look at the processes of learning as well as specific kinds of learning in science, and Chapter 5 provides insight into how specific science learning outcomes play out in citizen science contexts. Chapter 6 uses design theory to offer guidelines for project designers and educators to use in order to achieve learning outcomes in citizen science projects or in processes borrowed from citizen science. In Chapter 7, we conclude the report with a summary of the report's conclusions and offer recommendations for continued practice and further research. Appendix A presents a table that summarizes demographic trends in participation in citizen science. Appendix B includes a brief description of how design research can and has been used in educational contexts. The committee performed an ad hoc analysis of 28 citizen science projects to review their claims and efforts related to science learning outcomes, which we have included in Appendix C. Appendix D contains biographical sketches of committee members and staff.

# REFERENCES

Association of American Colleges and Universities. (2015). *Committing to Equity and Inclusive Excellence: A Campus Guide for Self-Study and Planning.* Washington, DC. Available: https://www.aacu.org/publications/committing-to-equity [July 2017].

Banks, J.A. (1997). *Educating Citizens in a Multicultural Society.* Multicultural Education Series. New York: Teachers College Press.

Cooper, C.B., Shirk, J., and Zuckerberg, B. (2014). The invisible prevalence of citizen science in global research: Migratory birds and climate change. *PloS ONE, 9*(9), e106508.

Foldit. (2018). *Foldit. Solve Puzzles for Science.* Available: https://fold.it/portal [September 2018].

Green Peas. (2018). *Green Peas. A Zooniverse Project Blog.* Available: https://blog.galaxyzoo.org/tag/green-peas/ [September 2018].

Malcom-Piqueux, L.E., Robinson, J., and Bensimon, E.M. (2017). Equity in higher education. In M. Klemenčič (Ed.), *International Encyclopedia of Higher Education.* Dordrecht: Springer.

National Academies of Sciences, Engineering, and Medicine. (2017). *Indicators for Monitoring Undergraduate STEM Education.* Washington, DC: The National Academies Press. doi: https://doi.org/10.17226/24943.

National Research Council. (2009). *Learning Science in Informal Environments: People, Places, and Pursuits.* Washington, DC: The National Academies Press.

Parmesan, C., Ryrholm, N., Stefanescu, C., Hill, J.K., Thomas, C.D., Descimon, H., Descimon, H., Huntley, B., Kaila, L., Kullberg, J., Tammaru, T., Tennent, W.J., Thomas, J.A., and Warren, M. (1999). Poleward shifts in geographical ranges of butterfly species associated with regional warming. *Nature, 399*(6736), 579-583.

Theobald, E.J., Ettinger, A.K., Burgess, H.K., DeBey, L.B., Schmidt, N.R., Froehlich, H.E., Wagner, C., Hill Ris Lambers, J., Tewksbury, J., Harsch, M.A., and Parrish, J.K. (2015). Global change and local solutions: Tapping the unrealized potential of citizen science for biodiversity research. *Biological Conservation, 181*, 236-244.

Washington Sea Grant. (2018). *2017 Crab Team European Green Crab and Pocket Estuary Monitoring, Infographic.* Available: https://wsg.washington.edu/v22017datasummary/ [November 2018].

Zuckerberg, B. (2010). *Citizen Science and Range Shifts: The Impacts of Climate Change on Birds.* Paper presented at the 96th annual meeting of the Ecological Society of America.

# 2

# Mapping the Landscape

The term "citizen science" is often applied to a wide range of projects with different goals, participants, and modes of participation. All involve people, typically not professional scientists, who participate in and make use of scientific processes, data, and knowledge. The fact that all citizen science includes participation in some form of science activity and thinking means that all citizen science projects have the potential to advance science learning. The range of citizen science opportunities also means that these possibilities vary by the project, and are influenced by the goals, participants, and modes of participation of the project.

Though the committee declined to specifically define citizen science and instead elected to describe citizen science activity (as discussed in Chapter 1), many scholars have attempted to create typologies that characterize and define citizen science. Understanding the evolution of these typologies helps to understand the differing goals, participants, and modes of participation, and how citizen science can support science learning. In this chapter, we describe the evolution of how scholars have defined and characterized citizen science in order to explain the breadth of contemporary understandings of citizen science. We then turn to our own description of similarities and variations in citizen science projects and kinds of participation in citizen science. By exploring these ideas, this chapter lays the groundwork for our later discussions that connect contemporary understandings of science learning and design to the diverse kinds of citizen science.

## THE HISTORY OF CITIZEN SCIENCE:
## EVOLVING DEFINITIONS AND TYPOLOGIES

Citizen science has antecedents in the desire to collect regular, repeated information about the natural world. In some ways, the idea of citizen science has roots in practices before science was professionalized: observations of nature as part of indigenous knowledge, agricultural and pastoral practice, and historical record keeping all bear similarities to citizen science. The notion of "gentleman" science, where people with privilege and means engaged in science and science activities as hobbyists, recalls citizen science. Officially, however, the field of citizen science emerged in reaction to the formal institution of science as a mechanism for engaging the public: A central tenet of citizen science is that science is not the sole providence of professional scientists.

The gathering of natural history data by both expert and nonexpert participants predates the development of "scientist" as a category in the mid-19th century (Jardine, Secord, and Spary, 1996), and many other historical antecedents can be found (e.g., Vetter, 2011). Miller-Rushing, Primack, and Bonney (2012, p. 286) point to deep historical traditions regarding the systematic collection of observations and information by publics, including millennia-old records documenting natural phenomena over time (referred to as phenological datasets):

> For instance, wine-growers in France have been recording grape harvest days for more than 640 years (Chuine et al., 2004), while court diarists in Kyoto, Japan have been recording dates of the traditional cherry blossom festival for 1,200 years (Primack et al., 2009). In China, both citizens and officials have been tracking outbreaks of locusts for at least 3,500 years (Tian et al., 2011). In the United States, among the oldest continuous organized datasets are phenological records kept by farmers and agricultural organizations that document the timing of important agronomical events, such as sowing, harvests, and pest outbreaks (Hopkins, 1918).

Likewise, indigenous peoples around the world have and continue to develop knowledge of the natural world through their own knowledge systems that utilize systematic observation and interaction with their environments (Cajete, 2000).

Citizen science also has antecedents in the desire to affect change, and in nonscientists using scientific methods and data, often data they collected, to motivate or guide that change. Community groups have long collected data in their neighborhoods and used that data to improve lives and livelihoods (Miller-Rushing, Primack, and Bonney, 2012). Recent advances in technology, including low-cost sensors and Internet-enabled data management and communication, have contributed to an explosion in community-led collection and analysis of data (Haklay, 2013). In the following section, we discuss the history of defining and characterizing citizen science in order to set the stage for our description of the diversity of citizen science projects and types of participation in citizen science.

## Definitions and Typologies

As described in Chapter 1 of this report, the field of citizen science has not yet codified into a discipline with clearly defined criteria for what "counts." Attempts to define the field have led in divergent directions, with multiple scholars positing different meanings and practices for the work of citizen science. In this section, we describe attempts to define and characterize citizen science. In unpacking the variation present in these efforts, the committee demonstrates the challenges inherent in trying to find a single, clear definition for citizen science. Along those same lines, by describing the variations in what citizen science signifies to different parties, the committee is setting the stage for our later discussions about how project designers can leverage variation in citizen science to support science learning.

The term citizen science has two distinct, but related root definitions. In *Citizen Science: A Study of People, Expertise and Sustainable Development,* Irwin (1995) employs the term "citizen science" in reference to the relationship people have to ongoing environmental concerns that benefit from a scientific understanding. Irwin employs the term as a critique of the institution of Western science, arguing that science must be accessible if it is to be useful to individuals and communities. In 1996, Bonney articulated a different use for the term: "Scientific work undertaken by members of the general public, often in collaboration with or under the direction of professional scientists and scientific institutions."

Eitzel and colleagues (2017) compare citizen science to crowdsourcing, where a large number of people are recruited to contribute "services, ideas or content" to a project through "microtasking," without necessarily understanding the full import of the work. For science projects, this may mean that participants are conducting tasks without engaging with the underlying science concepts, as in the gamification of a project.

Bonney and colleagues (2009b, p. 977) describe a kind of citizen science focused on large-scale data collection, where citizen participation is driven by the scales of space and time beyond any one individual that the data patterns describe:

> Studying large-scale patterns in nature requires a vast amount of data to be collected across an array of locations and habitats over spans of years or even decades. One way to obtain such data is through citizen science, a research technique that enlists the public in gathering scientific information.

These elements of scale have also been pointed out by Cooper and colleagues (2007) and by Danielsen and colleagues (2009) as seminal to the modern phenomena of citizen science, whether in service of encapsulating the geographic entirety of a scientific question or working at larger scales of data analysis and interpretation allowing enlightened decision making at both local and regional scales. Haklay (2013) defines "geographical citizen science" as projects explicitly collecting location information, often as part of the meta-data attached to the sample. For instance, the geolocation stamp a cell phone attaches to a photograph sent to iNaturalist (Bowser et al., 2014), a digital image data storage platform that houses more than 2,000 citizen science projects centered on crowdsourcing both image collection and subsequent species identification.

In working to define citizen science (within a youth-focused context but applying it more generally), Ballard, Dixon, and Harris (2017) emphasizes the contribution to basic research or resource management and distinguishes citizen science from projects that result only in new awareness, understanding, and skill development only on the part of the participant.

In terms of typologies that attempt to classify citizen science, one common way of describing the range of citizen science projects is to describe how the extent of control that project participants have over the direction of the project is correlated with the degree of participation (a concept often traced to Arnstein's [1969] "ladder of participation"). In *contributory* projects, participants focus on data collection; *collaborative* projects also include participants in data analysis, interpretation and/or dissemination; and *co-created* projects mix the involvement of scientists and participants throughout all aspects of the work (Bonney et al., 2009a, see also Shirk et al., 2012). Danielsen et al. (2009) and Haklay (2013) point out the degree of control over any-to-all aspects of the project as crucially important, referring variously to "autonomous local monitoring" and "extreme citizen science" to describe projects in which citizens control most aspects of the project.

Wiggins and Crowston (2011, p. 1) consider citizen science typologies derived from the goal(s) of citizen science projects and project participants, arguing that a singular focus on the level of participant engagement pays "little attention to sociotechnical and macrostructural factors influencing the design and management of participation." Thus, their schema incorporates goals of science, of individuals (via education), and of community in five mutually exclusive types identified through a cluster analysis of 80 possible attributes assessed more than 28 intentionally selected projects. They further link this schema to educational opportunities and posit the following:

- *Investigation* projects focus on physical data collection according to scientific standards and methods and often provide volunteers with scaffolded learning opportunities.
- *Virtual* projects adhere to scientific standards and methods but are entirely mediated through information and communication technologies.
- *Conservation* projects are primarily ecologically focused, support natural resource management or stewardship, are designed by content experts, and involve volunteers as data collectors.
- *Action* projects are grassroots, community projects that may employ participatory action research methods in service of addressing local concerns.
- *Education* projects span formal and informal learning providing youth learners with opportunities to engage in the practice of science in order to contribute data to a larger scientific effort. Within the latter type, Zoellick, Nelson, and Schauffler (2012) define Scientist-Teacher-Student Partnerships as engaging in authentic science practice, from study question through dissemination, with the students as the focus and with facilitated interaction with scientists and teachers at all stages.

Haklay (2013) divides citizen science projects involving technology into *"volunteered computing"* or projects using the computer resources of millions of individuals across the globe to process otherwise intractable problems without any direct interaction with the owner; *"participatory sensing"* in which the smart phone or other personal data-recording device is automatically used to collect environmental information with, or without additional direct input of the owner; and *"volunteered thinking"* or projects where the participant is trained to perform some task (e.g., image classification or analysis as in Zooniverse; Masters et al., 2016).

## Summary

Clearly, no single definition can encompass the broad range of activities that exist under the umbrella of citizen science. In this section, we have described several efforts to define citizen science in order to demonstrate the complexity of codifying on the activities that occur across this broad range of projects. For some, the term citizen science refers to people contributing observations and efforts to conducting science. Those holding this view may see citizen science as a new research tool, which facilitates larger scale research. For others, the term encompasses the democratization of science, allowing people outside of the mainstream scientific establishment to conduct and govern science. Still others see citizen science as including elements of civic education and expanding the public understanding of science (Eitzel et al., 2017). We do not attempt to define the term in a way that excludes projects; rather, we seek to understand the different projects to which the terms can apply and link those differences to different, and similar, opportunities for science learning.

Thinking about the way in which citizen science projects are constructed, the activities of the participants, and their different levels of engagement all help understand the learning that occurs in citizen science and how to design to influence learning. In the following section, the committee attempts to illuminate the complex landscape of citizen science activities by describing how projects may be similar or different across a range of axes. In describing this space, the committee found it most helpful to think in terms of the specific activities that are carried out by participants, how often those activities are carried out, and how those activities are supported. These activities in turn depend on the project's stated goal or desired outcome, and by the degree of public participation or project control by nonscientists.

## PROJECT SIMILARITIES AND VARIATIONS

For the purposes of analyzing learning, we focused on elements and attributes of citizen science that speak to advancing the educational, scientific, and community-action oriented goals of these activities. We divided these elements and attributes into two categories—those that were common across citizen science projects and those that varied among citizen science projects. Here, projects are our unit of analysis and are often identified by a specific name, a framing scientific question, a pool of participants, and multiple activities in which those participants engage. Broad similarities across projects seem to hint at necessary prerequisites for a project to be considered citizen science, and these prerequisites were validated against available research describing citizen science, including the definitions summarized above. In surveying research and projects, we also identified tensions or continua, which span the space that is collectively citizen science. All citizen science projects possess the common traits, but no single project can encompass all the tensions or exemplify the whole continuum. Like traditional science, citizen science is an inherently social phenomenon, with many actors, roles, and interactions, all of which bear on how each of these traits play out in project implementation.

### Common Traits of Citizen Science Projects

In the following section, we describe several of the traits the committee identified as largely common across citizen science projects. Again, it is important to note that the committee does not consider these traits to be inclusion or exclusion critieria; a project need not possess all these traits to "count" as citizen science. Rather, the committee describes these traits in order to help readers develop a general sense of commonalities across citizen science projects.

## Citizen Science Projects Actively Engage Participants

Active engagement refers to the personal effort from the participant required to either physically and/or intellectually take part in the science. This can include a myriad of activities, including defining the problem, issue, or question; developing hypothesis; designing the study or protocol; receiving training; collecting data or samples; advising on analysis; doing data analysis and interpreting results; drawing conclusions and disseminating results/conclusions; asking new questions and taking action. Passive activities such as allowing a software program to use one's personal computer for automated analysis (e.g., SETI at home, Anderson et al., 2002) or wearing sensors that automatically collect information about personal (Milenković, Otto, and Jovanov, 2006) or environmental health (Piedrahita et al., 2014) may be useful contributions to ongoing scientific endeavors, but the committee suggests that participating in citizen science involves active engagement and thus the possibility of learning through action. The committee also opted not to count projects where the participants are subjects of the research, even if they were contributing data (Reade et al., 2017).

## Citizen Science Projects Engage Participants with Data

Projects collect data in myriad forms and, in turn, may provide access to these data to support science learning opportunities and activities. These activities may include collecting and submitting data, formulating hypotheses based on data, asking and answering questions with data, data interpretation and analysis, and using data as evidence in decision making or to back a scientific claim. Projects where participants are solely engaged in science communication or science policy but do not have a direct connection to the data generation or analysis and application do not fall under our description of citizen science.

## Citizen Science Projects Use a Systematic Approach to Producing Reliable Knowledge

Citizen science projects meet widely recognized standards of scientific integrity and follow practices common in science. For example, hypotheses and interpretations are rigorously weighed against available evidence—data are not changed, ignored, or selectively subsampled to prove a certain idea. It is important to note that these values are not exclusive to science, which means a project could be considered citizen science even if the values are anchored in traditions, cultures, and epistemologies that are not part of what is sometimes referred to as Western[1] science.

## Participants in Citizen Science Projects Are Primarily Not Project-Relevant Scientists

Participants may range from children to adults. Many will not have degrees in science or extensive formal training in the content and skills of the project they elect to join; although many participants may have some scientific training or a desire for such training. Depending on the project, some participants may be classified as hobbyists (Jones et al., 2017), enthusiasts (Boakes et al., 2016), or amateurs with a high degree of expertise (Cooper and Smith, 2010). While professional scientists are typically involved in citizen science as project organizers, they may also be participants. Professional scientists involved as participants may be working outside their professional role or field of study and may be motivated by personal concerns rather than career interests.

## Citizen Science Projects Help Advance Science

Here, advancing science is broadly defined. Citizen science may lead to novel discoveries. However, just as with science conducted by professional scientists, advances can include documenting known phenomenon within a novel context, replicating findings, or using science to create a local impact. This means that citizen science projects are not designed solely to educate the participants about known scientific knowledge. Neither is the purpose of these projects solely to transform nonscientists into scientists, such as is the case for many internship programs. Citizen science projects include multiple shared goals between the organizers and the participants and advancing science may be only one of those goals.

## Participants in Citizen Science Can Benefit from Participation

Often, participants choose to become involved with a project because it provides tangible or intangible benefits aligning with their values and

---

[1]In the same way committee members are ambivalent about the term citizen science but used it because of its ubiquity, we are using Western science but noting that this term fails to acknowledge or make room for past and future contributions to science from Eastern, Islamic, and indigenous communities, among others.

motivations.[2] The project could simply be a venue to do something they thoroughly enjoy (e.g., "hobbyists"). The project may be personally meaningful in ways that lend intrinsic purpose to their effort. The project results could be useful to them, for example, satisfying intellectual curiosity or providing information that guides other activities and practices in their lives. The project may serve as a conduit to scientific data or information that can benefit a community or larger group more broadly. An example of this larger group value would be environmental monitoring that could impact environmental management and improve environmental conditions in the local area, for example, the Alliance for Aquatic Resource Monitoring ([ALLARM], 2018), or a project that allows people to share health information to improve their health outcomes (Wicks et al., 2010).

### Citizen Science Projects Communicate Results

To support both scientific and participant benefits, an important feature of citizen science projects is that the results are communicated. Participants are more likely to persist in participating if they are aware of how the results of their work are being used (Eveleigh et al., 2014). Citizen science projects can often hold relevance for communities, policies, and scientific advancement. The potential utility of the information learned from the project is a motivation for communicating it to community members, managers, policy makers, scientists, and other interested parties. It is worth noting that decisions about how project data are handled (i.e., the extent to which it is open and accessible to the public or blocked from public use) may inform how project results are communicated.

### Summary

The committee has attempted to describe above several of the common traits of citizen science. While a project does not need to possess all these traits in order to be considered citizen science (although many do), the committee noted these general trends across projects. In summary, citizen science projects tend to actively engage participants, engage participants with data, use a systematic approach to producing reliable knowledge, engage participants that are primarily not project-relevant scientists, help advance science, offer some kind of benefit to participants, and communicate results.

---

[2]In some cases, especially for youth, participants might join a citizen project because it is part of a formal or informal educational experience (e.g., Girl Scouts). The committee recognizes that this kind of participation can provide valuable contributions to citizen science projects, regardless of whether participants have complete autonomy or agency over the nature of their participation. We discuss the role of choice in participation later in this chapter in our section on Free-Choice, Voluntary, and Compensated Participation.

## VARIATION IN CITIZEN SCIENCE PROJECTS

Though citizen science projects largely possess the common traits listed above, there is also considerable variation across projects. The committee delineated a number of axes across which citizen science might vary. In this section, we discuss several types of variation that we encountered in citizen science projects. In Chapter 6 of this report, we discuss the ways that these variations can influence project design and learning outcomes.

### Duration of Participation

Some projects are designed to be a one-time only activity such as BioBlitzes (National Geographic Society, 2018), while others like monitoring streams (e.g., ALLARM, 2018; Dickinson et al., 2012; Wilderman, 2007) or weather (e.g., CoCoRHaS, Community Collaborative Rain, Hail, and Snow Network, 2018; Reges et al., 2016) request that participants engage multiple times over an extended period of time. Because of the regular meeting structure of formal educational contexts such as science classes, citizen science activities that can be conducted within these spaces may provide even more opportunities for repeated, sustained engagement with learners. Many citizen science projects effectively support a mix of one-time and repeated participation, as many participants drop out after a short time (Sauerman and Franzoni, 2015). This difference in time commitment can impact what participants learn and projects designed for one-time engagement are less likely to include extensive and in-depth training.

For this reason, it is worthwhile to consider the frequency or intensity of engagement in the project. Boakes and colleagues (2016, p. 2) use the terms "dabblers," "steady," and "enthusiasts" to categorize the likelihood that a participant will return more than once to a project. Many studies of participant involvement have found the majority of individuals spend little time—down to a single data collection session—involved in a given citizen science project. Sauerman and Franzoni (2015) analyzed the seven "most-played" Zooniverse projects and found that 90 percent of the players within each project contributed less than 20 percent of the classifications, and in some projects less than 10 percent. Jones and colleagues (2017) used interviews to characterize "hobbyists" (akin to the enthusiasts of Boakes et al., 2016) within citizen science (specifically birders and amateur astronomers) as individuals who have pursued their hobby for at least a decade; began their pursuit in childhood or early adolescence often sparked by parents, grandparents, or other family members; and continue to deepen their interest through a personalized learning ecology involving TV, the Internet, reading materials, interactions with experts or mentors, and other informal science education opportunities. Other taxonomies of participants can come from the "serious leisure" literature, where hobbies can be described as social worlds with four levels of participants: strangers, tourists, regulars, and insiders (Unruh, 1980). Similarly, Edwards (2014) distinguishes among "volunteers," "citizens," and "amateurs." These studies collectively suggest that citizen science provides opportunities for a range of different kinds of participants, from social individuals to those less interested in ongoing social interaction, and from individuals who sample widely to those who dive deeply into a single pursuit.

## Modes of Communication

Although communication of project results is a common trait of citizen science (as described in the preceding section), the modes for how projects can communicate with their participants and how participants communicate with one another are quite diverse, including but not limited to Web-based, social media, in-person, telephone, and print. Within each of these modes, the topics of communication with and among participants also vary, including recruiting, training, testing, project data and results, calls to action, and social interaction. With respect to participant training, the mode of communication may impact learning and/or engagement. For instance, Gallo and Waitt (2011) found that of the total pool of 338 participants recruited to a hands-on invasive species project (Invaders of Texas), 43 percent of those attending a training workshop went on to submit observations whereas only 9 percent of participants trained online followed through to begin observations. Opportunities for in-person communication are especially high for projects that are conducted in formal education settings, where regular attendance is the norm.

Finally, modes of project communication with participants can include written information, graphic displays of information or visualization, and audio or audio-visual presentation. Kermish-Allen (2017) suggested that fewer, and simpler, modes of communication are best for reliably conveying information to participants in an online project. However, a single mode of communication will be limiting when not all participants have equal access (e.g., Internet-based communications in locations where participants do not have easy, free, or reliable access to the Internet, social media platforms of which not all members are a participant, or in-person meetings where the participants are geographically dispersed or transportation is not universally accessible) and/or where different channels are used to convey different messages/information (Parrish et al., 2017). Multiple types of visual communication can be tuned to specific content and skills learning needs within the participant community (Snyder, 2017).

## Online, In-Person, and Hybrid Modes of Participation

An online project refers to one in which all aspects of the project occur virtually (e.g., projects in the Zooniverse, Masters et al., 2016). These projects can offer participants unique opportunities to investigate natural systems and phenomena that would typically be inaccessible to them, from the charismatic megafauna of East Africa (Wildcam Gorongosa, 2018) to the planets and solar systems beyond our own (Sungrazer, 2018) to the inner workings of cells and proteins (Foldit, 2018). In-person citizen science projects refer to those in which all participant-involved activities (usually training and data collection) are done physically rather than virtually. A hybrid program can mix elements from either. For example, training could be online for an in-person water monitoring project, where the samples are mailed to a lab for analysis (e.g., Global Microplastics Initiative, 2018), or training could be in person for a coastal monitoring project, in which data are later uploaded to an online database (e.g., COASST; Haywood, Parrish, and Dolliver, 2016). This variance in project type has implications for accessibility of the project to different groups of participants. Projects that have an outdoor component, for example, need to provide different things to be accessible to people with physical disabilities than do projects in online environments. Both projects, however, will benefit from improving all learners' ability to participate.

## Individual to Community-Scale Activities

Some activities may be conducted by a single person, while others require pairs, a small group, or an entire community. The level of social interaction can influence whether someone chooses to participate. Jones and colleagues (2017) reported that birders most often listed "environmental awareness" and the "opportunity to exercise" as their primary reasons for continuing to bird (~62% of the interview population), over "opportunities to socialize" (45% of the interviewees). By contrast, the Hudson River Estuary Program—a citizen science project that engages people in counting and releasing American eels along tributaries of the Hudson River—requires at least two people to monitor together and participants report that the social interactions are one of the most enjoyable aspects of the project as well as a great source of learning (Phillips, 2017).

Some projects are built around the participation of a large group of people. For social and environmental justice projects, a community focus is often paramount. For instance, the West Oakland Environmental Indicators Project—a community action program centered on issues of local air quality—explicitly focuses on bringing together community members to document and work toward eliminating toxic sources in their neighborhood (Environmental Protection Agency, 2018). Social interaction can also contribute to growing community beyond the citizen science project itself. Haywood, Parrish, and Dolliver (2016) reported that 18 percent of 80 interviewees in COASST—a beached bird monitoring project in the Pacific Northwest—called out the ability to come together as a community as valuable: "One of the things that has really been a benefit for us is the ability to get together and have these kinds of conversations and have this community that has grown out of it."

## Role of Location

Centralized projects operate in a specific location, such as a park, museum, zoo/aquarium, or other informal learning center, all of which allow dozens to thousands of participants to access science activities that are connected to the context in which they occur (e.g., FrogWatch USA [Association of Zoos & Aquariums, 2018]). Citizen science projects centered in a specific geographic or ethnographic community may encourage learning about particular interactions between science and society within that context. As a result, participants in these projects may take political or advocacy actions based on the science they learned through participation (Chari et al., 2017).

Decentralized citizen science activities are conducted over a wide geographic range, which may be habitat based, as in the coral reef fish project at the Reef Environmental Education Foundation (2018), more broadly taxon based as in the birding project eBird (Sullivan et al., 2009), or even process based as in the natural event timing project at the National Phenology Network (2018).

## Free-Choice, Voluntary, and Compensated Participation

Free choice occurs when participants actively and freely choose the what, where, when, and with whom of their participation. Free-choice learning (Falk, Storksdieck, and Dierking, 2007) is a concept linked to citizen science as part of informal science education, or science learning outside of the classroom. Citizen science as truly free-choice learning implies that all individuals can elect to join, stay, or leave a project. In reality, a range of challenges and barriers restrict choice. Joining requires awareness: Individuals must know about an opportunity to take advantage of it. Some projects may intentionally exclude individuals, for example not allowing the participation of minors (e.g., Patients Like Me, 2018); or unintentionally exclude individuals, for instance as a function of disability, language, or economic hardship (Conrad and Hilchey, 2011). The structure of a project or the training necessary to participate in the project may not be designed to be culturally responsive, and its leadership may not be culturally competent (Ladson-Billings, 1995). Some participants may be closely supervised or directed by someone else, as in students required to participate in a citizen science project as part of their class activities and for which they receive a grade. Another aspect of free choice is informed choice, for instance an activity that participants believe is purely educational and may be unaware that data are also being gathered on them (e.g., Project Implicit [Xu, Nosek, and Greenwald, 2014] or Perfect Pitch Test [Wiggins and Crowston, 2011]).

Most citizen participants are involved as volunteers. However, in some citizen science programs, participants may be compensated, either because the activity is woven into their job, or in recognition of their specialized expertise, as in traditional ecological knowledge. Finally, some individuals pay to participate in science projects, as in the small fee for Project FeederWatch or other eco-tourist and conservation tourism activities such as EarthWatch (Chandler, 2017; Halpenny and Caissie, 2003).

### Citizen Science vs. Using Citizen Science Practices and Activities

The practices that are common to citizen science such as creating data, using data, and displaying/analyzing data can also be used outside of citizen science. For example, an educator may teach his or her students to use a citizen science protocol to analyze water quality in a local stream, which presents a variety of opportunities for different kinds of learning but is not necessarily citizen science in itself. However, many classes take their participation to the next level by making contributions to citizen science projects when they not only collect data according to a prescribed protocol but also go on to share their data with a common project database. The use of these activities, whether fully participating in the common feature of contributing knowledge to a larger project or not, represents one way that the practices of citizen science can influence science education, so it is one of the ways the committee investigated learning from citizen science in this report.

Another mode of citizen science supports participants to act as apprentice scientists, with a goal of developing scientific skills and practices through participation in the overall activities of science, For example, Kids Survey Network at TERC (see https://www.terc.edu/display/Projects/Kids%27+Survey+Network [May 2018]) created a set of activities for youth in after school programs to ask and answer questions in social science by creating and taking surveys from each other (Kids Survey Network, 2018). The project provided opportunities to learn some of the activities of scientific inquiry, but with considerable support, and without any assumption that the results would be publishable. Again, the committee would not call this particular example citizen science, because the students did not contribute to a larger investigation, but we see the potential for similar apprentice models to be used in the context of citizen science (e.g., Freitag, Meyer, and Whiteman, 2016).

## Longitudinal Monitoring to Experimental Science

Many citizen science projects involve collecting measurements to monitor the state of something, as in many environmental quality projects. At the local level, monitoring projects may address specific environmental concerns, particularly where the issue is one of safety (i.e., environmental justice). At larger geographic scales, monitoring projects can be used to document patterns, as in the distribution and abundance of birds globally (eBird; Sullivan et al., 2009). Other projects are specifically designed to answer a particular question, and may involve an experimental design, even if the individual participant may be unaware of all aspects of the experimental work. These projects may be bounded in time, that is, they end when the question has been answered (Oliveira, Jun, and Reinecke, 2017).

## Community-Based Decision Making vs. Citizen Science

In terms of how projects are designed and resulting decisions are made, citizen science projects may be led by scientists or may be led primarily by citizens. The citizen science community seems to agree that citizen science includes community-based and community-driven projects that bring professional scientists into the project either to conduct or facilitate particular tasks (e.g., analysis advice within collaborative monitoring with local data interpretation, see Danielsen et al., 2009). There is less agreement that projects that engage in the discourse about or use of science findings in a decision-making capacity without engaging directly in science practices, such as data collection, knowledge creation, or priority setting are also citizen science. For the purposes of the report, the committee is not considering projects that focus entirely on science communication or science-based decision making, as citizen science, and so we did not investigate science learning in those projects.

## Summary

The preceding section describes variation across types of citizen science projects, all of which must be considered when project designers are making choices about how to set up and implement their projects. Later in this report, we will describe how decisions about these variations matter for what kinds of learning are possible through participation in citizen science, and how project designers might leverage these decisions to support specific learning outcomes.

## WHO IS INVOLVED AND HOW ARE THEY INVOLVED?

A second factor that influences whether and how learning might occur is the role of the participant, and how that role is perceived by other participants. In the section below, we discuss different types of roles often embodied by project participants, and some implications for how participating in that role could lead to science learning. We conclude with investigation into who participates in citizen science and discuss how the demography of participation can inform our understanding of how to support science learning through project participation.

### Variations in Types of Participation

The committee observed several different ways that an individual might enter into participation in citizen science. Given the variations in project type described above, participants must make a number of decisions about what kind of citizen science experience is important for them. In this section, we highlight a few different kinds of participations and offer insight into what that might imply about participants' experiences and opportunities for learning.

### Participants as Observer and Data Provider

Bonney and colleagues (2009a) identify one of the most common paradigms of participation: that of observer and data gatherer. Their examples, drawn from the field of ornithology, include highly structured, pre-digital projects such as the Audubon Christmas Bird Count, as well as more current work in which amateur birders enter their birding data collected via a variety of individualized methods online (e.g., eBird).

Data collection can involve minimal expertise on the part of participants or demand specialized training and the development of specific skills in order to acquire usable scientific data (Dickinson, Zuckerberg, and Bonter, 2010). Virtual observations are also possible, as in the annotation of digital files (still images, videos, and audio files). For example, the Galaxy Zoo project was able to categorize the morphology of nearly 1 million galaxies in the Sloan Digital Sky Survey with the assistance of online volunteers (Lintott et al., 2010).

Even within the participant as data collector, there is a huge range of ways to participate. Pocock and colleagues (2017) scored 509 environmental or ecological citizen science projects on 32 attributes and found a broad distribution of methodological approaches to data collection. They argued that there is a continuum from projects requiring regular monitoring and featuring elaborate approaches to data collection requiring written protocols and specialized equipment, to "mass participation" projects allowing one-off participation and featuring relatively simple tasks.

## Participants as Competitor or Gamer

In some scientific areas, gamification (Deterding et al., 2011) can allow people to participate in science as recreation or competition. For example, Foldit is an online game in which players construct portions of large, complex proteins of unknown structure according to a set of rules and with the goal of finding the lowest energy configuration (Khatib et al., 2011). In Phylo, participants align gene sequences with no knowledge of the underlying scientific questions and answers (Kawrykow et al., 2012). Here the main objective is often to solve a problem or challenge, rather than explicit science learning.

## Participants as Stakeholder/Partner

Some citizen science projects involve partnerships between the science community and nonscientists whose goals either instrumentally involve science or overlap with those of scientists. For example, the Nature's Notebook project, run by the USA National Phenology Network, engages groups who have instrumental needs for phenology data or findings. They partner with amateur scientists, but also with professional natural resource managers who might need phenology data for their environmental management, or hiking clubs such as the Appalachian Mountain Club whose members might need phenology data to help schedule long-distance treks (Schwartz, Betancourt, and Weltzin, 2012).

## Participants as Cultural Guides

Some projects engage participants not only as researchers or drivers of inquiry, but also as guides to a culture that is relevant to the project. One example is described by Charitonos and Kukulska-Hulme (2017) in which heritage learners in a language school conducted projects to study language and cultural heritage. The research model was one of action research, in which the learners were simultaneously studying and participating in the cultures and practices being examined. In these cases, participants have a critical role in not only conducting the research, but also interpreting it, and in bringing meaning-making (both personal and collective) to the work. As crisply pointed out by Medin and Bang (2014, p. 34), "If participation in cultural practices is central to our development as humans, then these practices will influence how we learn and practice science." They argue for the importance of engaging diverse participants in science not only out of some sense of fairness or equity but also because the diversity of cultural perspectives contributes to project outcomes.

## Summary

As with variations in types of projects, there are noteworthy distinctions in how participants can engage in citizen science activities. Each of these variations impact what participants may be likely to learn through participation in citizen science. In subsequent chapters, we will discuss how different kinds of participation may be leveraged in pursuit of specific learning outcomes.

## CONSIDERING THE DEMOGRAPHICS OF CITIZEN SCIENCE

In order to fully understand how citizen science can support science learning, it is essential to consider who has access to citizen science, especially in terms of groups that have been historically underrepresented in science. For this reason, the committee devoted considerable time and energy, including a review of participation literature (see Appendix A), to understanding who participates in citizen science. As Appendix A details, existing data are relatively limited, and the data we have undercount youth-focused projects and projects designed to advance community goals; the available data suggest that members of communities historically underrepresented in science, people with less formal education, and people of color are underrepresented in citizen science as well. Some projects also have an underrepresentation of women.

Despite the limited data described in Appendix A, the committee believes that it is possible to make some narrow observations about the demographics of citizen science, with the appropriate caveats. First, of course, it is important to note that more comprehensive demographic data would assist in a more comprehensive understanding of participation if more programs knew and shared who their participants were, even in an aggregate way, researchers could investigate trends in participation for a more diverse group of participants.

Second, the field of citizen science is in danger of reproducing the inequities, biases, and underrepresentation that has plagued science. Our interpretation of available evidence suggests that the majority of projects that are being studied/profiled in the peer-reviewed scholarly literature have a participant base that is well-educated, middle to upper class, older in age, and almost entirely white.

It is worth recalling the danger of underparticipation in science. A science community that is less diverse than society is less likely to engage in research relevant to the full diversity of society and less likely to do work reflecting the priorities of those groups underrepresented, or unrepresented, in the current scientific mainstream (Hurtado, Carter, and Kardea, 1998). Less diverse science settings marginalize cultural knowledge from members of underrepresented groups (Calabrese Barton, 2012) and privilege cultural knowledge and practices from dominant groups. Indeed, some indigenous people argue that science has been used to oppress their communities (Deloria and Wildcat, 2001). The committee's investigations suggest that these trends, all too common in professional science and formal and informal science education, reach into citizen science.

Moreover, there is *no* research to suggest that some groups of people are inherently less able to participate in citizen science projects because of some perceived deficit—cultural, social, educational, linguistic, or otherwise. Rather, the committee emphasizes that *all* participants need some encouragement or scaffolding to participate in citizen science, regardless of demography or prior experience. On the other hand, conducting citizen science in partnership with underrepresented groups, welcomed both as experts in their own culturally inflected perspectives and equal participants with something to contribute to scientific process, *does* allow a diversity of epistemologies, interpretations, and questions. For example, work by Bang and Medin (2010) illustrates how European-American and Native American learners interpret the relationship between self and nature differently, and how incorporating these differences can enhance ecological science work for all students. More generally, there is a robust literature from community science that confirms the educational value of respectfully welcoming participants' prior knowledge and experience (Ballard, Dixon, and Harris, 2017; Calabrese Barton, 2012; Carlone et al., 2015; Mueller, 2009; Rahm, 2002) and recognizing that experience for its contributions to scientific understanding.

Consideration of these questions—what kinds of scaffolding are necessary and in what context—all revolve around the fundamental question of who is designing citizen science experiences for whom. As we will discuss in Chapter 7, designing in ways that remove barriers connected to assumptions about physical ability, economic resources, linguistic ability, and neurodiversity is design that respects every individual's right to choose to engage in citizen science or science.

## Summary

The preceding sections have detailed the substantial differences and similarities across the range of citizen science projects and types of participation in citizen science. These descriptions are intended to demonstrate the complex landscape of citizen science, and set the stage for our later discussions of how project designers can make particular choices in order to achieve specific science learning outcomes.

Our analysis of the characteristics of citizen science mostly focuses on who participates and how participation takes place, and not on the kind of scientific questions that are asked in the projects. This is reflective of the state of research and practice in the field of citizen science: We know of no analysis that either looked at learning outcome explicitly in terms of the nature of the scientific question asked, nor have we seen a typology of learning in citizen science based on scientific question. Yet, as we will see in subsequent chapters on learning outcomes and design, there is strong evidence that the nature of scientific learning is influenced by the kind of question or investigation asked, and the questions asked are often part of the explicit or implicit design process. More research in this arena could shed light on a potential relationship between the kind of scientific question asked and the nature of participation and activity.

## REFERENCES

Alliance for Aquatic Resource Monitoring. (2018). *Alliance for Aquatic Resource Monitoring.* Available: https://www.dickinson.edu/allarm [May 2018].

Anderson, D.P., Cobb, J., Korpela, E., Lebofsky, M., and Werthimer, D. (2002). SETI@ home: An experiment in public-resource computing. *Communications of the ACM, 45*(11), 56-61.

Arnstein, S.R. (1969). A ladder of citizen participation. *Journal of the American Institute of Planners, 35*(4), 216-224. doi:10.1080/01944366908977225.

Association of Zoos & Aquariums. (2018). *FrogWatch USA.* Available: https://www.aza.org/frogwatch [December 2018].

Ballard, H.L., Dixon, C.G.H., and Harris, E.M. (2017). Youth-focused citizen science: Examining the role of environmental science learning and agency for conservation. *Biological Conservation, 208*, 65-75.

Bang, M., and Medin, D. (2010). Cultural processes in science education: Supporting the navigation of multiple epistemologies. *Science Education, 94*(6), 1008-1026.

Boakes, E.H., Gliozzo, G., Seymour, V., Harvey, M., Smith, C., Roy, D.B., and Haklay, M. (2016). Patterns of contribution to citizen science biodiversity projects increase understanding of volunteers' recording behaviour. *Scientific Reports, 6*, 33051. doi:10.1038/srep33051.

Bonney, R. (1996). Citizen science: A lab tradition. *Living Bird, 15*(4), 7-15.

Bonney, R., Ballard, H., Jordan, R., McCallie, E., Phillips, T., Shirk, J., and Wilderman, C.C. (2009a). *Public Participation in Scientific Research: Defining the Field and Assessing Its Potential for Informal Science Education.* A CAISE Inquiry Group Report. Washington DC: Center for Advancement of Informal Science Education.

Bonney, R., Cooper, C.B., Dickinson, J., Kelling, S., Phillips, T., Rosenberg, K.V., and Shirk, J. (2009b). Citizen science: A developing tool for expanding science knowledge and scientific literacy. *BioScience, 59*(11), 977-984. doi: 10.1525/bio.2009.59.11.9.

Bowser, A., Wiggins, A., Shanley, L., Preece, J., and Henderson, S. (2014). Sharing data while protecting privacy in citizen science. *Interactions, 21*(1), 70-73.

Broeder, L., Devilee, J., Van Oers, H., Schuit, J., and Wagemakers, A. (2016). Citizen science for public health. *Health Promotion International, 33*(3), 505-514. https://doi.org/10.1093/heapro/daw086 [May 2018].

Burgess H., DeBey L.B., Froehlich H., Schmidt, N., Theobald, E.J., Ettinger A.K., Hille Ris Lambers J., Tewksbury J., and Parrish, J.K. 2017. The science of citizen science: Exploring barriers to use as a primary research tool. *Biological Conservation, 208*, 113-120.

Cajete, G. (2000). Indigenous knowledge: The Pueblo metaphor of Indigenous education. In M. Battiste (Ed.), *Reclaiming Indigenous Voice and Vision* (pp. 181-191). Vancouver: University of British Columbia Press.

Calabrese Barton, A.M. (2012). Citizen(s') science. A response to "The Future of Citizen Science." *Democracy and Education, 20*(2), 12.

Carlone, H.B., Huffling, L.D., Tomasek, T., Hegedus, T.A., Matthews, C.E., Allen, M.H., and Ash, M.C. (2015). "Unthinkable" selves: Identity boundary work in a summer field ecology enrichment program for diverse youth. *International Journal of Science Education, 37*(10), 1524-1546.

Chandler, M., Rullman, S., Cousins, J., Esmail, N., Begin, E., Venicx, G., Eisenberg, C., and Studer, M. (2017). Contributions to publications and management plans from 7 years of citizen science: Use of a novel evaluation tool on Earthwatch-supported projects. *Biological Conservation, 208*, 163-173.

Chari, R., Matthews, L., Blumenthal, M., Edelman, A., and Jones, T. (2017) *The Promise of Community Citizen Science.* Santa Monica, CA: RAND Corporation. Available: https://www.rand.org/pubs/perspectives/PE256.html [May 2018].

Charitonos, K., and Kukulska-Hulme, A. (2017). *Community-Based Interventions for Language Learning among Refugees and Migrants.* Paper from the 8th International Conference on Communities and Technologies (CandT 2017). Available: http://oro.open.ac.uk/49677/4/ACM_HCI%20Refugees_Charitonos%2BKukulska-Hulme.pdf [November 2018].

Chuine, I., Yiou, P., Viovy, N., Seguin, B., Daux, V., and Ladurie, E.L.R. (2004). Historical phenology: Grape ripening as a past climate indicator. *Nature, 432*(7015), 289.

Community Collaborative Rain, Hail, and Snow Network. (2018). Available: https://www.cocorahs.org [September 2018].

Conrad, C.C., and Hilchey, K.G. (2011). A review of citizen science and community-based environmental monitoring: Issues and opportunities. *Environmental Monitoring and Assessment* 176(1-4), 273-291.

Cooper, C.B., and Smith, J.A. (2010). Gender patterns in bird-related recreation in the USA and UK. *Ecology and Society* 15(4), 4.

Cooper, C.B., Dickinson, J., Phillips, T., and Bonney, R. (2007). Citizen science as a tool for conservation in residential ecosystems. *Ecology and Society, 12*(2), 11-22.

Danielsen, F., Burgess, N.D., Balmford, A., Donald, P.F., Funder, M., Jones, J.P.G., Alviola, P., Balete, D.S., Blomley, T., Brashares, J., Child, B., Enghoff, M., Fjelds, J., Holt, S., Hübertz, H., Jensen, A.E., Jensen, P.M., Massao, J., Mendoze, M.M., Ngaga, Y., Poulsen, M.K., Rueda, R., Sam, M., Skielboe, T., Stuart-Hill, G., Topp-Jorgensen, E., and Yonten, D. (2009). Local participation in natural resource monitoring: A characterization of approaches. *Conservation Biology, 23*(1), 31-42.

Deloria, V., Jr., and Wildcat, D.R. (2001). *Power and Place: Indian Education in America.* Golden, CO: Fulcrum.

Deterding, S., Dixon, D., Khaled, R., and Nacke, L. (2011). From game design elements to gamefulness: Defining gamification. In *Proceedings of the 15th International Academic MindTrek Conference: Envisioning Future Media Environments* (pp. 9-15). New York: Association for Computing Machinery.

Dickinson, J.L., Zuckerberg, B., and Bonter, D.N. (2010). Citizen science as an ecological research tool: Challenges and benefits. *Annual Review of Ecology, Evolution, and Systematics*, 41, 149-172.

Dickinson, J.L., Shirk, J., Bonter, D., Bonney, R., Crain, R.L., Martin, J., Phillips, T., and Purcell, K. (2012). The current state of citizen science as a tool for ecological research and public engagement. *Frontiers in Ecology and the Environment*, 10(6), 291-297.

Edwards, R. (2014). The "citizens" in citizen science projects: Educational and conceptual issues. *International Journal of Science Education, Part B*, 4(4), 376-391. doi:10.1080/21548455.2014.953228.

Eitzel, M.V., Cappadonna, J.L., Santos-Lang, C., Duerr, R.E., Virapongse, A., West, S.E., Kyba, C.C. M., Bowser, A., Cooper, C.B., Sforzi, A., Metcalfe, A.N., Harris, E.S., Thiel, M., Haklay, M., Ponciano, L. Roche, J., Ceccaroni, L., Shilling, F.M., Dörler, D., Heigl, F., Kiessling, T., Davis, B.Y., and Jiang, Q. (2017). Citizen science terminology matters: Exploring key terms. *Citizen Science: Theory and Practice*, 2(1).

Environmental Protection Agency (2018). Available: https://www.epa.gov/c-ferst/california-west-oakland-environmental-indicators-project-former-epa-care-project [May 2018].

Eveleigh, A., Jennett, C., Blandford, A., Brohan, P., and Cox, A.L. (2014). Designing for dabblers and deterring drop-outs in citizen science. In *Proceedings of the SIGCHI Conference on Human Factors in Computing Systems* (pp. 2985-2994). New York: Association for Computing Machinery.

Falk, J.H., Storksdieck, M., and Dierking, L.D. (2007). Investigating public science interest and understanding: Evidence for the importance of free-choice learning. *Public Understanding of Science*, 16(4), 455-469.

Foldit. (2018). Available: http://dx.doi.org/10.5334/cstp.6https://fold.it/portal [September 2018].

Freitag, A., Meyer, R., and Whiteman, L. (2016). Strategies employed by citizen science programs to increase the credibility of their data. *Citizen Science: Theory and Practice*, 1(1) 2. doi: http://doi.org/10.5334/cstp.6.

Gallo, T., and Waitt, D. (2011). Creating a successful citizen science model to detect and report invasive species. *BioScience* 61(6), 459-465.

Global Microplastics Initiative. (2018). Available: http://www.adventurescientists.org/microplastics.html [May 2018].

Haklay, M. (2013). Citizen science and volunteer geographic information: Overview and typology of participation. In D.Z. Sui, S. Elwood, and M.F. Goodchild (Eds.), *Crowdsourcing Geographic Knowledge: Volunteered Geographic Information (VGI) in Theory and Practice* (pp. 105-122). Berlin: Springer.

Halpenny, E.A., and Caissie, L.T. (2003). Volunteering on nature conservation projects: Volunteer experience, attitudes and values. *Tourism Recreation Research*, 28(3), 25-33.

Haring M.J. (1999). The case for a conceptual base for minority mentoring programs. *Peabody Journal of Education*, 74, 5-14. doi: 10.1207/s15327930pje7402_2.

Haywood, B.K., Parrish, J.K., and Dolliver, J. (2016). Place-based and data-rich citizen science as a precursor for conservation action. *Conservation Biology*, 30(3), 476-486.

Hopkins, A.D. (1918). *Periodical Events and Natural Law as Guides to Agricultural Research and Practice* (No. 9). Washington, DC: U.S. Government Printing Office.

Hurtado, S., Carter, D.F., and Kardia, D. (1998). The climate for diversity: Key issues for institutional self-study. *New Directions for Institutional Research*, 98, 53-63.

Irwin, A. (1995). *Citizen Science: A Study of People, Expertise, and Sustainable Development*. New York: Routledge.

Jardine, N., Secord, J.A., and Spary, E.C. (1996). *Cultures of Natural History*. Cambridge, England: Cambridge University Press.

Jones, M.G., Corin, E.N., Andre, T., Childers, G.M., and Stevens, V. (2017). Factors contributing to lifelong science learning: Amateur astronomers and birders. *Journal of Research in Science Teaching, 54*(3), 412-433.

Kawrykow, A., Roumanis, G., Kam, A., Kwak, D., Leung, C., Wu, C., Zarour, E., Phylo players, Sarmenta, L., Blanchette, M., and Waldispühl, J. (2012). Phylo: A citizen science approach for improving multiple sequence alignment. *PloS ONE, 7*(3), e31362.

Kermish-Allen, R. (2017). Design principles of online learning communities in citizen science. *Maine Policy Review, 26*(2), 80-85, Available: https://digitalcommons.library.umaine.edu/mpr/vol26/iss2/16 [May 2018].

Khatib, F., Cooper, S., Tyka, M. D., Xu, K., Makedon, I., Popović, Z., Baker, D. and Foldit Players (2011). Algorithm discovery by protein folding game players. *Proceedings of the National Academy of Sciences of the United States of America, 108*(47), 18949-18953.

Kids Survey Network. (2018). Available: https://www.terc.edu/display/Projects/Kids%27+Survey+Network [May 2018].

Ladson-Billings, G. (1995). Toward a theory of culturally relevant pedagogy. *American Educational Research Journal, 32*(3), 465-491.

Lintott, C., Schawinski, K., Bamford, S., Slosar, A., Land, K., Thomas, D., Edmondson, E., Masters, K., Nichol, R.C., Raddick, M.J., Szalay, A., Andreescu, D., Murray, P., and Vandenberg, J. (2010). Galaxy Zoo 1: Data release of morphological classifications for nearly 900,000 galaxies. *Monthly Notices of the Royal Astronomical Society, 410*(1), 166-178.

Masters, K.L., Oh, E.Y., Cox, J., Simmons, B., Lintott, C., Graham, G., Greenhil, A., and Holmes, K. (2016). Science learning via participation in online citizen science. *Journal of Science Communication, Special Issue: Citizen Science, Part II, (15)*03. doi: https://doi.org/10.22323/2.15030207.

Medin, D.L., and Bang, M. (2014). *Who's Asking?: Native Science, Western Science, and Science Education.* Cambridge, MA: MIT Press.

Meymaris, K., Henderson, S., Alaback, P., and Havens, K. (2008, December). *Project Budburst: Citizen Science for All Seasons.* In the abstracts for the American Geophysical Union, Fall Meeting.

Milenković, A., Otto, C., and Jovanov, E. (2006). Wireless sensor networks for personal health monitoring: Issues and an implementation. *Computer Communications, 29*(13-14), 2521-2533.

Miller-Rushing, A., Primack, R., and Bonney, R. (2012). The history of public participation in ecological research. *Frontiers in Ecology and the Environment, 10*(6), 285-290.

Mueller, M.P. (2009). Educational reflections on the "ecological crisis": Ecojustice, environmentalism, and sustainability. *Science and Education, 18*(8), 1031-1056.

National Geographic Society. (2018). *BioBlitz.* Available: https://www.nationalgeographic.org/projects/bioblitz/ [November 2018].

National Phenology Network. (2018). Available: https://www.usanpn.org/ [September 2018].

Oliveira, N., Jun, E., and Reinecke, K. (2017) Citizen science opportunities in volunteer-based online experiments. In *Proceedings of the 2017 CHI Conference on Human Factors in Computing Systems* (pp. 6800-6812). New York: Association for Computing Machinery.

Parrish, J.K., Litle, K., Dolliver, J., Hass, T., Burgess, H., Frost, E., Wright, C. and Jones, T. (2017). Defining the baseline and tracking change in seabird populations: The Coastal Observation and Seabird Survey Team (COASST). In J.A. Cigliano and H.L. Ballard (Eds.), *Citizen Science for Coastal and Marine Conservation* (pp. 37-56). New York: Routledge.

Patients Like Me. (2018). Available: https://www.patientslikeme.com [May 2018].

Pfund, C., Maidl Pribbenow, C., Branchaw, J., Miller Lauffer, S., and Handelsman, J. (2006). Professional skills: The merits of training mentors. *Science, 311*(5760), 473-474.

Phillips, T.B. 2017. *Engagement and Learning in Environmentally Based Citizen Science: A Mixed-Methods Comparative Case Study.* (Doctoral dissertation.) Cornell University, Ithaca, NY.

Piedrahita, R., Xiang, Y., Masson, N., Ortega, J., Collier, A., Jiang, Y., Li, K., Dick, R.P., Lv, Q, Hannigan, M., and Shang, L. (2014). The next generation of low-cost personal air quality sensors for quantitative exposure monitoring. *Atmospheric Measurement Techniques, 7*(10), 3325-3336.

Pocock, M.J.O., Tweddle, J.C., Savage, J., Robinson, L.D., and Roy, H.E. (2017). The diversity and evolution of ecological and environmental citizen science. *PLoS One, 12*(4), e0172579.

Primack, R.B., Higuchi, H., and Miller-Rushing, A.J. (2009). The impact of climate change on cherry trees and other species in Japan. *Biological Conservation, 142*(9), 1943-1949.

Rahm, J. (2002). Emergent learning opportunities in an inner-city youth gardening program. *Journal of Research in Science Teaching: The Official Journal of the National Association for Research in Science Teaching, 39*(2), 164-184.

Reade, S., Spencer, K., Sergeant, J.C., Sperrin, M., Schultz, D.M., Ainsworth, J., Lakshminarayana, R., Hellman, B., James, B., McBeth, J., Sanders, C., and Dixon, W.G. (2017). Cloudy with a chance of pain: Engagement and subsequent attrition of daily data entry in a smartphone pilot study tracking weather, disease severity, and physical activity in patients with rheumatoid arthritis. *JMIR mHealth and uHealth, 5*(3), e37.

Reef Environmental Education Foundation. (2018). Available: https://www.reef.org [September 2018].

Reges, H.W., Doesken, N., Turner, J., Newman, N., Bergantino, A., and Schwalbe, Z. (2016). CoCoRHaS: The evolution and accomplishments of a volunteer rain gauge network. *Bulletin of the American Meteorological Society, 97*(10), 1831-1846.

Rose, D. (2000). Universal design for learning. *Journal of Special Education Technology, 15*(3), 45-49.

Russell, S.H., Hancock, M.P., and McCullough, J. (2007). Benefits of undergraduate research experiences. *Science, 316*, 548-549. doi: 10.1126/science.1140384.

Sauermann, H., and Franzoni, C. (2015). Crowd science user contribution patterns and their implications. *Proceedings of the National Academy of Sciences of the United States of America, 112*(3), 679-684.

Schwartz, M.D., Betancourt, J.L., and Weltzin, J.F. (2012). From Caprio's lilacs to the USA National Phenology Network. *Frontiers in Ecology and the Environment, 10*(6), 324-327.

Shirk, J.L., Ballard, H.L., Wilderman, C.C., Phillips, T., Wiggins, A., Jordan, R., McCallie, E., Minarchek, M., Lewenstein, B.V., Krasny, M.E., and Bonney, R. (2012). Public participation in scientific research: A framework for deliberate design. *Ecology and Society, 17*(2), 29.

Snyder, J. (2017). Vernacular visualization practices in a citizen science project. In *Proceedings of the 2017 ACM Conference on Computer Supported Cooperative Work and Social Computing* (pp. 2097-2111). New York: Association for Computing Machinery.

Sobel, D. (2004). Place-based education: Connecting classroom and community. *Nature and Listening, 4*, 1-7.

Stolle-McAllister, K. (2011). The case for summer bridge: Building social and cultural capital for talented black STEM students. *Science Educator, 20*(2), 12-22.

Sullivan, B.L., Wood, C.L., Iliff, M.J., Bonney, R.E., Fink, D., and Kelling, S. (2009). eBird: A citizen-based bird observation network in the biological sciences. *Biological Conservation, 142*(10), 2282–2292.

Sungrazer. (2018). Available: https://scistarter.com/project/529-The-Sungrazer-Project [May 2018].

Tian, H., Stige, L.C., Cazelles, B., Kausrud, K.L., Svarverud, R., Stenseth, N.C., and Zhang, Z. (2011). Reconstruction of a 1910-years-long locust series reveals consistent associations with climate fluctuations in China. *Proceedings of the National Academy of Sciences of the United States of America*, *108*(35), 14521-14526.

Tsui, L. (2007). Effective strategies to increase diversity in STEM fields: A review of the research literature. *The Journal of Negro Education*, 76(4), 555-581.

Unruh, D.R. (1980). The nature of social worlds. *Pacific Sociological Review*, 23(3), 271-296.

Vetter, J. (2011). Introduction: Lay participation in the history of scientific observation. *Science in Context*, 24(02), 127-141. doi:10.1017/S0269889711000032.

Wicks, P., Massagli, M., Frost, J., Brownstein, C., Okun, S., Vaughan, T., Bradley, R., and Heywood, J. (2010). Sharing health data for better outcomes on PatientsLikeMe. *Journal of Medical Internet Research*, 12(2), 124-135.

Wiggins, A., and Crowston, K. (2011, January). *From Conservation to Crowdsourcing: A Typology of Citizen Science*. Paper presented at the 44th Hawaii International Conference on System Sciences.

Wildcam Gorongosa. (2018). Available: https://www.wildcamgorongosa.org/#/ [May 2018].

Wilderman, C.C. (2007). *Models of Community Science: Design Lessons from the Field*. Presentation at the Citizen Science Toolkit Conference, June 20-23, Cornell Laboratory of Ornithology, Ithaca, NY. Available: http://www.birds.cornell.edu/citscitoolkit/conference/toolkitconference/proceeding-pdfs/Full%20Proceedings.pdf {December 2018}.

Xu, K., Nosek, B., and Greenwald, A. (2014). Psychology data from the Race Implicit Association Test on the Project Implicit Demo Website. *Journal of Open Psychology Data* 2(1).

Zoellick, B., Nelson, S.J., and Schauffler, M. (2012). Participatory science and education: bringing both views into focus. *Frontiers in Ecology and the Environment*, *10*(6), 310-313.

Zooniverse. (2018). Available: http://www.zooniverse.org [September 2018].

# 3

# Overview of Citizen Science as a Context for Learning

Human learning is a complex, multidimensional phenomenon. In everyday use and in professional research and educational contexts, the word "learning" is used to capture a multiplicity of processes and outcomes, and language is rich with related terms that are associated with learning: knowledge, know-how, competence, understanding, skill, expertise, and proficiency. Understanding the nature of different varieties of learning, the processes that support them, and the ways in which they are expressed requires considering factors at multiple levels and scales. Science learning inherits all of the complexity of learning, while at the same time possessing a distinctive character in some respects.

The next few chapters explore what is known about science learning and how it is possible to apply this knowledge to citizen science. This will set the stage for some design strategies that can maximize learning in citizen science and preface a research agenda that explores how to continue supporting learning in citizen science. In this chapter, we offer some preliminary insight into why citizen science is a useful place to pursue science learning. We do this by first explaining why citizen science provides a useful venue for supporting learning, and we then describe potential outcomes of science learning in the context of citizen science using a framework developed by an earlier National Research Council report (2009). We conclude with a few notes on who is learning in citizen science, and how to approach supporting learning for all learners.

## UNIQUE POSSIBILITIES FOR LEARNING
## THROUGH CITIZEN SCIENCE

Citizen science provides a rich and varied array of contexts in which to consider science learning. As shown in Chapter 2, the field of citizen science is characterized by many different participants in various roles. Those participants and stakeholders enter into their participation with wide ranging goals, motivations, backgrounds, and interests. Because citizen science projects offer participants the opportunity to play a role in a scientific investigation, they offer particular opportunities for learning science. As the committee considered the unique constellations of potentials, constraints, and challenges that citizen science offers for science learning, several distinct characteristics emerged as elements of citizen science that are especially fertile opportunities for learning. In particular, the committee considered the common traits and variations in citizen science projects and types of participation in citizen science identified in Chapter 2, with an eye toward how those similarities and differences are mobilized to support science learning. Based on these descriptions, the committee was able to identify elements of citizen science that can be leveraged to support science learning, which we cluster into the following three categories:

1. **Scientific context.** As investigations of natural phenomena, citizen science projects provide an entry point for learning about the science related to the phenomena under investigation, for learning to engage in the scientific practices involved in the investigation, and for learning about the nature of science.
2. **Nature of participation.** As detailed in Chapter 2, the committee identified a number of variations in how participants can take part in citizen science, ranging from the duration of participation to the mode of project participation (online or in person, etc.) to the kind of role a participant might assume. As participants make decisions about the nature of their participation, the kind of learning that is possible through their citizen science experience is apt to change.
3. **Project infrastructure.** Citizen science projects are supported by technological and social infrastructures. These infrastructures can be used to support learning.

In the following section, the committee describes how these elements of citizen science can be leveraged to support science learning.

## Scientific Context and Supporting Learning

As with all scientific efforts, every citizen science project exists in a scientific context, which can be defined in terms of the phenomenon under study and the reason that it is a focus of study. For example, the scientific context for the Monarch Larva Monitoring Project is "to better understand the distribution and abundance of breeding monarchs and to use that knowledge to inform and inspire monarch conservation" (Monarch Larva Monitoring Project, 2018). There are three ways that the scientific context of a citizen science project can support science learning:

1. **Authentic scientific endeavor.** By definition, citizen science projects are authentic scientific endeavors, meaning that they are ongoing investigations of a scientific phenomenon conducted for a purpose. Authenticity can serve as a motivator for participation, which provides an opportunity to learn. That citizen science is an authentic endeavor provides the additional opportunity to engage in scientific practices and to learn about the nature of science.
2. **Real-world context.** Most citizen science projects are investigations of phenomena in the natural or built environment that play out at observable scales, that is, they are investigations that play out in "real-world contexts." Taking place in a real-world context provides the opportunity to motivate learning based on relevance (Boullion and Gomez, 2001).
3. **Data-driven.** Citizen science opportunities generally engage participants in the collection or processing of data. The focus on data in citizen science projects creates the opportunity to learn about the role of data in scientific inquiry (nature of science) and the opportunity to learn to conduct data analysis (a scientific practice).

## The Nature of Participation and Supporting Learning

The participation of members of the public in a scientific investigation is the essential characteristic of citizen science. As described in Chapter 2, participation in citizen science can take many forms. In considering that variation, the committee noted three specific aspects of participation that present potential opportunities for learning.

1. **Interest- or concern-driven participation.** Participation in citizen science projects is often voluntary.[1] Research has shown that most citizen science participants are motivated by interest in the topic of the project or concern about the implications of the project (Geoghegan et al., 2016). Because interest- or concern-driven participation motivates learning about the context of the project, this interest or concern can be an opportunity for learning. The committee notes that the role of interest-driven participation is potentially complicated and/or enhanced when citizen science or practices in citizen science are used in a formal learning setting. For more on citizen science and formal learning, see Box 3-1.

2. **Social, communal activity.** Citizen science projects exist in a communal context insofar as participation is conducted in relationship to a scientific goal shared by participants and project designers. Even in projects where participants do not have direct interaction with organizers or other participants, participants are generally aware that they are participating in a project alongside others with a shared purpose. The social and communal nature of citizen science projects can be an affordance for social, communal learning.

3. **Longer-term participation.** While participation in some citizen science projects can be brief, many projects offer the opportunity for repeated activity over an extended period of time. For example, FrogWatch USA asks participants to make weekly observations of frog calls over a 6-month period, and many participants continue for multiple years (Association of Zoos & Aquariums, 2018). A longer duration of involvement creates the opportunity to develop deeper understanding and more sophisticated skills. Additionally, it creates the opportunity for learning through repetition and reinforcement. Our analysis, however, suggests that a minority of project participants engage in an extended way, which means that most people participating in citizen science cannot take advantage of learning opportunities afforded by repeated exposure.

## Project Infrastructure and Supporting Learning

What makes a citizen science project possible is its infrastructure. When committee members reviewed citizen science projects for this report,

---

[1]The committee notes that the term "voluntary," though intended to signify that participants elect to engage of their own volition, is necessarily contingent on an individual's or community's access to participate in a given project. Issues of access and how they may be mitigated through intentional project design are taken up in Chapter 7 of this report.

**BOX 3-1**
**Learning Through Citizen Science in**
**Formal Education Settings**

As the committee discusses later in this report, one of the settings in which citizen science appears to have substantial potential for learning is in formal education spaces such as K–2 science classrooms. Citizen science can be used in formal settings in all three of the ways described in Chapter 1: It can be designed specifically with particular learning outcomes and the constraints of formal settings in mind, educators may adapt existing projects to meet specific learning goals, or they may borrow practices of citizen science to support a desired learning outcome.

Formal education settings provide an environment explicitly designed for learning, but educators in formal settings must consider a few specific issues prior to making use of citizen science. First, to the extent that engaging out of one's independent interest is central to a person's citizen science experience, the degree of choice may be constrained in formal settings. Students who are compelled to participate may not reap the same benefits that accrue when participation is entirely voluntary. However, even when choice is limited, there may be considerable learning gains due to the additional support, resources, and sustained engagement that is possible in formal environments. Educators should consider the extent to which these benefits are part of their desired outcomes and calibrate accordingly.

Similarly, educators in formal settings are often pursuing specific learning outcomes. These outcomes may or may not align with the potential goals of a citizen science project. Further, to the extent that educators need to be involved in the early and iterative design of a project in order to elicit specific outcomes (see Chapter 7 of this report), it may be challenging to involve individuals in the midst of competing professional and educational obligations.

For formal education to make effective use of citizen science in supporting learning, project designers and educators must pay attention to the unique opportunities as well as constraints associated with formal settings. Later in this report, we offer thoughts on how to address these concerns.

we noted two infrastructures distinctive to citizen science that specifically support learning.

1. **Social infrastructure.** The social infrastructure includes the people who organize the project, provide direction to participants, and are available to assist them. The social infrastructure also includes the network of participants engaged with and learning from one another, either in person or virtually. The social infrastructure for a project can provide support for learning by developing educational resources or by facilitating learning directly.

2.  **Technology infrastructure.** The technology infrastructure includes the computing and communication technologies that enable participants to learn about and fulfill their roles in the project, as well as the specialized equipment that contributes to scientific investigations such as telescopes and DNA sequencing technology. The technology infrastructure can support learning by providing access to educational resources and specialized equipment, database platforms that house, maintain, and disseminate data, or by providing the communications platform that enables participants to learn from each other and other individuals that make up the social infrastructure of the project.

As articulated above, the characteristics of citizen science outlined here create particular and special opportunities for learning. The committee discusses how these opportunities may be identified and utilized in the design of citizen science projects in Chapter 6, with an eye toward how they might be leveraged to support specific learning goals.

## WHAT ARE THE GOALS OF SCIENCE LEARNING?

To understand *what* people learn, the committee turned to the National Research Council's 2009 report on *Learning Science in Informal Environments: People, Places, and Pursuits* (hereafter referred to as *LSIE*). That report synthesized multiple bodies of evidence to propose a framework of six complementary strands of science learning, conceived as intertwined strands of a rope. Four of the strands had been previously developed to capture aspects of science learning in K–8 school settings (National Research Council, 2007); two additional strands (Strands 1 and 6 in Box 3-2) were added to capture some of the distinctive aspects of learning in informal environments (i.e., settings outside of school such as museums, clubs, or nature centers), which typically reflect a greater emphasis on personal interest, growth, and free-choice engagement, often over extended periods of time and across different phases of participants' lifespans. Many settings for citizen science projects can be naturally characterized as informal or nonformal, and, as described below, the kinds of learning outcomes possible in citizen science projects align with one or more of the six strands of informal science learning.

*   **Strand 1: Sparking Excitement and Interest.** *Learners experience excitement, interest, and motivation to learn about phenomena in the natural, physical, constructed, and social worlds.*

    This strand captures the affective component of learning, including the sense of fun and curiosity that citizen science can engender, and the way that scientists get excited by the ability to answer a question. It also encompasses the social motivations that may drive or be driven by citizen science, such as desires for cleaner environments or more diverse ecosystems. There is evidence that citizen science can produce excitement, interest, and motivation (Everett and Geoghegan, 2016; Frensley et al., 2017; Geoghegan et al., 2016; Rotman et al., 2012), thus we can conclude that this kind of learning takes place. This kind of learning is also aligned with goal- and interest-driven learning, in which a learner needs to know something to accomplish a goal or because one enjoys learning more about something one is interested in. An additional effect of this strand of learning is that when participants are motivated and excited, this engagement improves recruitment and retention, leading to higher quality scientific data (Gollan et al., 2012; Shirk et al., 2012).

- **Strand 2: Understanding Scientific Content and Knowledge.** *Learners come to generate, understand, remember, and use concepts,*

---

**BOX 3-2**
**Strands of Informal Science Learning**

Learners who engage with science in informal environments . . .

Strand 1: Experience excitement, interest, and motivation to learn about phenomena in the natural and physical world.

Strand 2: Come to generate, understand, remember, and use concepts, explanations, arguments, models, and facts related to science.

Strand 3: Manipulate, test, explore, predict, question, observe, and make sense of the natural and physical world.

Strand 4: Reflect on science as a way of knowing: on processes, concepts, and institutions of science, and on their own process of learning about phenomena.

Strand 5: Participate in scientific activities and learning practices with others, using scientific language and tools.

Strand 6: Think about themselves as science learners and develop an identity as someone who knows about, uses and sometimes contributes to science.

SOURCE: National Research Council (2009, p. 43).

*explanations, arguments, models, and facts related to science (including both technical content and broader social, political, and cultural contexts of science).*

This strand includes the traditional "disciplinary knowledge" associated with a citizen science project such as knowledge about project-relevant science content. This knowledge includes knowledge that learners acquire through their participation and the new or cutting-edge knowledge that professional scientists will acquire through the project, such as novel data that are collected by participants. Disciplinary knowledge may also include an enhanced understanding of the interaction of science and society, such as the political contexts, needs, and potential actions that result from a community engaging in environmental issues. This type of learning is further discussed by the National Academies of Sciences, Engineering, and Medicine report on science literacy (2016), and people across all levels of technical expertise can learn about these issues. The various participant groups within a project (nonscientists, scientists and researchers, community activists) bring different preexisting knowledge to the table, and thus both contribute and receive different content.

- **Strand 3: Engaging in Scientific Reasoning.** *Learners manipulate, test, explore, predict, question, observe, and make sense of the natural, physical, constructed, and social worlds.*

  This strand includes learning traditional scientific methods, which in the context of citizen science may include well-established research methods that are learned by participants, as well as cutting-edge research methods that are collectively developed through cooperative efforts of all groups, including professional scientists. As scientists learn to use the citizen science "method" for conducting their own research, they also learn how novel methods can improve data, analysis, the formulation of questions, etc.

  Citizen science offers a venue where people who are not training to be scientists—whether school students or adults—gain access to learning how to think in scientifically sophisticated ways. The evidence here is mixed; many studies show that participants learn only specific methods or tools, and do not engage in the full panoply of scientific methods and reasoning (Phillips et al., in review).

- **Strand 4: Reflecting on Science.** *Learners reflect on science as a way of knowing: on processes, concepts, and institutions of science; and on their own process of learning about phenomena.*

  This strand captures the need for learners to improve their

understanding of the nature of the scientific enterprise. As *LSIE* explains, "The outcomes targeted in this strand address issues related to how scientific knowledge is constructed, and how people, including the learner herself, come to know about natural phenomena and how the learner's ideas change" (National Research Council, 2009, p. 68). In order to achieve these outcomes, the learner needs to understand that people are responsible for making sense of theories and evidence and that, as a result, science changes as understandings of the relationships between theory and evidence evolve with the construction of new knowledge.

In the context of citizen science, this may include considering one's own identity as a participant (whether as expert or as new researcher) and understanding the value and rewards to self from the activity. Through whatever role a person plays within a project, they may come to understand how collaboration among many different kinds of people leads to new knowledge. Participants may also reflect on the social, political, and cultural contexts of the activity. Participants may also come to recognize the broader implications, applications, and meaning of a project, both through their activities, as well as through the new knowledge generated, and ultimately wonder, "Where do I/we go from here?" This strand is particularly important for identifying learning about the social context of science, including issues of history and social power that affect learning, the multiple ways of understanding what counts as reliable knowledge, and the ways that communities learn and use learning to advance their priorities.

- **Strand 5: Engaging in Scientific Practices.** *Learners participate in scientific activities and learning practices with others, using scientific language and tools, and engaging in collective activities.*

This strand captures the need for learners to participate "in normative scientific practices akin to those that take place in and govern scientific work" (National Research Council, 2009, p. 70). Mastery in this area includes recognition of the hallmarks of scientific culture and the ability to participate in its codes and mores, specifically in regard to scientific argumentation.

Within citizen science, learning outcomes from this strand may include learning specific skills associated with a project or activity, such as political or organizational skills in collective or community projects. For scientists, a few things that may be learned through practice include project leadership and management, communication skills, reporting and review of data, as well as project design and implementation.

- **Strand 6: Identifying as a science learner.** *Learners think about themselves as science learners—that is, as ones who CAN learn science—and develop an identity as someone who knows about, uses, and sometimes contributes to science.*

  This strand captures the change in identity that can occur when people recognize that they are capable of learning in science. This shift or change in identity is accompanied by increased feelings of self-efficacy and agency in relation to science. Taken together, the issues of identity, self-efficacy, and agency do not necessarily indicate that people develop identities as scientists, but rather they come to the understanding that they can learn and contribute to the process by which reliable scientific knowledge is produced. For some participants, an identification with science preceded their participation in citizen science, and this part of their identity may have motivated their engagement with citizen science (Phillips et al., in review).

The strands helped the committee address the challenging task of organizing potential learning outcomes for citizen science and linking them to important knowledge about how people learn science. Each strand describes and organizes a whole range of outcomes of science learning, for a variety or learners, in a variety of contexts including cultural contexts. In light of the many opportunities for learning potentially supported through citizen science, the committee was able to use the strands to better consider how participation in citizen science can maximize specific learning outcomes.

## WHO IS LEARNING IN CITIZEN SCIENCE?

As the committee broached the subject of supporting learning in citizen science, it became clear that it was first important to introduce a few considerations about learners in citizen science: that is, who is it that is doing the learning in citizen science, and what do we need to know about the learner in order to begin to support learning outcomes. In Chapter 4, we summarize the committee's approach to understanding learning in order to provide a theoretical foundation for the committee's discussion of learning processes and outcomes. In advance of that discussion, we offer perspective on how our understanding of the learners themselves informs our later discussion of supporting learning in citizen science.

### Broadening Understandings of Who Is Learning in Citizen Science: Learning in Communities

Many research literatures and theoretical perspectives, including developmental, social, organizational, and cultural psychology; cognitive science, neuroscience, and the learning sciences; and education, have contributed to nuanced and comprehensive frameworks for understanding and facilitating learning in individuals. Citizen science has, in large part, remained close to that research tradition and, as we will discuss in Chapters 4 and 5, much of the existing research on learning in citizen science focuses on individual learners and their learning outcomes. Given the nature of citizen science projects and activities, however, the committee also observed that "the learner" in citizen science may, in fact, be broader than individual participants. In 2016, the National Academies' report on science literacy demonstrated a different perspective on learning by highlighting an emerging idea in the literature on learning in science: community science literacy (National Academies of Sciences, Engineering, and Medicine, 2016).

Community literacy is more than the sum of knowledge held by individuals in the community. Rather, community literacy is distributed among many individuals, but comes together through established networks of trust, behavior, relationships, power, and mechanisms of sharing. As the 2016 report documented, community (or communal) science literacy is ubiquitous: for example, it can occur in families (Borun, Chambers, and Cleghorn, 1996; Borun et al., 1997), in groups facing health crises (Epstein, 1996), or in communities addressing issues of toxic wastes or water quality (Brown, 1992; Brown and Mikkelsen, 1990; Fagin, 2013; Lee and Roth, 2003c; Ottinger, 2010a, 2010b; Ottinger and Cohen, 2011; Roth and Calabrese Barton, 2004; Roth and Lee, 2004). Community science literacy is particularly evident in the understandings of science held by marginalized communities, such as suspicion of the health care system in the African American community, based on historical and contemporary patterns evident in the Tuskegee syphilis study and in the contamination of water in Flint, Michigan (Armstrong et al., 2007; Benjamin, 2014; Dula, 1994; George, Duran, and Norris, 2014; Markowitz and Rosner, 2016; Thomas and Quinn, 1991). As described in Ann Fadiman's book, *The Spirit Catches You and You Fall Down* (2012), the Hmong community demonstrates a set of beliefs about health and healthcare that conflict with the American medical system; the conflict is not between the knowledge of individuals, but between different community understandings of what constitutes and creates health. Other researchers have found community-level differences in knowledge, reasoning, and practice between fisherpeople and hunters from different cultural communities, primarily Native American and European

American, that have at times resulted in policy and community level conflict (Medin and Atran, 2004; Atran and Medin, 2008).

An important aspect of community science literacy is that it highlights an issue that the committee will discuss in Chapter 4: Learning science means more than learning the content of specific topical domains. It also covers learning the processes of science (both idealized and in practice) and the epistemological bases of science (including the implications of different epistemological stances) and the ability to act on science. Learning theorists have provided several ways of thinking about the learning process that address community learning (Bela et al., 2016), described in Box 3-3.

Given these expanding conceptions of who is learning, the committee wishes to highlight that communities also have the potential to learn in citizen science, though research in this area is nascent. We will return to these ideas later in this report in Chapter 5, where we look at examples of learning in citizen science, and in Chapter 6 of this report, where we offer some thoughts on how to design citizen science in support of community science literacy.

## An Asset-Based Approach to Learners in Citizen Science

As noted in Chapter 1 of this report, the committee believes that in order to address this study's statement of task, it is critical that we consider how people of all backgrounds can learn through citizen science. In order to truly address these questions, the committee feels that it is first necessary to understand who learners in citizen science are: that is, what backgrounds and experiences do they bring to their encounters with citizen science that undergird what and how they will learn. In this section, we unpack the importance of honoring the prior knowledge and experiences that learners (individual learners *and* community learners) bring into their participation in citizen science by treating these backgrounds as assets that support learning.

In the past decade, research that devotes scholarly attention to the learning processes of nondominant communities and learners has illuminated the tendency for educational interventions to assume that people, and especially people from historically underrepresented communities in science, have minimal relevant prior knowledge (Bang et al., 2012). This research shows that these interventions fail to provide opportunities for learners to connect new learning to prior experiences. Even the choice of what content to learn is often constrained by applying a deficit model that presumes that learners do not have the ability to chart their own learning goals. Research has demonstrated that the assumption of a "deficit" on the part of some individuals and communities is invalid and that people the world over have experiences and exposure to phenomena that can be taken up in scientific study (National Research Council, 2012).

**BOX 3-3**
**Processes of Community Learning**

**Distributed Cognition**

Perhaps the fundamental theoretical perspective on community learning is distributed cognition, developed by computer scientist Edwin Hutchins in the 1980s (Hutchins, 1995). It draws on a Vygotsky-inspired tradition that recognizes knowledge in social and cultural context, and places knowledge across an extended network of people and objects. Through the interactions and relations of individuals, the network learns more than any one individual (or technological device) can learn (Hutchins, 1995; Salomon, 1997). For example, when citizen scientists in Zooniverse or similar projects use tags or labeling procedures, the collective knowledge of what is contained in the database exceeds the knowledge of any one individual (Fu, 2016).

**Transactive Memory/Collective Mind**

In the 1980s, communication scholars Daniel Wegner and others developed an understanding of shared knowledge called "transactive memory systems" (TMS) (Lewis and Herndon, 2011; Wegner, Giuliano, and Hertel, 1985). Jackson and Moreland (2009, p. 509) defined TMS as a "form of socially shared cognition [that] can lead to greater information sharing in groups." One of the consequences of transactive memory is the development of a "collective mind" that creates meaning out of the communally held knowledge (Weick and Roberts, 1993; Yoo and Kanawattanachai, 2001). For example, in community-led environmental citizen science (such as groups addressing local water quality or impacts of hydraulic fracturing), each individual may have a special knowledge—technical data, public speaking, political organizing—but the collective group knows how to mesh all those knowledges to create social action (Tallapragada, 2016).

**Communities of Practice**

The literature on communities of practice is particularly concerned with how groups build and maintain their core set of knowledge (Lave and Wenger, 1991). Although much of the work in the community of practice tradition focuses on how individuals become part of the community, that work is all based on the recognition that the group itself learns and collectively manages the knowledge of the group. The rise of social media as a tool in citizen science has been particularly important for these communities of practice, as research has demonstrated the power of social media for creating collective intelligence (Gunawardena, 2009).

As the committee will describe in Chapters 4 and 5, the processes of learning are always situated within the context of what learners already know and understand. It is easy to think that learners enter projects with a deficit and project activities fill that deficit. But adopting this perspective can undermine other sources of knowledge and other ways of knowing, alienate learners, and impede learning: ultimately, this perspective fails to recognize that learners enter projects with a variety of relevant prior knowledge and experience, some of it cultural, and that engaging that knowledge and experience actually empowers learners in the ways described above. Alternatively, learning environments that work to connect those experiences to the focal phenomena of new learning have demonstrated increased learning, retention, and sustained interest for learners (Moll and Gonzalez, 2004). Further, creating environments in which learners are positioned to see their own experiences and knowledge as resources has also been associated with increased persistence (Brossard, Lewenstein, and Bonney, 2009).

In our review of research on science learning specifically, the committee noted that the scholarly community is moving toward understanding science learning in ways that are attuned to learners' prior knowledge and their many ways of knowing. This has led to a shift away from deficit models toward a more refined understanding of alternative conceptions and epistemologies and their role in supporting science learning, referred to as an asset-based approach to supporting learning. In order to support learning, asset-based approaches seek to connect and query disciplinary (science) knowledge with and against a broader store of knowledge, and leverage that knowledge in ways that advance scientific disciplines.

In thinking about learning in the context of citizen science, the committee stresses the importance of adopting an asset-based perspective in regard to participants' prior knowledge and experience. We return to this idea in Chapter 5, where we attempt to highlight examples of how this asset-based approach is supporting specific learning outcomes in citizen science, as well as in Chapter 6, where we discuss how to design for learning in citizen science.

## SUMMARY

In summary, this chapter seeks to set the stage for our in-depth conversations about science learning in citizen science. By identifying what it is about citizen science that makes it a desirable vehicle for supporting learning, we lay a foundation for our later discussions about how citizen science can be leveraged in support of specific learning outcomes. Also, by calling out the strands of learning and their associated learning outcomes, we set the stage for what kinds of learning outcomes are possible; we discuss these processes of learning in greater depth in Chapter 4. Finally, by exploring who is learning—whether an individual or community—and considering the knowledge and experience that learners bring with them into citizen science, we prepare for subsequent analysis and recommendations that leverage sociocultural conceptions of learning.

## REFERENCES

Armstrong, K., Ravenell, K.L., McMurphy, S., and Putt, M. (2007). Racial/ethnic differences in physician distrust in the United States. *American Journal of Public Health*, 97(7), 1283-1289.

Association of Zoos & Aquariums. (2018). *Welcome to FrogWatch USA*. Available: http://frogwatch.fieldscope.org [September 2018].

Atran, S., and Medin, D.L. (2008). *The Native Mind and the Cultural Construction of Nature*. Cambridge, MA: MIT Press.

Bang, M., Warren, B., Rosebery, A.S., and Medin, D. (2012). Desettling expectations in science education. *Human Development*, 55(5-6), 302-318.

Bela, G., Peltola, T., Young, J.C., Balázs, B., Arpin, I., Pataki, G., and Bonn, A. (2016). Learning and the transformative potential of citizen science. *Conservation Biology*, 30(5), 990-999. doi:10.1111/cobi.12762.

Benjamin, M.M. (2014). *Water Chemistry*. Long Grove, IL: Waveland Press.

Borun, M., Chambers, M., and Cleghorn, A. (1996). Families are learning in science museums. *Curator: The Museum Journal*, 39(2), 123-138.

Borun, M., Chambers, M.B., Dritsas, J., and Johnson, J.I. (1997). Enhancing family learning through exhibits. *Curator: The Museum Journal*, 40(4), 279-295.

Boullion, L., and Gomez, L. (2001). Connecting school and community partnerships as contextual scaffolds. *Journal of Research in Science Teaching*, 38(8), 899-917.

Brossard, D., Lewenstein, B., and Bonney, R. (2005). Scientific knowledge and attitude change: The impact of a citizen science project. *International Journal of Science Education*, 27(9), 1099-1121.

Brown, P. (1992). Popular epidemiology and toxic waste contamination: Lay and professional ways of knowing. *Journal of Health and Social Behavior*, 267-281.

Brown, P., and Mikkelsen, E.J. (1990). *No Safe Place: Toxic Waste, Leukemia, and Community Action*. Berkeley: University of California Press.

Dula, A. (1994). African American suspicion of the healthcare system is justified: What do we do about it? *Cambridge Quarterly of Healthcare Ethics*, 3(3), 347-357.

Epstein, S. (1996). *Impure Science: AIDS, Activism, and the Politics of Knowledge*. Berkeley: University of California Press.

Everett, G., and Geoghegan, H. (2016). Initiating and continuing participation in citizen science for natural history. *BMC Ecology*, 16(1), 13.

Fadiman, A. (2012). *The Spirit Catches You and You Fall Down: A Hmong Child, Her American Doctors, and the Collision of Two Cultures*. New York: Farrar, Straus and Giroux.

Fagin, D. (2013). *Toms River: A Story of Science and Salvation*. New York: Bantam Books.

Frensley, T., Crall, A., Stern, M., Jordan, R., Gray, S., Prysby, M., Newman, G., Crall, A.C. Hmelo-Silver, and Huang, J. (2017). Bridging the benefits of online and community supported citizen science: A case study on motivation and retention with conservation-oriented volunteers. *Citizen Science: Theory and Practice*, 2(1), 4, 1-14.

Fu, W. (2016). From distributed cognition to collective intelligence: Supporting cognitive search to facilitate online massive collaboration. In U. Cress, J. Moskaliuk, and H. Jeong (Eds.), *Mass Collaboration and Education* (pp. 125-140). New York: Springer.

Geoghegan, H., Dyke, A., Pateman, R., West, S., and Everett, G. (2016). Understanding motivations for citizen science. In *Final report on behalf of UKEOF*. University of Reading, Stockholm Environment Institute (University of York) and University of the West of England.

George, S., Duran, N., and Norris, K. (2014). A systematic review of barriers and facilitators to minority research participation among African Americans, Latinos, Asian Americans, and Pacific Islanders. *American Journal of Public Health, 104*(2), e16-e31.

Gollan, J., de Bruyn, L.L., Reid, N., and Wilkie, L. (2012). Can volunteers collect data that are comparable to professional scientists? A study of variables used in monitoring the outcomes of ecosystem rehabilitation. *Environmental Management, 50*, 969-978.

Gunawardena, C.N., Hermans, M.B., Sanchez, D., Richmond, C., Bohley, M., and Tuttle, R. (2009). A theoretical framework for building online communities of practice with social networking tools. *Educational Media International, 46*(1), 3-16. doi:10.1080/09523980802588626.

Hutchins, E. (1995). *Cognition in the Wild*. Cambridge, MA: MIT Press.

Jackson, M., and Moreland, R.L. (2009). Transactive memory in the classroom. *Small Group Research, 40*(5), 508-534.

Lave, J., and Wenger, E. (1991). *Situated Learning: Legitimate Peripheral Participation*. Cambridge, England: Cambridge University Press.

Lee, S., and Roth, W.M. (2003). Science and the "good citizen": Community-based scientific literacy. *Science, Technology, and Human Values, 28*(3), 403-424.

Lewis, K., and Herndon, B. (2011). Transactive memory systems: Current issues and future research directions. *Organization Science, 22*(5), 1254-1265.

Markowitz, G., and Rosner, D. (2002). *Deceit and Denial: The Deadly Politics of Industrial Pollution*. Berkeley: University of California Press.

Medin, D.L., and Atran, S. (2004). The native mind: Biological categorization and reasoning in development and across cultures. *Psychological Review, 111*(4), 960.

Moll, L.C., and González, N. (2004). Engaging life: A funds-of-knowledge approach to multicultural education. *Handbook of Research on Multicultural Education, 2*, 699-715.

Monarch Larva Monitoring Project. (2018). *About the Monarch Larva Monitoring Project*. Available: https://monarchlab.org/mlmp/about-us/ [September 2018].

National Academies of Sciences, Engineering, and Medicine. (2016). *Science Literacy: Concepts, Contexts, and Consequences*. Washington, DC: The National Academies Press.

National Research Council. (2007). *Taking Science to School*. Washington, DC: The National Academies Press.

National Research Council. (2009). *Learning Science in Informal Environments: People, Places, and Pursuits*. Washington, DC: The National Academies Press.

National Research Council. (2012). *A Framework for K-12 Science Education: Practices, Crosscutting Concepts, and Core Ideas*. Washington, DC: The National Academies Press.

Ottinger, G. (2010a). Constructing empowerment through interpretations of environmental surveillance data. *Surveillance and Society, 8*(2), 221-234.

Ottinger, G. (2010b). Buckets of resistance: Standards and the effectiveness of citizen science. *Science, Technology, and Human Values, 35*(2), 244-270.

Ottinger, G., and Cohen, B.R. (Eds.). (2011). *Technoscience and Environmental Justice: Expert Cultures in a Grassroots Movement*. Cambridge, MA: MIT Press.

Phillips, T.B., Ballard, H., Lewenstein, B.V., and Bonney, R. (In review). Examining engagement in science through citizen science: Moving beyond data collection. *Science Education*.

Roth, W.M., and Calabrese Barton, A. (2004). *Rethinking Scientific Literacy*. New York: RoutledgeFalmer.

Roth, W.M., and Lee, S. (2004). Science education as/for participation in the community. *Science Education, 88*(2), 263-291.

Rotman, D., Preece, J., Hammock, J., Procita, K., Hansen, D., Parr, C., Lewis, D., and Jacobs, D. (2012, February). Dynamic changes in motivation in collaborative citizen-science projects. In *Proceedings of the ACM 2012 Conference on Computer Supported Cooperative Work* (pp. 217-226). New York: Association for Computing Machinery.

Salomon, G. (Ed.). (1997). *Distributed Cognitions: Psychological and Educational Considerations*. Cambridge, England: Cambridge University Press.

Shirk, J.L., Ballard, H.L., Wilderman, C.C., Phillips, T., Wiggins, A., Jordan, R., McCallie, E., Minarchek, M., Lewenstein, B.V., Krasny, M.E., and Bonney, R. (2012). Public participation in scientific research: A framework for deliberate design. *Ecology and Society*, 17(2).

Tallapragada, M. (2016). *Activists, Learning, and Relating to the Controversial Technology of Hydraulic Fracturing*. (Doctoral dissertation.) Cornell University, Ithaca, NY.

Thomas, S.B., and Quinn, S.C. (1991). The Tuskegee Syphilis Study, 1932 to 1972: Implications for HIV education and AIDS risk education programs in the black community. *American Journal of Public Health*, 81(11), 1498-1505.

Wegner, D.M., Giuliano, T., and Hertel, P.T. (1985). Cognitive interdependence in close relationships. In W. J. Ickes (Ed.), *Compatible and Incompatible Relationships* (pp. 253-276). New York: Springer.

Weick, K.E., and Roberts, K.H. (1993). Collective mind in organizations: Heedful interrelating on flight decks. *Administrative Science Quarterly*, 357-381.

Yoo, Y., and Kanawattanachai, P. (2001). Developments of transactive memory systems and collective mind in virtual teams. *The International Journal of Organizational Analysis*, 9(2), 187-208.

# 4

# Processes of Learning and Learning in Science

## INTRODUCTION

Understanding both the depth and breadth of scholarship on learning is central to addressing the committee's charge of investigating how citizen science can be poised to support science learning. In this chapter, we review the complex landscape of scholarship on learning in a way that highlights concepts relevant to the design of citizen science for learning. The concepts lay the groundwork for Chapter 5, which delves into how citizen science can advance specific science learning outcomes. We begin with an explanation of the committee's perspective on learning in the context of the history and evolution of learning theories. This discussion will set the stage for a description of some of the central cognitive processes involved in learning generally. We conclude the chapter with descriptions of some of the specific kinds of learning that happen in science content domains.

Although we describe the different theoretical perspectives on how learning occurs, contemporary scholars of learning generally recognize that learning is a complicated, interactive phenomenon. Individuals are nested within communities that are nested within societies, and these contexts matter for how knowledge is acquired and engaged. Different theories of learning are not mutually exclusive and can be used in complementary ways to attend to the multifaceted nature of learning, even in a single environment such as a citizen science project. Moreover, participants in citizen science project are also learning in a wide variety of other contexts and may even participate in multiple citizen science projects. It is helpful in both design of citizen science projects and in research about learning to

71

remember that all learning is happening with a larger ecosystem of citizen science opportunities and other science education experiences, both formal and informal.

This chapter is not intended as a comprehensive review of scholarship on learning; rather, we attempt to lay out central principles of learning, particularly with respect to science, for readers new to the field of science learning.

## PERSPECTIVES ON LEARNING

The committee has elected to take an expansive view of learning in general and science learning more specifically: Both what the learning is and the many contextual factors that influence it. Historically, most learning research focuses on individuals, and as we discussed in our section on community science literacy in Chapter 3, many research literatures and theoretical perspectives (including developmental, social, organizational, and cultural psychology; cognitive science, neuroscience, and the learning sciences; and education) have endeavored to construct frameworks for understanding and facilitating learning in individuals. As we discuss the processes of learning (both in general and in science) later in this chapter, the committee recognizes that these processes are aimed at characterizing what the individual learner knows and is able to do.

Over the past few decades, the study of human learning and development has moved beyond the examination of individual characteristics to understand learning as dependent on sociocultural contexts, even when examining a single individual's learning. In order to explain why and how people think and act in the world the way they do, scholars employing sociocultural perspectives often study and characterize how people in places interact with each other toward goals and use materials to mediate and support their interactions and goals.

From a sociocultural perspective, culture, learning, and development are seen as dynamic, contested, and variably distributed and transformed within and across groups, and involve a reciprocal and evolving relationship between individuals' goals, perspectives, values, and their environment (Cole, 2000; Gutiérrez and Rogoff, 2003; Hirschfeld, 2002; Lave, 1988; Lave and Wenger, 1991; Nasir and Hand, 2006; Rogoff, 2003). Culture, in this sense, is both historically constituted and dynamically changing through participation in social practices and making sense of life. More simply put, all people explore, narrate, and build knowledge about their worlds, but they do so in varied ways that are dynamically linked to particular contexts and depend on interaction with others (e.g., Bang et al., 2012; National Research Council, 2009; Rogoff, 2003).

While there remain important distinctions between individual and sociocultural perspectives, it is increasingly accepted that what and how people think are interdependent, and that both are sculpted by the daily activities, discursive practices, participation structures, and interactional processes over the course of a person's life. Sociocultural perspectives have expanded our foundational knowledge of human learning as well as led to important practice-based innovations in learning environments. While we acknowledge that much of the research on specific processes of learning mentioned in this chapter are concerned with individual learners, the committee believes that given the explicitly social nature of many citizen science projects, it is critically important to consider learning in citizen science through a sociocultural lens.

Given this perspective, the committee wishes to highlight three major principles of learning that undergird our discussion of how learning happens—both in science and in general. First, as we discussed in Chapter 3: Learners come to their learning experiences with prior knowledge experiences that shape what they know, their skills, their interests, and their motivation. Constructivist frameworks explain how this prior knowledge and experience matter for learning, positing that learning involves an interplay of the learner's prior knowledge and current ways of thinking with new ideas introduced by instruction or through interactions in the world (e.g., Piaget, Carey, Vosniadou, Chi, Posner, et al.) Second, learners actively construct their own understanding of the world; they are not passive recipients of knowledge, and transmitting knowledge is not equivalent to learning. Later in this chapter, we will discuss this principle in relationship to conceptual development, and how educators must actively engage learners in the process of developing conceptual understandings of science. Finally, some learning objectives in science are more challenging to achieve than others, so more intentional supports for learning are necessary. We will discuss this in the context of citizen science in Chapter 5, as we review how the existing literature describes different learning outcomes in citizen science.

In summary, the committee recognizes that learning is inherently social. It is situated in, and dependent upon, social interactions among people as well as their social and cultural tools and practices. In the following discussions of learning processes and kinds of learning in science, the committee emphasizes this sociocultural perspective on learning while also considering the insights gained from many decades of research from other theoretical perspectives.

We begin our discussion of learning by considering the processes of learning in individuals; specifically, the processes of memory, activity, and developing expertise. Then, the chapter narrows in on the specifics of science learning, including learning disciplinary content; using scientific tools; understanding and working with data; developing motivation, interest, and identity; and developing scientific reasoning, epistemological thinking, and the nature of science.

## PROCESSES OF LEARNING

This section considers the dominant cognitive processes that contribute to learning—that is, those processes that can be understood at the level of the individual and relate to content knowledge and reasoning. Because the charge of this study is specific to science learning, wherever possible the committee elects to discuss how these learning processes happen in the context of the domain of science. It is critical to note that these processes are not unique to science learning. Indeed, much of the general scholarship on learning has emerged in relationship to other academic disciplines, each with their own scholarly research traditions.

### The Role of Memory in Learning

Learning depends fundamentally on memory. Well over a century of research has delved into the properties of human memory in action, detailing the remarkable role memory plays in both developing and sustaining learning over time. From this research, there are several themes that are helpful to keep in mind.

Durable, long-term learning is best accomplished by repeated experience with the material one seeks to remember. Many researchers of memory and learning would caution against relying on a training program that involves a one-time introduction and immediate assessment of proficiency, which tends to result in short-term performance that predictably deteriorates over time, rather than long-term learning (Soderstrom and Bjork, 2015). Further, learning episodes are most efficient when they are spread out over multiple sessions rather than crammed together—a phenomenon known as the spacing effect (Cepeda et al., 2006; Rawson and Dunlosky, 2011). That is, the same amount of time invested in studying material one wants to remember will generally result in longer-lasting learning if it is distributed over time rather than performed all at once.

Learning can be enhanced by strategies that promote cognitive engagement with and elaboration of the material one is attempting to learn. Knowledge and skills that are densely interconnected to other information have better storage strength in long-term memory and also have links to more potential retrieval cues. Examples of beneficial strategies include such activities as concept mapping, note-taking, self-explanation, and representing material in multiple formats (e.g., text and graphics). Learning researchers Michelene Chi and Ruth Wylie (2014) have proposed a framework that differentiates cognitive engagement during learning into four modes: *interactive, constructive, active,* and *passive* (presented in decreasing order of the intensity of engagement), with interactive and constructive modes having the greatest impact on learning and conceptual development.

*Constructive* engagement is defined as activities where learners generate some kind of additional externalized product beyond the information they were originally provided with, such as generating inferences and explanations or constructing a new representational format (e.g., a diagram). *Interactive* engagement goes one step further and occurs when two or more partners (peers, teacher and learner, or intelligent computer agent and learner) together contribute to a mutual dialogue in a constructive mode.

Learning is improved when people are asked to actively apply or construct material from long-term memory, as opposed to passively restudying or being re-told the content, a phenomenon known as the "testing effect" (Karpicke and Blunt, 2011; Karpicke and Roediger, 2008; Rowland, 2014). Providing regular opportunities to generate active responses, such as through informal assessments or practice in the field, helps learners reinforce their learning while at the same time providing information about current states of proficiency. As these examples suggest, corrective feedback is another tool that can help to promote accurate learning and reinforce retention over time (Lyster and Ranta, 1997).

Learning opportunities that are deliberately designed with these principles of learning and memory in mind often show significant learning gains over traditional instructional practices such as lecture and rote memorization or self-organized learning (Bjork and Bjork, 2011; Bjork, Dunlosky, and Kornell, 2013). Although it was developed primarily to improve studying and instructional practices in school learning, the IES Practice Guide on Organizing Instruction and Study to Improve Student Learning (Pashler et al., 2007) provides a concise summary of these and several other principles of learning that are supported by substantial bodies of research and are relevant across learning contexts (see Box 4-1).

In Chapter 6, we will discuss the choices that project designers need to make in order to support science learning in citizen science. As with the all the processes of learning described below, designers of citizen science projects can leverage the role of memory in learning to support specific science learning outcomes.

## The Importance of Activity

As noted above, human thinking, learning, and behavior is fundamentally shaped by the need to engage in purposeful activity within social systems involving other people. As active agents, humans engage with the objective world in ways that infuse it with meaning. Activity theory (e.g., Engestrom, Miettinen, and Punamaki, 1999) takes a systems approach, treating as the unit of analysis a community of interacting individuals, such as a team or an organization, who have a common object of their activity.

**BOX 4-1**
**Recommended Principles for Organizing Instruction and Study to Improve Student Learning with Corresponding Levels of Supporting Evidence**

| Recommendation | Level of Evidence |
|---|---|
| 1. Space learning over time. *Arrange to review key elements of course content after a delay of several weeks to several months after initial presentation.* | **Moderate** |
| 2. Interleave worked example solutions with problem-solving exercises. *Have students alternate between reading already worked solutions and trying to solve problems on their own.* | **Moderate** |
| 3. Combine graphics with verbal descriptions. *Combine graphical presentations (e.g., graphs, figures) that illustrate key processes and procedures with verbal descriptions.* | **Moderate** |
| 4. Connect and integrate abstract and concrete representations of concepts. *Connect and integrate abstract representations of a concept with concrete representations of the same concept.* | **Moderate** |
| 5. Use quizzing to promote learning. *Use quizzing with active retrieval of information at all phases of the learning process to exploit the ability of retrieval directly to facilitate long-lasting memory traces.* | **5a. Low** |
| 5a. *Use pre-questions to introduce a new topic.* 5b. *Use quizzes to re-expose students to key content.* | **5b. Strong** |
| 6. Help students allocate study time efficiently. *Assist students in identifying what material they know well, and what needs further study, by teaching children how to judge what they have learned.* | **6a. Low** |
| 6a. *Teach students how to use delayed judgments of learning to identify content that needs further study.* 6b. *Use tests and quizzes to identify content that needs to be learned.* | **6b. Low** |
| 7. Ask deep explanatory questions. *Use instructional prompts that encourage students to pose and answer "deep-level" questions on course material. These questions enable students to respond with explanations and supports deep understanding of taught material.* | **7. Strong** |

SOURCE: Pashler et al. (2007).

For example, members of a team of health care providers in a hospital are the individual subjects in a community and their patients are the objects.

Activity systems are characterized by rules and conventions, which evolve historically and culturally, as well as divisions of labor and participation structures, which may include social strata or a hierarchical structure to the activity, with different actors taking on distinctive roles. A key insight of activity theory is that "tools," which may be culturally created artifacts or concepts (e.g., machines, software interfaces, information systems, protocols, etc.) that evolve over time, mediate behavior in the system, including learning and transmitting knowledge (Jonassen and Rohrer-Murphy, 1999).

Individuals may participate in multiple activity systems, and more recent work on activity theory has brought out the importance of considering interactions among multiple activity systems, which raises issues of individual and cultural identity, power, motivation, and difference (Bakhurst, 2009; Gutiérrez and Rogoff, 2003) and also points back to the need to consider citizen science learning in the context of a larger ecosystem of learning experiences. Activity systems are often used as a way of modeling practice in various contexts, including educational practice, in such a way that systems-level relations and dynamics are highlighted. In the context of citizen science, activity theory offers ways to think about the complex set of roles, objectives, values, and activities that can emerge when volunteer participants are simultaneously members of other communities, such as master naturalists and conservationists, community activists, hobbyists, students or teachers in formal or informal education, or workers engaged in related economic activity (e.g., fishing or harvesting). Actors may come from distinctly different groups, each with its own set of objectives, tools, customs, discourse patterns, role structures, and ways of doing things. Activity theory suggests that participants and organizers may advance collaborative goals by paying deliberate attention to recognizing or designing appropriate role structures, shared tools, and systems of communication to take advantage of the resources that different activity systems can potentially contribute while promoting common action and understanding.

Another example that lends itself to an activity systems analysis comes from Ottinger (2016), who presents the case of a multisite study and report completed by a coalition of environmental and community groups working in parallel with credentialed scientists (Coming Clean and Global Community Monitor, 2014). The study entails the development and deployment of modified instruments and protocols for sampling air quality in ways that were scientifically credible but more affordable and responsive to the concerns and questions of community groups. They allowed project participants to collect data at time intervals and in locations associated with community health concerns, and they provided data that pushed beyond prior standards that focused primarily on long-term averages. Ottinger's account also illustrates the tensions and interplay among the roles taken by community activists, scientists, and regulatory authorities around issues such as authorship and dissemination of reports, setting standards, and critiquing standard scientific practices vs. aligning with them for the sake of credibility. In summary, activity theory provides a way of identifying, analyzing, and modifying the elements—such as communities, actors and roles, objects of activity, tools, and practices—that both mediate and represent learning.

## Developing Expertise

Competence in any domain, and specifically in science, requires the ability to recognize relevance and potential applications of knowledge in varying contexts. While individuals new to the field (known as novices) tend to focus on superficial aspects of a situation and may have correspondingly shallow problem solving methods, experts quickly and accurately perceive higher-order relations, deep structure, and meaningful patterns (Chi, Feltovich and Glaser, 1981; Kellman and Massey, 2013). Experts tend to be fast and accurate, in large part because they process available information selectively—ignoring information that is irrelevant and registering information that is not noticed by novices. They are also better able to make fine discriminations and to apply their knowledge to novel cases. Experts are particularly good at recognizing conditions of application of knowledge—that is, knowing which principles and concepts are relevant in a particular situation (Chi, Feltovich and Glaser, 1981; Kellman and Garrigan, 2009).

In this subsection, we discuss the role of conceptual change and perceptual learning in the development of expertise. It is important to note that in science, development of expertise hinges on the ability to utilize scientific tools and practices. We discuss this particular aspect of developing expertise—using scientific tools and participating in science practices—later in this chapter, where we discuss specific kinds of learning in science.

### Conceptual Change and Development

One way of understanding how people develop expertise in content areas—specifically in the domain of science—explores the evolution of foundational ideas from the perspective of conceptual development over time. Theorists of conceptual development have noted repeatedly that mature concepts are often qualitatively different from concepts held by children or by uninstructed adults (Duit and Treagust, 2003; National Research Council, 2007). Acquiring sophisticated understanding of concepts is not merely a matter of accumulating more factual knowledge.

A common idea in theories of conceptual development is that concept learning varies in the degree to which knowledge must be restructured to move from naïve to more expert understanding. Some early understandings can be readily nurtured in thoughtful learning settings (Gelman et al., 2010). On the other hand, strong restructuring is required when novice and expert conceptual structures are fundamentally incompatible or incommensurate (Carey, 1988). In this case, rather than refining individual concepts or adding new concepts to existing ones, the nature of the concepts themselves and the explanatory structures in which they are embedded undergo change. Chi and her colleagues (Chi, Slotta, and de Leeuw, 1994) argue that some science learning is particularly difficult because learners' initial conceptions belong to a different *ontological category* than corresponding scientific conceptions. For example, many novices think of heat, gravity, and force as types of material substances, or properties of matter, rather than interactive processes. This can lead learners to misconstrue instruction, as happens when a learner who thinks of electrical current as similar to flowing water draws on matter-based conceptions, like volume or mass, to try to understand electrical phenomena.

The degree to which scientific concepts displace naïve knowledge during the process of strong restructuring is a subject of much debate. Strike and Posner (1982) show how conceptual change *can* occur when a learner begins to be sufficiently dissatisfied with a prior conception (e.g., by being confronted with anomalous information) and comes to see a new alternative conception as intelligible, plausible, and fruitful in its ability to explain and understand other problems. However, a number of studies indicate that intuitive ideas are also persistent and learners may ignore, reject or distort anomalous information. Even experts do this, as is illustrated by the history of science (Chinn and Brewer, 1993). Further, intuitive beliefs and alternative frameworks can continue to be activated in particular contexts even after an individual shows evidence of understanding and using a scientific concept.

Importantly, people can hold multiple conceptions about phenomena as they engage in rapid reorganization of knowledge and respond to the demands of a particular context. Even experts will shift their reasoning and understanding about a phenomenon depending upon the context (e.g., Hogan and Maglienti, 2001). When confronted with novel activities or practices, learners may need to create their own alternative pathways to reconcile conflicting cultural, ethnic, and academic identities (Nasir and Saxe, 2003).

Learning environments that only see learners' alternative conceptions as wrong can produce conflicts between learners' cultural, ethnic, and academic identities (Nasir and Saxe, 2003), and this approach can also leave narrow the possibilities of generative engagements between community ways of knowing and scientific ways of knowing (e.g., Bang and Medin, 2010). Instead, research shows that many phenomena of interest in scientific study are intimately related to people's everyday experiences and knowledge systems of cultural communities historically underrepresented in science can, and should, be regarded as assets for learning (Cajate, 1999; National Research Council, 2007). Educators can do this in a variety of ways. The use of culturally relevant examples, analogies, artifacts, and community resources that are familiar to learners can make science more relevant and understandable (Barba, 1993), and integrated approaches that rely on the input of community member participation (e.g., input from elders, use of traditional language, respect of cultural values) help learners navigate between Western modern scientific thinking and other ways of knowing (Bang and Medin, 2010). Sconiers and Rosiek (2000) point out that science inquiry demands patience, skepticism, and a willingness to embrace uncertainty and ambiguity—which demands trust between teachers and students. Accordingly, the development of trust and caring relationships between teachers and students may be necessary in order to develop deep understandings of science content and practices. In short, research demonstrates that conceptual learning is advanced in contexts and with instructors that recognize learners are simultaneously developing expertise in multiple knowledge systems (Bang and Medin, 2010; Levine Rose and Calabrese Barton, 2012).

## Perceptual Learning

Another process by which people develop domain expertise is perceptual learning, defined as an increase in the ability to extract relevant information from the environment as a result of experience (Adolph and Kretch, 2015; Gibson, 1969). Perceptual learning happens at all ages from infancy through mature adulthood, and has been studied in many professional and academic domains, including medical learning, aviation, mathematics, and chemistry, as well as in everyday learning (Kellman and Massey, 2013). Perceptual learning is often implicit and can be seen as a fundamental complement to more familiar ways of knowing, such as factual and procedural knowledge. Common instructional techniques emphasizing explicit didactic instruction or procedural practice typically do not advance perceptual learning very effectively (Kellman and Massey, 2013). Instead, perceptual learning often results from extended experiences with many examples as individuals participate in a meaningful activity. Recent research demonstrates that perceptual learning can be accelerated by providing systematic opportunities for learners to practice making relevant discriminations and classifications with feedback (Kellman, Massey, and Son, 2010). Learning software is an efficient and cost-effective way to do this. However, it is important for learners to experience a full range of variation in the examples they work with, so that the critical features, patterns, and structures involved in the activity are observed repeatedly across many different situations. Deliberate training tutorials can also ensure that participants have sufficient exposure to unusual or rare cases or difficult discriminations that they might not otherwise encounter often enough to gain proficiency. This kind of repeated classification activity across a range of examples is a central feature of many citizen science projects, like Zooniverse or COASST, suggesting that citizen science projects may be a particularly rich venue for perceptual learning.

Although the term "perceptual" may give the impression that it applies only to simple sensory tasks and discriminations, recent work drawing on modern theories of perception emphasizes that perceptual learning is abstract and adaptive, working synergistically with other cognitive processes (Kellman and Massey, 2013). Rather than conceiving of learning as the acquisition of discrete mental contents, the focus is on how human minds attune themselves to meaningful patterns, relations, and structures in the environment, typically in the context of a purposeful task or activity (Bereiter and Scardamalia, 1996; Goldstone, Landy, and Son, 2010). In addition to enabling the selective pick up of information in natural settings, as when a geologist effortlessly sees complex structure and patterns in natural rock formations, it also applies to processing of image representations, such as medical images read by a radiologist, and to symbolic representations, such as equations perceived by a mathematician or chemical formula notations read by a chemist. (Indeed, fluent reading in everyday life relies heavily on automatic information pick up obtained through perceptual learning).

Other approaches to the development of expertise have also emphasized how gaining experience in a domain or sphere of activity changes how one "sees." Working from an anthropological perspective and drawing on activity theory, Goodwin (1994) introduced the term "professional vision" to describe how members of a professional community engage in discursive practices that shape how they perceive relevant entities and phenomena. Goodwin's concept of professional vision focuses on practices within professions that create and operate on highly mediated representations of experience. For example, professional practices may highlight specific phenomena in a complex scene to make them salient, and they may apply verbal codes to classify phenomena and relate them to each other in an articulated framework. Professionals also produce shared material representations, such as graphs, charts, images, and annotated records. For example, teams of archeologists excavating a site use shared procedures to create profile maps of dirt that capture spatial relations among distinctive layers. Novices typically gain experience with these practices and tools as apprentices and, over time, develop the professional vision characteristic of their profession.

Similarly, Stevens and Hall (1998), has introduced the term "disciplined perception" to describe forms of visual interaction that develop among people as they engage in practice or in teaching and learning in a discipline such as mathematics. People create, coordinate, and behaviorally interact with aspects of visual displays to make objects or conditions of interest visible to themselves and to each other. For example, a student working with a tutor on graphs of linear functions develops a set of visual practices specific to the graphing of points and lines on grids representing the Cartesian plane. In Stevens' analysis, embodied action (e.g., gesture), visual perception, and talk work together in specific and coordinated ways throughout the teaching and learning process, both enabling and constraining the understanding that the student develops.

## KINDS OF LEARNING IN SCIENCE

This section focuses on the kinds of learning in science: learning disciplinary content; using scientific tools; understanding and working with data; developing motivation, interest, and identity; and developing scientific reasoning, epistemological thinking, and an understanding of the nature of science. Throughout this section, we refer back to the strands of informal science learning outlined in Chapter 3 to provide a framework for understanding the outcomes that result from these different kinds of learning in science. As emphasized in that chapter, we note that focusing on strands in insolation is an analytic convenience to help understand science learning; in practice strands are inextricably interwoven and projects that effectively advance science learning outcomes often advance and connect multiple strands. In the next chapter, we see examples of these kinds of learning in the context of citizen science.

### Learning Specific Scientific Disciplinary Content

Learning science content and developing expertise in a scientific discipline involve several types of knowledge, which are acquired through multiple learning processes. Following standard practice, we refer to this kind of learning as "developing expertise in a scientific content area" or "science content learning." Science content learning may be a stand-alone goal of the project and/or it may be part of achieving other scientific or community goals. With respect to the *Learning Science in Informal Environments: People, Places, and Pursuits* (*LSIE*; National Research Council, 2009) strands, science content learning is most closely related to understanding scientific content and knowledge (Strand 2) and using the tools and language of science (Strand 5).

The learning processes that help develop specific disciplinary knowledge and associated competencies, which can be quite sophisticated, go well beyond simple rote memorization of facts. Although the acquisition of specific knowledge is sometimes contrasted with conceptual understanding and the two are treated as if they are competing learning priorities, evidence shows that they play complementary and mutually supportive roles in learning. Specific knowledge and skills that are not incorporated into coherent conceptual organizations tend to exist as isolated "factoids"— difficult to remember, recognize in context, or apply in a productive way. At the same time, a rich foundation of specific knowledge animates abstract concepts and provides accessible, meaningful instantiations of important relations and patterns.

Expertise in specific disciplinary content requires *declarative* knowledge—concepts that can be verbalized. This kind of learning is sometimes described as "knowing that." Declarative knowledge can be thought of as facts that can be reliably and accurately retrieved and applied. A budding geologist, for instance, must learn the names and composition of different types of rocks and minerals and the processes by which they are formed. A volunteer monitoring invasive or endangered species must learn their typical habitats and the properties by which each type is identified. However, as described above in the section on conceptual change, a rich body of factual knowledge is not simply an accumulation of independent facts.

To be functional, science content knowledge must be organized and integrated through conceptual frameworks that provide coherence and explanatory power. Facility in this arena supports the evolution of learners' relationships to foundational ideas that have broad importance for conceptual development over time. As discussed above, theorists of conceptual development in science learning have noted repeatedly that mature science concepts are often qualitatively different from concepts held by children or by uninstructed adults.

One strong example of how this conceptual change can play out in science domains can be observed through the implementation of *A Framework for K–12 Science Education's* core disciplinary ideas, which aim to focus science learning around fewer science topics but to develop them in more depth across multiple years while simultaneously integrating them with science practices, described in the following sections (National Research Council, 2012). The NGSS Framework lays out a small, focused set of core disciplinary ideas in the physical sciences, life sciences, earth and space sciences, engineering, technology, and applications of science. Box 4-2 presents an example of how core disciplinary ideas in life sciences can set the stage for learners' conceptual change over time.

Not only are specific knowledge and conceptual understanding mutually supportive but also they are both situated in existing knowledge and understanding that learners bring into their experience in citizen science. It can be tempting to think of developing conceptual understanding and specific knowledge as an almost remedial process, where learners enter projects with a deficit and project activities fill that deficit. It is important to note that this approach can undermine other sources of knowledge and other ways of knowing, alienate learners, and impede learning. Learners enter projects with a variety of relevant prior knowledge and experience, some of it cultural, and the research shows that providing opportunities to connect new knowledge and emerging understandings with previous knowledge and experience advances learning.

---

**BOX 4-2**
**Example of Core Disciplinary Ideas**

An example of a core disciplinary idea in life sciences is an organized, inter-connected cluster of concepts related to the interactions, energy, and dynamics in ecosystems:

- Ecosystems are characterized by interdependent relations among organisms and the nonliving elements of the environment.
- Interactions in ecosystems can be understood as involving cycles of matter and energy transfer like the carbon cycle, which includes processes such as photosynthesis, digestion, respiration, decomposition, and gas exchange.
- Ecosystems are dynamic and change in response to disruption, and more diverse ecosystems tend to be more resilient.
- Within an ecosystem, many organisms are part of interactive groups, which can increase the likelihood of survival of individual members.

SOURCE: Adapted from National Research Council. (2012).

---

## Using Scientific Tools and Participating in Science Practices

Another way that science learning occurs is by using scientific tools and methods to engage in scientific reasoning (Strand 3) and to engage in scientific practices and discourse (Strand 5). Gaining competence with the scientific tools and practices related to a given content domain is known as *procedural knowledge*, sometimes described as "knowing how." In science, "knowing how" enables one to perform procedures and tasks in the service of scientific protocols. This competency might involve developing laboratory skills, measurement techniques, field methods, or analytic skills, such as how to organize, analyze, and present data. While procedural knowledge is sometimes condensed into a fixed set of rote behaviors—and there is certainly scientific value in maintaining consistent methods and protocols—functional competence and active problem solving in science typically require adaptability and flexibility in application, which in turn requires a deeper understanding of why procedures and practices take the form that they do and what the implications of contextual variations might be. It is important to note that the use of tools and scientific practices is strongly influenced by cultural and social norms (e.g., what is a valid practice, how tools are judged) and the interaction of groups. Indeed, learning is mediated through the tools, artifacts, and discourse structures that are used to frame, create, and convey knowledge. The cultural construction of tools[1] profoundly influences how people learn and how knowledge is organized and communicated, but more local and individualized tools play similar roles in particular contexts. For example, data collection protocols, maps, databases, online interfaces, and computer simulations may all shape how knowledge is produced and how learning occurs in a given setting. Social norms and conventions—whether at a scientific conference, in a classroom, or among a self-organized community group—may also serve as tools that mediate learning and knowledge sharing.

Along those same lines, it can take time for learners who are new to science to understand that measures and the evidence that they provide are developed according to community norms, rather than being direct, self-evident representations of the world (Manz, 2016). It can take even longer for learners to feel like they can contribute to those norms, especially if those norms are presented as the exclusive providence of professional scientists or are grounded in cultural norms from dominant communities. For example, the vigorous questioning that is a norm in discourse among practicing scientists can be discouraging when it is extended, often without thinking about it, to people new to science (Pandya et al., 2007). It is particularly dissonant compared to values of welcoming people to a field and affirming their identity as valued contributors.

## Understanding and Working with Data

Many of the tools and practices of science are linked to bodies of data and the associated practices for collecting, organizing, representing, modeling, and interpreting data. The power of data to enhance our understanding of the natural world and to address meaningful problems in our local and global communities is one of the factors that inspires people to participate in science. Though understanding and working with data is technically a subset of participating in scientific practices, the committee chooses to highlight these particular practices because of their centrality to citizen science.

Opportunities to learn to understand science and do science through active engagement with data are rich, plentiful, and multifaceted. In everyday thinking, most people are accustomed to interacting with whole objects embedded in naturalistic contexts. In contrast, framing scientific questions and designing methods to investigate them typically requires a more precise focus on the specific attributes of the objects or phenomena that

---

[1]The committee wishes to clarify that, in this case, "tools" is defined broadly. Written language, for example, is a tool constructed to transmit ideas. In science, tools are the apparatuses that facilitate the work and process of science: a tool might be a methodological protocol or a mechanism for measuring data.

are relevant to the question and the intentional development of a method for measuring or classifying those attributes. Most people have practical experience with measures of spatial dimensions, such as length, volume, area, and weight, but many measured attributes in science may take less familiar forms, such as rates and ratios (e.g., parts per million, radioactive decay rates) or involve magnitudes—either very large or very small—that fall outside everyday experience (e.g., geologic time, light years, microns, nanometers). Science may also involve developing ways of measuring or classifying behavioral phenomena (e.g., aggressive behavior), which must be *operationally defined* in the context of a scientific investigation—that is, the investigators and participants have to share a definition of what counts as an occurrence of the behavior of interest in the context of the study and specify how to reliably rate its intensity or frequency.

Data collection also provides a gateway for learning about issues related to measurement and variability, especially when learners have opportunities to reflect on and reason about what they are doing. Repeated measurement often creates conditions for noticing variability and for beginning to think about the sources of that variability. Representing and visualizing variability in a variety of ways can help people see data in the aggregate and to recognize distributions that have central tendencies (e.g., mean, mode, median) and variability or spread, as well as shapes of various sorts (Lehrer and Schauble, 2004). Repeated experience representing variability in data and thinking about different possible explanations for observed variability can help people better explore what drives good practice in designing and implementing data collection. They may become more responsive to or even spontaneously suggest procedures such as improving conditions of observation, using reliable instruments, training multiple data collectors to be consistent, and using multiple samples to reduce error variation in data being collected.

Lehrer and English (2018) wrote a comprehensive overview of methods for introducing young learners to central ideas related to measurement, sampling, variability, and distributions through data modeling activities. In this review, they propose a framework for organizing key concepts and the practices through which they are expressed and understood. Although this framework is aimed at younger learners in classrooms, such an approach could be applied to learners of all ages in various settings. The learning-focused road map starts with forming questions, and then moves into making decisions about relevant attributes and how they will be measured, organizing data and representing variability in distributions of data, and ultimately making inferences, which will in turn stimulate new questions (see Figure 4-1). Similar to other inquiry-driven approaches to science education that emphasize doing science as engaging in interrelated practices (e.g., Manz, 2016; National Research Council, 2007, 2012; Schwartz et

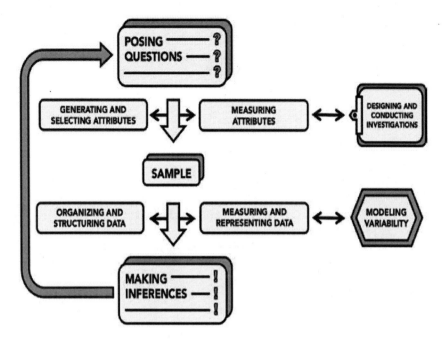

**FIGURE 4-1** Components of data modeling.
SOURCE: Lehrer and English (2018).

al., 2009), data collection and data modeling can be connected in iterative cycles. This cycle begins with forming questions, and then moves into
making decisions about relevant attributes and how they will be measured,
organizing data and representing variability in distributions of data, and
ultimately making inferences, which will in turn stimulate new questions.

Several projects have looked more closely at how students learn to
engage in practices related to scientific modeling; these projects offer field-
tested strategies and curricular resources for supporting this learning with
topics such as genetics, Darwinian evolution, plant growth, light and
shadows, and evaporation and condensation (Lehrer and Schauble, 2004;
Schwarz et al., 2009; Stewart, Cartier, and Passmore, 2005). Some common features have appeared across these various projects. One feature is
that learners generally need some prior knowledge in a topic or domain to
ground their thinking. As has been demonstrated in many studies of cognition and learning, it is difficult for people to engage in sophisticated, productive thinking and problem solving without a sufficient knowledge base
to think with. For example, in scientific modeling, students working in the
domain of genetics should already have some background in topics such as

meiosis. Modeling activities would be aimed at deepening this knowledge further, integrating it with new concepts, and using it to develop specific models. This background knowledge may come from a variety of sources—provided by instructors and curricular materials, gathered through online or library research, and so forth. At the same time, it is important to set up the learning situation to encourage learners to be able to probe their own understanding of established knowledge, to raise questions about it, and to evaluate the credibility of their sources rather than passively accepting everything on authority.

A second common feature across a variety of projects is providing sufficient time for repeated cycles of data collection, modeling, and revision. Many of the projects reported in the literature played out over multiple months or even entire academic years. A third common feature is that teachers or teams of teachers and researchers provided systematic facilitation to help guide students toward more and more sophisticated ways of thinking about and engaging in modeling. They did this through the types of assignments they made and how they sequenced them, how they modeled and managed classroom discourse, and the physical and representational resources they provided for conducting investigations and for organizing and representing data and models.

## The Importance of Motivation, Interest, and Identity

Motivation, interest, and identity can be thought of as inputs to, mediators for, and outcomes of participation in science. For example, interest in a science topic can motivate people to seek out information; people whose whole identities are welcomed and appreciated are more likely to participate in science learning activities (Rahm et al., 2003); and building identity as someone with something to contribute to science (Ballard, Harris, and Dixon, 2017) can deepen an individual's interest in science (Bonney et al., 2009).[2]

Learning research suggests that motivation, interest, and identity are important touchstones for learning. An individual's identity plays an important role in learning—both through shaping what is of interest, as well as what people find motivating. A spark of curiosity can develop into an interest, but to support long-term learning and eventual identification with the scientific enterprise, learners must demonstrate sustained and persistent motivation (Hidi and Renninger, 2006). Underdevelopment of these compe-

---

[2]As a note, the committee wishes to acknowledge issues around motivation, interest, and identity are not specific to science, and are important to learning in any disciplinary context. For the purposes of this report, however, the committee is interested in how to support these outcomes in science and is discussing research with that specific focus.

tencies present substantial obstacles to learning, while support for the development of these competencies can lead to achievement of science learning outcomes. In the "free-choice" contexts of citizen science, these constructs are particularly important as they are integral to the drive to participate, as well as the choice to stay engaged in the work. The committee finds it particularly important to call out this interplay of identity, motivation, and interest, as it is critical to support learning in citizen science.

Learning experiences can be purposefully designed in ways that support or constrain development in these arenas. In this chapter, we discuss these competencies as mediators for learning and their subsequent role(s) in learning processes. In the following chapter, we consider how citizen science can support their development as outcomes in science learning.

## Motivation

Two primary theories support contemporary understandings of motivation. Expectancy value theory posits that people are goal oriented and that behavior is driven by the relationship between an individual's expectations or perceptions and the value they place on the goal they are working toward. Such an approach predicts that when more than one behavior is possible, the behavior chosen will be the one with the largest combination of expected success and value (Palmgreen, 1984). An alternative theory, achievement goal theory, was developed in order to understand the unfolding or development of engagement in a task. Achievement goals generally refer to the purposes or reasons an individual is pursuing a task as well as the standards or criteria used to judge successful performance (Pintrich, 2000; Pintrich and Schunk, 1996). This theory identifies two types of comingled achievement goals: mastery, sometimes called competence, and performance. Mastery goals have been labeled task-goals (Nicholls, 1984) and learning goals (Dweck and Leggett, 1988; Elliott and Dweck, 1988), whereas performance goals have been labeled ego-goals (Nicholls, 1984) and ability goals (Ames and Ames, 1984). However, mastery and performance goals may also comingle.

An individual who adopts a performance goal toward learning is generally more concerned with the outcome and demonstrating his or her competence to others. A person who adopts mastery goals toward learning is often more focused on the process of learning rather than the outcome and often experiences learning to be a rewarding in and of itself. In the domain of education, mastery goals have been articulated to focus on what learners should know, understand, and be able to do. Thus, mastery requires that individuals understand concepts, have background knowledge (content), and can address tasks that require critical thinking, inference, induction, deduction, and application of knowledge—to solve problems and address issues in novel situations. In schools, students with mastery orientations show consistent, positive learning outcomes, engage in deeper cognitive strategies, and are intrinsically motivated to learn (Anderman and Young, 1994; Lee and Brophy, 1996; Meece, Blumenfeld, and Hoyle, 1988).

An important development in the field of motivation has been focused on the ways in which goals and forms of motivation are variable and context dependent—that is, how the social context impacts motivation, goals, and participation (Nolen and Ward, 2008). Part of this social context is the ways in which tasks and forms of participation are intertwined. For individuals that have mastery-oriented goals, a task that does not afford continual mastery goals can lead to disengagement—if something is too easy, a mastery-oriented person may lose interest and seek other opportunities.

Another important finding in the field of science education has been the interlocking of motivation and learning with opportunities to participate in the full range of scientific practices and sense-making (e.g., Chin and Brown, 2000). That is, motivation and learning increase when individuals have opportunities to develop explanations, carry out investigations, and evaluate knowledge claims (Blumenfeld et al., 1991). Importantly, the different forms of practice and activity tend to mutually reinforce each other—learning in one area tends to promote learning and engagement in another (Eveleigh et al., 2014). Furthermore, scholarship has demonstrated the need to carefully attend to the variation in factors that motivate or fail to motivate students from particular demographic groups when designing instruction.

Motivation is a central component of the ability to develop self-efficacy (i.e., feelings of "I can do this"). There is considerable evidence that people will work harder, perform better, and persist in the face of challenges—all central components in learning—if they have some sense of control and believe that they are capable of success (Atkinson, 1964; Eccles et al., 1983; Hidi and Ainley, 2008; Sansone, 2009; Wigfield et al., 2006). People generally develop feelings of self-efficacy from past experiences, observations of others, performance feedback, emotional or physiological states, and social influences. As such, feelings of self-efficacy can evolve with new experiences.

## Interest

When people are interested in a topic or task, they are more likely to be attracted to challenges, use effective learning strategies, and make appropriate use of feedback (Csikszentmihalyi, Rathunde, and Whalen, 1993; Lipstein and Renninger, 2006; Renninger and Hidi, 2002). With increased interest, participants will begin to develop and seek out answers to questions as they work on a project (Renninger, 2000), and they are also more likely to use systematic approaches to answer these questions (Engle and Conant, 2002; Kuhn and Franklin, 2006; Renninger, 2000). Having an interest in a subject helps individuals to pay attention, learn, and retain more information for longer periods of time (Beier and Ackerman, 2003; Hidi and Renninger, 2006; National Research Council, 2000; Renninger and Hidi, 2011). Learning contexts that engage participants' personal interests have demonstrated increased participation, particularly by people from underrepresented groups (Barton and Tan, 2018).

A person's interest in a topic may be an enduring connection to a domain (e.g., they have a concern about water quality and public health) or connection to specific features of a task (e.g., they enjoy hiking and being outdoors with their family). Interest is not fixed but rather develops over time. Interest begins with sparks of curiosity, extends to voluntary re-engagement, and if supported, can develop into a part of a person's identity (Hidi and Renninger, 2006; Renninger and Hidi, 2011). Vocational interests in children often change with age and seem to be particularly aligned with one's social class at ages 9–13 (Cook et al., 1996), whereas beyond age 13, children develop differentiated and individualized career interests based on their internal, unique selves (Schoon, 2001). Learners of all ages can be supported to develop specific interests (Renninger, 2010). Beyond changes associated with getting older, interests are also influenced by other mutable factors, such as gender, race, ethnicity, and social class, all of which are discussed in the identity section of this chapter, below.

## Identity

Part of learning involves the construction of identities, including viewing one's self as a member or part of an enterprise. We discuss two primary ways of understanding issues of identity and science learning including: (1) disciplinary identities—who develops, and how, an identity as someone who does science and contributes to science learning, and (2) social and cultural identities—how socially and culturally constructed identities such as racial and gendered identities intersect with learning, as well as how power dynamics and processes such as racialization impact learning and engagement.

**Disciplinary identity.** In science, one particularly important aspect of learning is developing a disciplinary identity as someone who actually does science and can contribute to science more broadly. Developing an identity as someone who does and can contribute to science is shaped by an individual's long-standing perceptions and experiences with science (Atwater et al., 2013), some of which may not be very positive. For example, more than 60 years of research has demonstrated that young people, as well adults, tend to think about science as a body of facts or as a rigid, largely laboratory-based process that white males engage in (Finson, 2002; Mead and Metraux, 1957). However, this perception is changing; a recent meta-analysis of more than 50 years of "draw-a-scientist" surveys collected from more than 20,000 children in the United States shows drawings depicted more female scientists in later decades, especially among younger children (Miller et al., 2018).

**Social and cultural identities.** This research also highlights the ways in which individuals develop, even if implicitly, gendered and racialized perspectives about who does science; thus, social identities and disciplinary identities are intertwined, which we explore in the following section. It is important to note the ways in which these issues exclude people and influence the progress and relevance of science. For example, the increased participation of women and scientists from nondominant backgrounds has led to important new foundational knowledge in several fields of science. The environmental justice community draws a link between the historical exclusion of certain communities from science and the prevalence of toxic areas within communities of color.

The ways in which researchers have investigated the construction, reinforcement, and interaction of social and cultural identities with learning has shifted over time. An individual's social and cultural identity shapes how he or she will engage with science and what each will learn from these experiences. Similarly, these identities will influence the extent to which they come to identify with science or as someone who can contribute to science. The next chapter will explore the ways in which these identities intersect with, influence, and are influenced by science learning outcomes in citizen science.

### Scientific Reasoning, Epistemological Thinking, and the Nature of Science

The concepts covered in this subsection—scientific reasoning and epistemological thinking[3]—correspond to Strand 2 (using arguments and fact related to science) and Strand 4 (reflecting on science as a way of knowing). Critical thinking and reasoning in science involve a number of factors that must be coordinated in complex ways. Learners need to develop an understanding of how to differentiate among facts, hypotheses, theories, and evidence, and how data can gain meaning as they are used to evaluate potential explanations (King and Kitchener, 1994; Kuhn, 1999; Smith et al., 2000). Further learning objectives involve knowledge of how research

---

[3]Epistemological thinking understands the nature of building knowledge in science and the use of the methods of science to develop knowledge through scientific inquiry and argumentation.

designs, sampling, and measurement methodologies provide frameworks by which research questions and hypotheses are related to data, and how these methodologies can enable or limit the strength of the inferences that can be drawn from data. A central example of this is distinguishing when patterns of evidence do and do not warrant conclusions about causality (Kuhn et al., 1995; Schauble, 1996). Closely related to these abilities is the process of scientific argumentation, whereby people construct knowledge claims, justify them with evidence, consider and critique alternative claims, and revise claims (Berland and McNeill, 2010). There is general consensus among learning scholars that acquiring competence in scientific reasoning, argumentation, and discourse requires rich and extended opportunities to engage actively in these as practices (National Research Council, 2007, 2012).

Scientific reasoning entails learning to coordinate knowledge claims with evidence, but this, in turn, depends on understanding that there *is a difference* between claims and evidence or between facts and beliefs. Researchers who study epistemological development in children and adults in Western cultures typically propose that there is a general progression in the development of epistemological understanding (Hofer and Pintrich, 1997; King and Kitchener, 1994; Kuhn, 1999; Perry, 1970). An early view takes a dualistic stance toward knowledge, believing that all knowledge is unproblematically true or false and can be known with certainty by authorities. Facts are seen as a direct representation of reality, and experts should not disagree unless one knows less, has made a mistake, or is intentionally lying. Further in the progression, some uncertainty may be admitted, but it is seen as temporary. Eventually, an individual may recognize that knowledge is uncertain and that different people can have different subjective views, but he or she may still not fully distinguish between theory and evidence and may not feel that how well a belief is justified by evidence can or should be adjudicated, because it is a matter of personal opinion. Evidence may be seen more as an illustration of a belief than a justification for it. At more advanced levels, knowledge is viewed as something that is actively constructed and must be supported and justified by evidence. Differing interpretations of evidence vary in how well-grounded they are, and even experts' judgments can be productively questioned. One's own beliefs and conclusions are also open to revision based on new evidence or new interpretations of evidence. Individuals with this stance see knowledge as constructed and view themselves as active meaning-makers.

Both longitudinal and cross-sectional studies indicate that the most advanced levels are uncommon even among graduating college seniors (King and Kitchener, 1994), and are most often seen among advanced graduate students. However, older adults, noncollege-educated adults, and non-Western populations have not been well-represented in research samples (for an exception, see Belenky et al., 1986). It is possible that older individuals may bring more sophisticated critical thinking skills and more advanced beliefs about what they think knowledge is and how it is generated as a result of work and life experience.

While there are clear developmental progressions in epistemological thinking, current theories generally do not conceive of them in terms of fixed all-or-nothing stages, and the same individual may show somewhat more or less sophisticated reasoning or may draw on alternative views of knowledge and knowing as a function of the situation and the types of supports available in the environment. There is also evidence of the importance of structured learning opportunities: younger learners are capable of advancing in their epistemological reasoning and their use of evidence to support arguments in appropriate science contexts (Berland and McNeill, 2010; Smith et al., 2000); at the same time, adults may not commonly achieve higher levels of sophistication spontaneously without such learning opportunities (King and Kitchener, 1994). Kuhn (1999) argues that, in addition to epistemological knowledge, critical thinking also involves *metacognitive* knowledge—that is, an individual becomes more aware of his or her own thinking and is able to intentionally reflect on it and also control it by monitoring it and selecting strategies to manage critical thinking. Constructing a rebuttal in science, for example, requires this kind of complex, controlled thinking to evaluate the strengths and weaknesses of counterclaims and to generate and evaluate support for one's own claims.

Sociocultural perspectives are an important additional lens for understanding how epistemologies and scientific reasoning develop. They also call attention to variations in how people from different cultural backgrounds think about knowledge and the sources and processes that create and validate knowledge (e.g., Bang and Medin, 2010). Globally, many different cultures have developed sophisticated epistemologies based in systematic observations of nature. The traditional ecological knowledge of Indigenous communities is one example. The interplay of indigenous epistemologies and more mainstream scientific disciplines has been productive for a range of topics including, but not limited to, ecosystem management, fisheries, agroforestry, animal behavior, medicine, and pharmacology. Traditional knowledge not only brings diverse ideas to these areas of study, but also is associated with a cultural framework of respect, reciprocity, and responsibility (Kimmerer, 1998; Pierotti and Wildcat, 2000). Although traditional ecological knowledge has recently been formally recognized as having an equal status with Western scientific knowledge (United Nations Environment Programme, 1998), it has historically been marginalized or ignored in the scientific community (Salmon, 1996).

While European and Western scientific epistemologies have been productive in many contexts, history is rife with examples in which it has been used to oppress certain peoples. For example, colonists have utilized biased, ethnocentric tests to support racist ideals and assert their cultural superiority over colonized people, resulting in a legacy of persistent distrust and alienation of some cultures or communities from scientific research. Sociocultural analyses emphasize that the ways of knowing associated with Western science are not culturally neutral, and they have been privileged in part because they have been associated with power and dominant culture (Agrawal, 1995).

Some recent projects have attempted to develop new approaches to community participation in and support for science and science education by taking an explicitly integrative approach toward epistemological differences. In formal education contexts, for learners who recognize differences in the orientations of their home culture and that of western science, effective instructors can help students negotiate "border crossings" between the different ways of thinking (Aikenhead and Jegede, 1999; Costa, 1995). For example, Bang and Medin (2010) describe how a large project collaborating with urban and rural Native American communities blends the practice of science with elements of culturally based epistemological orientations, such as the stance that humans are an interconnected part of the natural world rather than independent and external from it. An integrated approach that relies on the participation of community members (e.g., elder input, use of traditional language, community participation in the research agenda, respect of cultural value, informed consent) may be useful to remove the implicit privileging of Western scientific thinking and recognize the importance of different cultural values and orientations. Place-based educational programs that are co-created and implemented with members of indigenous communities have demonstrated success in helping Native American learners to navigate multiple epistemologies and deepen their understanding of science related to plants, animals, and ecology while also appreciating the historic legacy and contemporary relevance of their own communities' knowledge and experience of the natural world.

Fluency in science also includes an understanding of the nature of science, which includes an in-depth understanding of the histories, philosophies, and sociologies of the institution of science. This metacognition also requires an awareness of the values implicit in scientific endeavors that shape the products of science, and an awareness of the ways in which science is not neutral and subject to constant review. It also includes an understanding of how science knowledge is built and the notion that there is a community of scientists working together to build knowledge through the use of scientific practices. Mastery of these concepts is embodied in Strand 4, reflecting on science as a way of knowing.

There is general agreement about the important concepts that are part of the nature of science (McComas and Olson, 1998; National Research

Council, 2007; Osborne, Simons, and Collins, 2003). First and foremost, understanding the nature of science recognizes that science is an empirical way of knowing about the world that utilizes transparent methods to make evidence-based claims. Science is an ongoing enterprise: Knowledge acquired scientifically is subject to continued review and revision. It is also important to understand that scientific knowledge is partially based on human inference, human imagination and creativity, and the social and cultural contexts in which it is formed. Data are collected and interpreted in context: current scientific perspectives, cultural influences, and the experiences and values of individual scientists all matter in the building of scientific knowledge. Third, there is no unitary scientific method. Instead, science is built on a number of methods, which like scientific knowledge in general, are subject to constant innovation, creativity, and revision. Finally, science can be understood as an epistemological framework, and even that framework is subject to revision as new ideas. In fact, thinking about the way in which learners approach science can yield insight into how the nature of science itself evolves over time.

It has been argued that engaging students in authentic science experiences contributes to their understanding of the nature of science (Schwartz et al., 2004), but evidence suggests that it is important to explicitly teach students about the nature of science (Abd-El-Khalick and Lederman, 2000). Because citizen science engages directly in scientific activity, it has the potential—though largely unrealized and not without significant supports— to provide opportunities to learn about the nature of science.

## SUMMARY

This chapter outlines some of the most current understandings of how people learn, and how people learn science. As we explain throughout this chapter, individuals learn, they learn through interaction with others, and their learning occurs in a broad landscape that is influenced by culture, practice, and history. Historically, inequities in society have affected people's opportunity to learn by discounting or neglecting cultural knowledge and prior experience. Attending to those prior experiences and providing learning opportunities that welcome the individual, social, and sociocultural aspects of learning are especially effective for addressing these inequities and provide enriched opportunities for all learners.

As we will see in the next chapter, awareness of the multiple factors that influence learning provide opportunities to build rich learning experiences that leverage and build out from citizen science. At the same time, research on learning reveals that any learning, including learning is citizen science, occurs in a larger ecosystem of learning opportunities and experiences. That means design and practice of citizen science for learning should be considered within a broader landscape of learning experiences, which can inform, enrich, and extend learning opportunities in citizen science. The next chapter will discuss these learning processes in the specific contexts of citizen science projects.

## REFERENCES

Abd-El-Khalick, F., and Lederman, N.G. (2000). Improving science teachers' conceptions of nature of science: A critical review of the literature. *International Journal of Science Education, 22*(7), 665-701.

Adolph, K.E., and Kretch, K.S. (2015). Gibson's theory of perceptual learning. In J.D. Wright (Ed.), *International Encyclopedia of the Social and Behavioral Sciences* (pp. 127-134). New York: Elsevier.

Agrawal, A. (1995). Dismantling the divide between indigenous and scientific knowledge. *Development and Change, 26*(3), 413-439.

Aikenhead, G.S., and Jegede, O.J. (1999). Cross-cultural science education: A cognitive explanation of a cultural phenomenon. *Journal of Research in Science Teaching, 36*(3), 269-287.

Ames, C., and Ames, R. (1984). Systems of student and teacher motivation: Toward a qualitative definition. *Journal of Educational Psychology, 76*(4), 535.

Anderman, E.M., and Young, A. (1994). Motivation and strategy use in science: Individual differences and classroom effects. *Journal of Research in Science Teaching, 31*, 811-831.

Atkinson, J.W. (1964). *An Introduction to Motivation.* Princeton, NJ: Van Nostrand.

Atwater, M.M., Lance, J., Woodard, U., and Johnson, N.H. (2013). Race and ethnicity: Powerful cultural forecasters of science learning and performance. *Theory into Practice, 52*(1), 6-13.

Bakhurst, D. (2009). Reflections on activity theory. *Educational Review, 61*(2), 197-210.

Ballard, H.L., Harris, E.M., and Dixon, C.G. (2017). *Science Identity and Agency in Community and Citizen Science: Evidence and Potential.* Paper commissioned by the Committee on Designing Citizen Science to Support Science Learning at the National Academies of Sciences, Engineering, and Medicine.

Bang, M., and Medin, D. (2010). Cultural processes in science education: Supporting the navigation of multiple epistemologies. *Science Education, 94*(6), 1008-1026.

Bang, M., Warren, B., Rosebery, A.S., and Medin, D. (2012). Desettling expectations in science education. *Human Development, 55*(5-6), 302-318.

Barba, R.H. (1993). A study of culturally syntonic variables in the bilingual/bicultural science classroom. *Journal of Research in Science Teaching, 30*, 1053-1070.

Barton, A.C., and Tan, E. (2018). A longitudinal study of equity-oriented STEM-rich making among youth from historically marginalized communities. *American Educational Research Journal, 55*(4), 761-800.

Beier, M.E., and Ackerman, P.L. (2003). Determinants of health knowledge: An investigation of age, gender, abilities, personality, and interests. *Journal of Personality and Social Psychology, 84*(2), 439-448.

Belenky, M.R, Clinchy, B.M., Goldberger, N.R., and Tarule, J.M. (1986). *Women's Ways of Knowing: The Development of Self, Voice, and Mind.* New York: Basic Books.

Bereiter, C., and Scardamalia, M. (1996). Rethinking learning. In D.R. Olson and N. Torrance (Eds.), *The Handbook of Education and Human Development: New Models of Learning, Teaching and Schooling* (pp. 485-513). Oxford, England: Blackwell.

Berland, L.K., and McNeill, K.L. (2010). A learning progression for scientific argumentation: Understanding student work and designing supportive instructional contexts. *Science Education, 94*, 765-793.

Bjork E.L., Bjork R.A. (2011). Making things hard on yourself, but in a good way: Creating desirable difficulties to enhance learning. In M.A. Gernsbacher, R.W. Pew, L.M. Hough, and J.R. Pomerantz (Eds.), *Psychology and the Real World: Essays Illustrating Fundamental Contributions to Society*. New York: Worth.

Bjork, R.A., Dunlosky, J. and Kornell, N. (2013). Self-regulated learning: Beliefs, techniques, and illusions. *Annual Review of Psychology, 64*, 417-444.

Blumenfeld, P.C., Soloway, E., Marx, R.W., Krajcik, J.S., Guzdial, M., and Palincsar, A. (1991). Motivating project-based learning: Sustaining the doing, supporting the learning. *Educational Psychologist, 26*(3-4), 369-398.

Bonney, R., Ballard, H., Jordan, R., McCallie, E., Phillips, T., Shirk, J., and Wilderman, C.C. (2009). *Public Participation in Scientific Research: Defining the Field and Assessing Its Potential for Informal Science Education. A CAISE Inquiry Group Report*. Washington DC: Center for Advancement of Informal Science Education.

Cajete, G.A. (1999). *Igniting the Sparkle: An Indigenous Science Education Model*. Skyland, NC: Kivaki Press.

Carey, S. (1988). Conceptual differences between children and adults. *Mind & Language, 3*(3), 167-181.

Cepeda, N.J., Pashler, H., Vul, E., Wixted, J.T., and Rohrer, D. (2006). Distributed practice in verbal recall tasks: A review and quantitative synthesis. *Psychological Bulletin, 132*, 354-380.

Chi, M.T.H., Feltovich, P.J., and Glaser, R. (1981). Categorization and representation of physics problems by experts and novices. *Cognitive Science, 5*, 121-152.

Chi, M.T.H., Slotta, J.D., and de Leeuw, N. (1994). From things to processes: A theory of conceptual change for learning science concepts. *Learning and Instruction 4*, 27-43.

Chi, M.T., and Wylie, R. (2014). The ICAP framework: Linking cognitive engagement to active learning outcomes. *Educational Psychologist, 49*(4), 219-243.

Chin, C., and Brown, D.E. (2000). Learning in science: A comparison of deep and surface approaches. *Journal of Research in Science Teaching, 37*(2), 109-138.

Chinn, C.A., and Brewer, W.F. (1993). The role of anomalous data in knowledge acquisition: A theoretical framework and implications for science instruction. *Review of Educational Research, 63*(1), 1-49.

Cole, M. (2000). Struggling with complexity: *The Handbook of Child Psychology* at the millenium. Essay Review of *The Handbook of Child Psychology* by W. Damon. *Human Development, 6*, 369-375.

Coming Clean and Global Community Monitor. (2014). *Warning Signs: Toxic Air Pollution Identified at Oil and Gas Development Sites. Results from Community Air Monitoring Reveal Chemicals Linked to Health Hazards*. Available: https://comingcleaninc.org/assets/media/images/Reports/Warning%20Signs%20Report.pdf [December 2018].

Cook, T.D., Church, M.B., Ajanaku, S., Shadish,W.R., Jr., Kim, J., and Cohen, R. (1996). The development of occupational aspirations and expectations of inner-city boys. *Child Development, 67*(6), 3368-3385.

Costa, V.B. (1995). When science is "another world": Relationships between worlds of family, friends, school, and science. *Science Education, 79*(3), 313-333.

Csikszentmihalyi, M., Rathunde, K., and Whalen, S. (1993). *Talented Teenagers: The Roots of Success and Failure*. Cambridge, UK: Cambridge University Press.

Duit, R., and Treagust, D.F. (2003). Conceptual change: A powerful framework for improving science teaching and learning. *International Journal of Science Education, 25*(6), 671-688.

Dweck, C.S., and Leggett, E.L. (1988). A social-cognitive approach to motivation and personality. *Psychological Review, 95*(2), 256.

Eccles, J., Adler, T., Futterman, R., Goff, S., Kaczala, C., Meece, J., and Midgley, C. (1983). Expectancies, values, and academic behaviors. In J.T. Spence (Ed.), *Achievement and Achievement Motivation* (pp. 75-146). San Francisco, CA: W.H. Freeman.

Elliott, E.S., and Dweck, C.S. (1988). Goals: An approach to motivation and achievement. *Journal of Personality and Social Psychology, 54*(1), 5.

Engeström, Y., Miettinen, R., and Punamäki, R.L. (Eds.). (1999). *Perspectives on Activity Theory*. Cambridge, UK: Cambridge University Press.

Engle, R.A., and Conant, F.R. (2002). Guiding principles for fostering productive disciplinary engagement: Explaining an emergent argument in a community of learners classroom. *Cognition and Instruction, 20*(4), 399-483.

Eveleigh, A., Jennett, C., Blandford, A., Brohan, P., and Cox, A.L. (2014, April). Designing for dabblers and deterring drop-outs in citizen science. In *Proceedings of the SIGCHI Conference on Human Factors in Computing Systems* (pp. 2985-2994). New York: Association for Computing Machinery.

Finson, K.D. (2002). Drawing a scientist: What we do and do not know after fifty years of drawings. *School Science and Mathematics, 102*(7), 335-345.

Gelman, R., Brenneman, K., MacDonald, G., and Román, M. (2010). *Preschool Pathways to Science: Facilitating Ways of Doing, Thinking, Communicating, and Knowing About Science*. Baltimore, MD: Brookes.

Gibson, E.J. (1969). *Principles of Perceptual Learning and Development*. New York: Appleton-Century-Crofts.

Goldstone, R.L., Landy, D.H., and Son, J.Y. (2010). The education of perception. *Topics in Cognitive Science, 2*(2), 265-284.

Goodwin, C. (1994). Professional vision. *American Anthropologist, 96*(3), 606-633.

Gutiérrez, K.D., and Rogoff, B. (2003). Cultural ways of learning: Individual traits or repertoires of practice. *Educational Researcher, 32*(5), 19-25.

Hidi, S., and Ainley. M. (2008). Interest and self-regulation: Relationships between two variables that influence learning. In D.H. Schunk and B.J. Zimmerman (Eds.), *Motivation and Self-Regulated Learning: Theory, Research, and Application* (pp. 77-109). Mahwah, NJ: Erlbaum.

Hidi, S., and Renninger, K.A. (2006). The four-phase model of interest development. *Educational Psychologist, 41*(2), 111-127.

Hirschfeld, L.A. (2002). Why don't anthropologists like children? *American Anthropologist, 104*(2), 611-627.

Hofer, B.K., and Pintrich, P.R. (1997). The development of epistemological theories: Beliefs about knowledge and knowing and their relation to learning. *Review of Educational Research, 67*(1), 88-140.

Hogan, K., and Maglienti, M. (2001). Comparing the epistemological underpinnings of students' and scientists' reasoning about conclusions. *Journal of Research in Science Teaching, 38*(6), 663-687.

Karpicke, J.D., and Roediger, H.L. (2008). The critical importance of retrieval for learning. *Science, 319*(5865), 966-968.

Karpicke, J.D., and Blunt, J.R. (2011). Retrieval practice produces more learning than elaborative studying with concept mapping. *Science, 331*(6018), 772-775.

Kellman, P.J., and Garrigan, P. (2009). Perceptual learning and human expertise. *Physics of Life Reviews, 6*(2), 53-84.

Kellman, P.J., and Massey, C.M. (2013). Perceptual learning, cognition and expertise. *Psychology of Learning and Motivation, 58*, 117-165.

Kellman, P.J., Massey, C.M., and Son, J.Y. (2010). Perceptual learning modules in mathematics: Enhancing students' pattern recognition, structure extraction and fluency. *Topics in Cognitive Science, 2*(2), 285-305.

Kimmerer, R. (1998). Intellectual diversity: Bringing the native perspective into natural resources education. *Winds of Change, 13*(3), 14-18.

King, P.M., and Kitchener, K.S. (1994). Developing *Reflective Judgment*. San Francisco: Jossey-Bass.

Kuhn, D. (1999). A developmental model of critical thinking. *Educational Researcher, 28*(2), 16-26.

Kuhn, D., and Franklin, S. (2006). *The Second Decade: What Develops (and How)*. New York: John Wiley and Sons.

Kuhn, D., Garcia-Mila, M., Zohar, A., and Andersen, C. (1995). Strategies of knowledge acquisition. *Monographs of the Society for Research in Child Development, 245*(60), 4.

Lave, J. (1988). *Cognition in Practice: Mind, Mathematics and Culture in Everyday Life*. Cambridge, UK: Cambridge University Press.

Lave, J., and Wenger, E. (1991). *Situated Learning: Legitimate Peripheral Participation*. Cambridge, UK: Cambridge University Press.

Lee, O., and Brophy, J. (1996). Motivational patterns observed in sixth-grade science classrooms. *Journal of Research in Science Teaching, 33*(3), 303-318.

Lehrer, R., and Schauble, L. (2004). Modeling natural variation through distribution. *American Educational Research Journal, 41*(3), 635-679.

Lehrer R., and English L. (2018) Introducing children to modeling variability. In D. Ben-Zvi, K. Makar, and J. Garfield (Eds.), *International Handbook of Research in Statistics Education* (pp. 229-260). New York: Springer.

Levine Rose, S., and Calabrese Barton, A. (2012). Should Great Lakes City build a new power plant? How youth navigate socioscientific issues. *Journal of Research in Science Teaching, 49*(5), 541-567.

Lipstein, R., and Renninger, K.A. (2007). "Putting things into words": The development of 12-15-year-old students' interest for writing. In P. Boscolo and S. Hidi (Eds.), *Motivation and Writing: Research and School Practice* (pp. 113-140). New York: Elsevier.

Lyster, R., and Ranta, L. (1997). Corrective feedback and learner uptake: Negotiation of form in communicative classrooms. *Studies in Second Language Acquisition, 19*(1), 37-66.

Jonassen, D.H., and Rohrer-Murphy, L. (1999). Activity theory as a framework for designing constructivist learning environments. *Educational Technology Research and Development, 47*(1), 61-79.

Manz, E. (2016). Examining evidence construction as the transformation of the material world into community knowledge. *Journal of Research in Science Teaching, 53*(7), 1113-1140.

McComas, W.F., and Olson, J.K. (1998). The nature of science in international science education standards documents. In W.F. McComas (Ed.), *The Nature of Science in Science Education: Rationales and Strategies* (pp. 41-52). Dordrect, The Netherlands: Springer.

Mead, M., and Metraux, R. (1957). Image of the scientist among high-school students. *Science, 126*(3270), 384-390.

Meece, J.L., Blumenfeld, P.C., and Hoyle, R.H. (1988). Students' goal orientations and cognitive engagement in classroom activities. *Journal of Educational Psychology, 80*, 514-523.

Miller, D.I., Nolla, K.M., Eagly, A.H., and Uttal, D.H. (2018). The development of children's gender–science stereotypes: A meta-analysis of 5 decades of US Draw-A-Scientist studies. *Child development*. [Epublication ahead of print.] doi: 10.1111/cdev.13039.

Nasir, N.I.S., and Hand, V.M. (2006). Exploring sociocultural perspectives on race, culture, and learning. *Review of Educational Research, 76*(4), 449-475.

Nasir, N.I.S., and Saxe, G.B. (2003). Ethnic and academic identities: A cultural practice perspective on emerging tensions and their management in the lives of minority students. *Educational Researcher, 32*(5), 14-18.

National Research Council. (2007). *Taking Science to School: Learning and Teaching Science in Grades K–8.* Washington, DC: The National Academies Press.

National Research Council. (2009). *Learning Science in Informal Environments: People, Places, and Pursuits.* Washington, DC: The National Academies Press.

National Research Council. (2012). *A Framework for K–12 Science Education: Practices, Crosscutting Concepts, and Core Ideas.* Washington, DC: The National Academies Press.

Nicholls, J.G. (1984). Achievement motivation: Conceptions of ability, subjective experience, task choice, and performance. *Psychological Review, 91*(3), 328.

Nolen, S.B., and Ward, C.J. (2008). Sociocultural and situative approaches to studying motivation. *Advances in Motivation and Achievement, 15,* 425-460.

Osborne, J., Simon, S., and Collins, S. (2003). Attitudes towards science: A review of the literature and its implications. *International Journal of Science Education, 25*(9), 1049-1079.

Ottinger, G. (2016). Social movement-based citizen science. In D. Cavalier and E.G. Kennedy (Eds.), *The Rightful Place of Science: Citizen Science* (pp. 89-104). Tempe, AZ: Consortium for Science, Policy and Outcomes.

Palmgreen, P. (1984). Uses and gratifications: A theoretical perspective. *Annals of the International Communication Association, 8*(1), 20-55.

Pandya, R.E., Henderson, S., Henderson, R.A. Anthes, and Johnson, R.M. (2007). BEST Practices for Broadening Participation in the Geosciences: Strategies from the UCAR Significant Opportunities in Atmospheric Research and Science (SOARS) Program. *Journal of Geoscience Education, 55*(6), 500-506.

Perry, W.G. (1970). *Forms of Intellectual and Ethical Development in the College Years: A Scheme.* New York: Holt, Rinehart and Winston.

Pierotti, R., and Wildcat, D. (2000). Traditional ecological knowledge: the third alternative. *Ecological Applications, 10*(5), 1333-1340.

Pintrich, P.R. (2000). Multiple goals, multiple pathways: The role of goal orientation in learning and achievement. *Journal of Educational Psychology, 92*(3), 544.

Pintrich, P., and Schunk, D. (1996). *Motivation in Education: Theory, Research and Applications.* Englewood Cliffs, NJ: Prentice-Hall.

Rahm, J., Miller, H.C., Hartley, L., and Moore, J.C. (2003). The value of an emergent notion of authenticity: Examples from two student/teacher–scientist partnership programs. *Journal of Research in Science Teaching, 40*(8), 737-756. doi: 10.1002/tea.10109.

Rawson, K.A., and Dunlosky, J. (2011). Optimizing schedules of retrieval practice for durable and efficient learning: How much is enough? *Journal of Experimental Psychology: General, 140*(3), 283-302.

Renninger, K.A. (2000). Individual interest and its implications for understanding intrinsic motivation. In *Intrinsic and Extrinsic Motivation: The Search for Optimal Motivation and Performance* (pp. 373-404). San Diego, CA: Academic Press.

Renninger, K.A. (2010). Working with and cultivating interest, self-efficacy, and self-regulation. In D. Preiss and R. Sternberg (Eds.), *Innovations in Educational Psychology: Perspectives on Learning, Teaching and Human Development* (pp. 107–138). New York: Springer.

Renninger, K.A., and Hidi, S. (2002). Student interest and achievement: Developmental issues raised by a case study. In A. Wigfield and J. Eccles (Eds.) *Development of Achievement Motivation* (pp. 173-195). Cambridge, MA: Academic Press.

Renninger, K.A., and Hidi, S. (2011). Revisiting the conceptualization, measurement, and generation of interest. *Educational Psychologist, 46*(3), 168-184.

Rogoff, B. (2003). *The Cultural Nature of Human Development.* Oxford, UK: Oxford University Press.

Rowland, C.A. (2014). The effect of testing versus restudy on retention: A meta-analytic review of the testing effect. *Psychological Bulletin, 140*(6), 1432-1463.

Salmon, E. (1996). Decolonizing our voices. *Winds of Change.* Summer, 70-72.

Sansone, C. (2009). What's interest got to do with it?: Potential trade-offs in the self-regulation of motivation. In J.P. Forgas, R. Baumeister, and D. Tice (Eds.), *Psychology of Self-Regulation: Cognitive, Affective, and Motivational Processes* (pp. 35-51). New York: Psychology Press.

Schauble, L. (1996). The development of scientific reasoning in knowledge-rich contexts. *Developmental Psychology, 32*(1), 102-119.

Schoon, I. (2001). Teenage job aspirations and career attainment in adulthood: A 17-year follow-up study of teenagers who aspired to become scientists, health professionals, or engineers. *International Journal of Behavioral Development, 25*(2), 124-132.

Schwarz, R.S., Lederman, N.G., and Crawford, B.A. (2004). Developing views of nature of science in an authentic context: An explicit approach to bridging the gap between nature of science and scientific inquiry. *Science Education, 88*(4), 610-645.

Schwartz, C.V., Reiser, B.J., Davis, E.A., Kenyon, L., Acher, A., Fortus, D., Shwartz, Y., Hug, B., and Krajcik, J.S. (2009). Developing a learning progression for scientific modeling: Making scientific modeling accessible and meaningful for learners. *Journal of Research in Science Teaching, 46*(6), 632-654.

Sconiers, Z.D., and Rosiek, J.L. (2000). Voices inside schools-historical perspective as an important element of teachers' knowledge: A sonata-form case study of equity issues in a chemistry classroom. *Harvard Educational Review, 70*(3), 370-405.

Smith, C.L., Maclin, D., Houghton, C., and Hennessey, M.G. (2000). Sixth-grade students' epistemologies of science: The impact of school science experiences on epistemological development. *Cognition and Instruction, 18*(3), 349-422.

Soderstrom, N.C., and Bjork, R.A. (2015). Learning versus performance: An integrative review. *Perspectives on Psychological Science, 10*(2), 176-199.

Stevens, R., and Hall, R. (1998). Disciplined perception: Learning to see in technoscience. *Talking Mathematics in School: Studies of Teaching and Learning,* 107-149.

Stewart, J., Cartier, J.L., and Passmore, C.M. (2005). Developing understanding through model-based inquiry. In M.S. Donovan and J.D. Bransford (Eds.), *How Students Learn: Science in the Classroom* (pp. 515-565). Washington, DC: The National Academies Press.

Strike, K.A., and Posner, G.J. (1982). Conceptual change and science teaching. *European Journal of Science Education, 4*(3), 231-240.

United Nations Environment Programme. (1998). *Report on the Fourth Meeting of the Parties to the Convention on Biodiversity,* UNEP/CBD/COP/4/27. Nairobi, Kenya.

Wigfield, A., Schiefele, U., Eccles, J., Roeser, R.W., and Davis-Kean, P. (2006). Development of achievement motivation. In W. Damon and N. Eisenberg (Eds.), *Handbook of Child Psychology: Social, Emotional, and Personality Development* (6th ed., vol. 3). New York: Wiley.

# 5

# Citizen Science as an Opportunity for Science Learning

Having discussed in depth the processes of learning and the specific kinds of learning that occur in science in the previous chapter, we now turn to a discussion of how citizen science can be an opportunity for supporting, facilitating, and extending science learning. Each section in this chapter represents a learning outcome in science; for each, we will discuss how citizen science can address the outcome, with examples from citizen science projects of the strategies and practices used to advance those outcomes. As mentioned in Chapter 4 and illustrated here, learning outcomes in citizen science are intertwined: learning related to one outcome can reinforce, build on, or set the stage for learning related to other outcomes. Application of a single practice or strategy in citizen science may advance learning across several outcomes; and a single learning outcome may be advanced through the interplay of several elements of citizen science.

Given these observations, the committee chose to organize this chapter around learning outcomes: Because the framework of the strands has utility and widespread use beyond citizen science, it allowed the committee an opportunity to consider how the field of citizen science can fit into an established scholarly landscape. The sections presented here are organized by how "proximal" citizen science is to each learning outcome, that is, how easily participation in citizen science can be leveraged toward achieving the outcome described. Where achieving an outcome through citizen science is more challenging, we aim to offer examples of how those challenges can be mitigated.

In order to identify the examples of learning in citizen science highlighted below, the committee first conducted an ad hoc review of 28 typical citizen science projects (see Appendix D of this report). In executing this review, the committee was able to identify trends in how citizen science projects provide supports for learning, as well as what evidence for learning these projects cite when describing their work. This review is also critical to our discussion of project design in Chapter 6; so that we may be useful to the field in offering assistance related to how to leverage design for learning, we wanted to first ensure that we fully understood the existing landscape of what projects are currently doing to support learning.

As we describe below, there is evidence that many kinds of science learning can occur through participation in citizen science. This chapter represents the science learning outcomes where research in citizen science currently exists: As a note, the committee did not find enough research to effectively discuss the role of citizen science in supporting the development of the understanding of the nature of science, and as a result we have not discussed that learning outcome below. More research on this and other learning outcomes is certainly needed, an issue discussed in depth in the final chapter of this report.

One final note: it is important to note that not all citizen science projects are poised to support all kinds of science learning outcomes. In fact, participation in a project may not necessarily lead to learning on any front. With that said, some projects may be well-suited to pursue one particular outcome or another, while other projects may need some adaptation in order to get at the more challenging, less proximal learning outcomes. Where we use examples below, they are intended to serve as case examples of how pursuing one learning outcome might look in action. As we will describe in the following chapter, context and design choices are critically important factors in determining the extent to which a project supports science learning. These factors and others must be considered in the design of citizen science intended to achieve science learning.

## PROXIMAL LEARNING OUTCOMES IN CITIZEN SCIENCE LEARNING

In the following sections, we will discuss science learning outcomes that are proximal to citizen science; that is, outcomes that are relatively easy to achieve through participation in a citizen science project. In each section, we will discuss how these outcomes manifest in existing citizen science projects, and unpack how specific project activities support participants' development in each outcome. Where appropriate, we also attempt to identify how mastery of specific outcomes improves individual performance in the citizen science project, thereby improving the quality of participation.

## Motivation and Interest as Science Learning Outcomes in Citizen Science

In Chapter 4, we discussed the role of identity, interest, and motivation as mediators for learning science. Given these different but interrelated constructs, we turn now to how citizen science can support the development of these competencies as learning outcomes. Though these constructs may act similarly when serving as mediators in the learning process, fostering interest and motivation as learning outcomes through participation in science is very different from cultivating identity. For this reason, we turn to the outcome of identity later in this chapter, as the committee views identity development as more distal to the work of citizen science.

As discussed in Chapter 4, when people are interested in a subject area, they are more likely to attack challenges, use effective learning strategies, and make appropriate use of feedback (Csikszentmihalyi, Rathunde, and Whalen, 1993; Lipstein and Renninger, 2006; Renninger and Hidi, 2002). The EyesOnALZ citizen science project leverages interest in order to motivate participants and improve participant performance in the project (EyesOnALZ, 2018). This project relies on crowdsourcing data analysis to accelerate the pace of research into the links between blocked blood vessels in the brain (stalls) and Alzheimer's disease. In an online game-like environment, participants learn to use a virtual microscope to analyze blood flow to identify stalls in mouse blood vessels. Participants are also offered support and encouragement, which are included with all training materials in the form of a 1-minute video, online help guides, instant feedback from experts, and other "catchers" who are available to support learning.

Other citizen science projects have also found competition and gamification to contribute to motivation for participants, for example, Old Weather (Eveleigh et al., 2013) and Zooniverse (Greenhill et al., 2014). An analysis of gamification in Biotracker suggested that this was a particularly important attractor for millennials (Bowser et al., 2013), while in-depth interviews with participants in Foldit and EyeWire suggested gamification was more effective at sustaining the interest of participants than attracting new participants (Iacovides et al., 2013).

Citizen science projects may also choose to focus more on performance-oriented goals, especially if there is an emphasis on externally determined and validated data collection. For example, the Vital Signs Experience presents multiple "missions" through which participants can investigate the presence of native and invasive species in different habitat types throughout Maine (Vital Signs Experience, 2018). It is essential that documentation of invasive species is accurate and precise for this investigation, so the online data submission process includes an evaluation of evidence, with quality control and peer review steps. Online profiles of the program's professionals include detailed explanations on how citizen data are utilized, which serve to remind participants of the need for quality control. In this case, the outcome for the project (high-quality data) hinges on the interest of participants: Project designers are able to capitalize on participants' commitment to the project content in pursuit of accurate, high-quality project data.

It is also important to consider how participation that occurs in a nonvoluntary context (such as a formal education setting where a grade might hinge on participation) might influence learning outcomes. The resources and structure available in a formal education setting may positively support the development of motivation and interest, but negative consequences associated with lack of participation or "incorrect" participation could also have deleterious impacts on participant motivation. To the extent that free choice is one important mechanism in developing interest in science, it is important to consider the extent to which that free choice may be eroded for potential participants.

For participants who choose sustained participation in a project, there can be multiple, repeating opportunities to work on a progression of goals, during which regular performance feedback can serve to nurture the participant interest. Even for people who choose less frequent participation, activities can be presented with incremental performance goals to align with participant abilities and desires. Projects can capitalize on individuals perceiving some inherent worth in the focal phenomena or questions, where those individuals believe that participating in answering these questions are likely to yield successful outcomes. In EyesOnALZ, for example, participants are often reminded that they are contributing to finding a cure for Alzheimer's disease, which may speak to and serve to extend any manner of personal motivation for participating.

Projects can also support individuals who have some degree of mastery-oriented goals. Avid birdwatchers may be attracted to citizen science programs such as Project FeederWatch, which relies on observations from birdwatchers to track broad-scale movements of winter bird populations and long-term trends in bird distribution and abundance (Project FeederWatch, 2018). Participants can choose to take their bird knowledge to the next level by accessing online tools that describe how to identify bird species, how to recognize bird diseases, and how participant data are utilized across the study.

## Using Scientific Tools and Participating in Science Practices in Citizen Science

Citizen science can also provide a useful context for learning about the use of scientific tools and practices. Indeed, the "real-life" feature of many citizen science projects facilitates a space in which participants are often able to immerse themselves directly in the use of project-specific tools, protocols, and methods, enabling an up-close experience with "doing" science. The discrete skills that may be gained through participation in citizen science map directly onto this particular learning outcome.

As discussed in Chapter 2, although activity in citizen science may involve any number of scientific activities, data collection and observation are the most common kinds of citizen science activities available for participation. The skills necessary to perform these functions are not unsophisticated: they rely on sufficient knowledge to distinguish significant features of a data set or object from less significant features, as well as mastery of the procedural knowledge necessary to perform the tasks at hand. Participation in citizen science can build in an opportunity to extend these skills through initial training, practice, and regular feedback.

One example of how citizen science can provide a context for learning related to scientific tools and practices (along with science content knowledge) is a project known as the Coastal Observation and Seabird Survey Team (COASST, 2018), which has focused on monitoring beached birds since the year 2000. Currently, there are approximately 800 participants involved in data collection at hundreds of beaches on the West Coast of the United States. COASST staff lead training workshops for volunteers to learn the skills they need to collect rigorous data for coastal monitoring and management, with some training materials available on the project website as well. Volunteers learn how to safely and accurately take measurements of beached seabirds, use keys and field guides to identify bird species, and then tag carcasses so that future survey efforts will not recount them. Volunteers are guided through proper data entry on standardized forms, and then instructed to upload all data and photos to the data entry portal following the survey. After initial training, participants are actively engaged in their recently acquired project skills during monthly beach surveys. COASST participants are also asked to engage in the same scientific practices as experts in order to classify specimens at the species level. After a single 5-hour training, participants can correctly identify species 85 percent of the time (Parrish, 2013). With extended participation, volunteers can see how their individual contributions are aggregated and used to establish baseline temporal patterns of carcass occurrence and then investigate whether and how systems are changing, both locally and at larger scales (Jones et al., 2017).

Another project where citizens learn how to collect data to answer research questions is the West Oakland Environmental Indicators Project (WOEIP, 2018). This project, which has been ongoing for more than 17 years, was developed after West Oakland residents identified diesel traffic as an issue of concern in their neighborhoods. In this community-based participatory research project, local residents collaborate with academic partners from the Pacific Institute in order to evaluate the air quality of residential areas in West Oakland, California. Residents learn how to use professional air monitoring equipment and Global Positioning System (GPS) devices to collect data as they walk around their houses and schools. In addition to learning about how to use project equipment, the project's formal training program offers 12 hours of leadership training on topics of the development of the Port of Oakland, the impact of the freight transportation industry on local development, the health impacts of diesel exhaust and air pollution, technological solutions to air pollution, how the air quality regulation works, and how to advocate successfully for social justice and community health. In learning how to use the equipment, participants can collect enough firsthand data to support their own community leadership: In the past, residents have also surveyed streets to estimate traffic volume as well as the routes and speeds of heavy-duty trucks along the surface streets and freeways in West Oakland, which led to strategic partnerships between diverse stakeholders and ultimately policy-level changes in truck route ordinances (Gonzalez et al., 2011). In this case, mastery of project tools is a precursor to engaging in other community activities.

The Acadia Learning Project is an example of a citizen science project developed exclusively to form partnerships among teachers, students, and scientists (Acadia Learning Project, 2018). There are multiple projects within the overarching program (e.g., investigating snowpack, mercury in watersheds, and nitrogen cycling in watersheds) with data collection and analysis activities designed to align with many different educational standards. For example, to learn more about the prevalence of mercury in the environment, students and teachers collect samples of invertebrates, fish, plants, and soil. They may take measurements of mass or weight, size, or species abundance, and collect samples to send to a lab where mercury concentrations will be analyzed. The identified requirements of scientists, teachers, and students were notably different, which created some conflict in the program initially (Zoellick, Nelson, and Schauffler, 2012). For example, teachers and students needed assistance developing skills to create and interpret graphs of data from the project, and the learning outcomes specified in state educational standards did not mesh with the research questions of interest to the scientists. The Acadia Learning Project and their teacher partners navigated these tensions by implementing professional development for teachers focused on helping students develop good research questions and facilitating opportunities for the students to be of service to scientists by carefully following field protocols related to the scientists' research. Zoellick, Nelson, and Schauffler (2012) suggest that it can be helpful to have a third party, such as a university-based project team, who understands the needs of all of the participants to take responsibility for the overall success of the project and to manage both parallel and intersecting efforts.

### Learning Project-Specific Disciplinary Content in Citizen Science

Participation in citizen science regularly requires some facility with the science content at hand, and often asks participants to engage with new or unfamiliar content. The committee found evidence that scientific domain content learning occurs in citizen science. Many ecologically focused scientific and community projects, such as projects engaged in species observation or air and water quality monitoring, require participants to develop expertise in identifying and documenting species or other natural phenomena and gathering and organizing related data. This can range from making simple visual observations or routine measurements at fixed times or locations to more complex activities such as identifying and providing scientific evidence of observed instances; to discerning and predicting patterns to optimize the likelihood that irregular or unusual cases will be sampled; to solving nonroutine problems that may arise under changing conditions in the field. In order to conduct these activities, participants require sufficient relevant disciplinary content knowledge. In the examples below, we identify how projects supported the development of relevant disciplinary content knowledge.

In the Wildcam Gorongosa project, a network of motion-sensitive trail cameras snap photos of animals throughout the Gorongosa National Park in Mozambique (Wildcam Gorongosa, 2018). Participants contribute to the massive species identification efforts by identifying and classifying animals that appear in the images. For unfamiliar species, the online identification tool allows users to develop enough content knowledge to make decisions based on body shape, pattern, color, and the presence of horns. Users are encouraged to make their best guess with the reassurance that many people review the same photo and experts will verify any cases of substantial disagreement.

While there may be a tendency to dismiss or undervalue species identification tasks as involving "simple fact learning," such an attitude often belies the nature of the learning that needs to occur and sheds little light on how to improve performance and outcomes. For example, accurate species identification is typically more complex than merely checking off whether a specimen has a couple of distinguishing features. Considerable within-species variation (e.g., juvenile versus adult forms, gender differences, and seasonal and individual variation) is not uncommon. At the same time, instances from other categories may share many similarities. Identification may also involve degraded samples (e.g., carcasses, partial or blurred photographs, instrument calibration issues) or nonvisual evidence, such as auditory calls, such that experienced participants must develop enough content knowledge to be able to recognize and discriminate species. In Wildcam Gorongosa, successful participation hinges on mastery of these content details, and the project is specifically designed to help participants get to that level of mastery through participation.

An example of a project that developed content knowledge in the field of biochemistry is Foldit (2018). Foldit[1] is a multiplayer online game in which players work in the computationally challenging domain of protein structure prediction. Experienced human players—most of whom do not have prior experience in molecular biology—have been able to match or outperform state-of-the-art automated computational methods in both their ability to remodel complex protein structures and their ability (both individual and collective) to generate and refine creative strategies for exploring this very large and complex problem space (Cooper et al., 2010). Foldit players have independently discovered new algorithms that parallel those developed by professional scientists (Khatib et al., 2011a), and they have generated successful models for structures that had eluded prior attempts in research labs, such as the crystal structure of a monomeric retroviral protease, which is now providing insights for the design of antiretroviral drugs (Khatib et al., 2011b). Foldit players who come to perceive the organization of complex protein structures are demonstrating the often-impressive results of successful learning processes, such as perceptual learning described in Chapter 4. With extended experience, Foldit players fine-tune their three-dimensional spatial reasoning skills and their problem-solving strategies to the particular requirements of this domain and the entities they encounter in it.

## Summary

It is clear from these examples that sophisticated learning occurs in citizen science projects. However, research exploring *learning processes* in citizen science, such as how participants acquire the expertise needed for a particular project, has been noticeably absent. Attending more deliberately to learning is a promising strategy for improving the consistency and quality of learning in citizen science, and for contributing to other project outcomes that depend on learning, such as collecting high-quality data.

---

[1]The committee notes that Foldit is on the boundary of what the committee considered as citizen science, as it is possible to participate in Foldit without any awareness of the underlying scientific content or the project's larger-scale scientific goals. Nevertheless, the committee includes this example here as it provides a well-documented example of how one might learn content through citizen science practices.

## DISTAL LEARNING OUTCOMES IN SCIENCE

In considering all of the science learning outcomes discussed in Chapter 4, the committee noted several learning outcomes that were distal to citizen science in that they are possible to achieve, but need more conscious planning or effort on the part of project designers. In the following sections, we discuss these distal outcomes. As noted in Chapter 4, these outcomes are distal in any learning context, not just citizen science: achieving mastery in these arenas requires intentionality on the part of educators. As with the sections above, we will discuss how specific project activities can be leveraged in support of participants' development in each outcome.

### Developing Understanding of Explanatory
### Scientific Concepts in Citizen Science

Chapter 4 discusses the import of conceptual change in learning generally, and specifically in science. As mentioned in our discussion in Chapter 1 about what kinds of citizen science projects we considered in our investigation, the committee looked at projects beyond those solely focused on achieving scientific goals. As conceptual change is not necessarily one of the easiest learning outcomes for citizen science, much of the evidence reviewed in this section is from approaches inspired by citizen science that have been successfully applied in more focused educational contexts. Learning goals involving conceptual change and development typically depend on more active facilitation, structuring, and sequencing of learning materials and opportunities over substantial periods of time. As such, learning outcomes involving conceptual change and development may be easier to achieve in formal educational settings because of the opportunities for more extensive and sustained support for learning.

Designers should not be surprised if participants bring intuitive or naïve knowledge that is not consistent with scientific explanations of the natural world. The conceptual change literature has documented common misconceptions in the physical sciences related to matter, force, and energy (Chi, Feltovich, and Glaser, 1981; Chi, Slotta, and deLeeuw, 1994; Clark, 2006; McCloskey et al., 1980); in the life sciences related to variability and natural selection in evolution, ecology (Munson, 1994), the operation of the circulatory system, and processes such as photosynthesis and respiration (Anderson, Sheldon, and Dubay, 1990); and in earth and space sciences related to explanations of day/night cycles, seasons, the solar system, and planetary rotation and orbits (Borun, Massey, and Lutter, 1993; Vosniadou and Brewer, 1992, 1994). Scientific phenomena that involve extreme scales of time and space are also challenging for naïve individuals to process (Jones et al., 2007; Libarkin, Kurdziel, and Anderson, 2007).

Partial change or changes in thinking that are confined to some contexts are also not uncommon.

Although there is virtually no direct research on conceptual change as an outcome of citizen science learning experiences, we speculate that aspects of some citizen science activities may support conceptual change. For example, some participants engage in citizen science over a long period of time and have successive opportunities to broaden and deepen their involvement (e.g., by seeing patterns of data over time, by participating in intensive workshops with scientists and scientifically trained facilitators, by becoming a mentor or trainer, or by engaging in more phases of a project) (Bonney et al., 2009). Also, many science educators see potential opportunities to enhance existing citizen science projects with additional learning activities and curricular resources or incorporate citizen science–style activities within a curricular sequence.

For projects interested in positioning citizen science activities as part of an intentional effort to promote conceptual change, a more recent approach termed "learning progressions" may be of interest (Corcoran, Mosher, and Rogat, 2009; National Research Council, 2012). Learning progressions focus on core concepts, such as the core disciplinary ideas and associated science practices outlined in *A Framework for K–12 Science Education* (National Research Council, 2012) and use empirical research on students' learning to pose testable hypotheses about how learning progresses over multiple years. Learning progressions describe coherent pathways and sequences so that learners' ideas can be developed and reconceptualized over time to achieve mature, scientific understanding (Wiser, Smith, and Doubler, 2012). Several learning progressions have already been systematically developed for key science topics, such as water, energy, and carbon cycling in socioecological systems (Gunckel et al., 2012; Jin and Anderson, 2012; Mohan, Chen, and Anderson, 2009); genetics (Duncan, Rogat, and Yarden, 2009); the nature of matter and atomic molecular theory (Smith et al., 2006; Stevens, Delgado, and Krajcik, 2010); force and motion (Alonzo and Steedle, 2009); and evolution (Catley, Lehrer, and Reiser, 2005). Active efforts are under way in other scientific domains.

The "iEvolve with STEM" program (iEvolve, 2018) presents an example of how citizen science activities can support learning progressions and the related conceptual change. In this program, two school districts present science teachers with the option of participating in a variety of citizen science projects for students in grades 3–5 and grades 6–8. To support science learning, curriculum is developed by a team of lead teachers: Curriculum development experts who generate structured templates, curriculum maps, and cross-curricular lesson planners. A 3-year program of teacher professional development, involving summer workshops and monthly meetings, begins by ensuring that teachers are comfortable and confident leading hands-on inquiry-based learning, and knowledgeable in specific science content knowledge. The second year focuses on understanding the true nature of scientific research by refining skills and methodologies related to data collection, analysis, and reporting. The third year focuses on optimizing teaching methods, improving assessment, and ensuring the sustainability of projects in subsequent years. This intensive approach may not be necessary to support all learning outcomes, but programs that can bring together researchers, educators, and curriculum professionals are much more likely to be able to support longer term learning outcomes associated with conceptual change.

Citizen science may also appeal to educators who are interested in supporting conceptual change and development of a deep understanding of core disciplinary ideas in science (e.g., those ideas described in the National Research Council's 2012 report) within a formal education setting. Because some citizen science activities can be productively sustained over longer periods of time (which is important when the goals of science learning involve conceptual change and development), it can be leveraged in support of gradual processes requiring extended learning opportunities. While a concern with developing deeper conceptual understanding of foundational ideas in science is typically thought of as a goal for school students, it is worth noting that citizen science could potentially provide unique and uncommon opportunities for adults who wish to do this but who do not have access to or who are not involved in formal education settings. Moreover, because citizen science–style projects and activities can provide a natural way to infuse the learning of core concepts with science practices (as is strongly advocated in the NGSS Framework and Standards), tools, and resources provided by a citizen science project can support an enriched set of practices, such as data analysis, modeling, and interpretation. Mastery of these outcomes can in turn spur deeper understanding of science concepts and how they are related.

## Identity in Science

Chapter 4 discusses the complexity of identity as both a mediator and an outcome in science learning. These constructs are tricky to untangle: An identity as someone whose ideas are welcome in science and as someone who has the ability to contribute to science mediates participation, and those identities can be reinforced by positive experiences participating in science.

Participation in citizen science is poised to support the development of both disciplinary identities (someone who actually does science and can contribute to science) and social and cultural identities (the extent to which participants are able to integrate their cultural selves into the culture of science). This is particularly true for participants who come to science from nondominant communities that are not always widely represented or visible within the institution of science. As discussed in Chapter 4, researchers have documented how recognizing and honoring different identities in learning, for example by inviting elders to share indigenous knowledge in the course of the project, can open new learning opportunities for learners from nondominant backgrounds (Aikenhead and Jegede, 1999; Bang et al., 2010; Morris, Chiu, and Liu, 2015). Indeed, this becomes particularly important with respect to developing disciplinary identities for learners from underrepresented groups because of the historical trends with respect to who does science, and to what extent their contributions are recognized—or not.

The contributors to the broad range of scientific knowledge are diverse, with important innovations and insights coming from all over the world, and reflecting many cultures, but the culture of modern science is dominated by Euro-American norms and emphasizes Western contributions. Learning environments concerned with equity need to include deliberate interventions in dominant narratives and perspectives by including multiple, diverse forms of relevance and contributions as part of peoples' experiences. Further, while this is especially important to successfully engaging more underrepresented groups, highlighting a diversity of perspectives can lead to better social interactions for all learners (Rosenthal and Levy, 2010). Additionally, intentionally showing respect for and engagement with multiple perspectives can lead to more rigorous learning and problem solving (Rosenthal and Levy, 2010).

Through participating in citizen science, individuals as well as communities can be empowered to make decisions about what to study, how research should be conducted, and who should be involved in scientific matters. Informal science experiences, such as those offered through citizen science projects can provide people, especially those from underrepresented backgrounds, valuable opportunities to practice and develop their connections to science (Farland-Smith, 2012; Rahm and Ash, 2008). These opportunities may be especially valuable for learners who are navigating conflicting identities from their home culture, as they look for activities that align with the values and practices of their home communities and the scientific community. It is important to recognize that individuals first need to be made aware of opportunities to engage in science, including citizen science projects. To this end, SciStarter embeds its project database on the Websites of partners including the National Science Teachers Association, PBS, *Discover* magazine, libraries, museums, and more (SciStarter, 2018). The contexts surrounding citizen science projects are filled with opportunities to engage with families and diverse communities.

As discussed in Chapter 3, considering *who* is learning through participation in citizen science and adopting an asset-based approach to supporting that learning can ultimately facilitate mastery of desired learning outcomes: the multiple ways of knowing within a citizen science project should be considered a source of the creative perspectives and approaches necessary for progress in the scientific endeavor. One example of a program using a foundation of traditional indigenous knowledge is the Urban Explorers Program designed by the American Indian Center in Chicago; this program helps the community cultivate the land in alignment with indigenous land management practices (American Indian Center, 2018). Indigenous Science Days encourage participants of all backgrounds to gather in different outdoor locations throughout Chicago to learn about culturally relevant seasonal activities (e.g., harvesting, land restoration and management, invasive species removal, planting) through traditional indigenous practices. Although the program was not designed or facilitated by professional scientists, it provided an opportunity for community members of all backgrounds to become familiar with Indigenous ways of knowing.

A different community-based summer science education program in Wisconsin and Illinois focused on supporting student's navigation among multiple epistemologies, with the participation of community members (Bang and Medin, 2010). While not a typical citizen science project, the program used an integrated approach to increase autonomy of community members, including the use of traditional knowledge, elder involvement, community participation in the research agenda, and respect of cultural value and informed consent. Through participation in the program, students became more engaged in school science as they learned to view it as more relevant and useful to their communities. Pre- and post-interviews showed a consistent increase in the ways that students identified with science, through their willingness to endorse the statement, "My tribe has been doing science for a long time."

These examples are useful because they capitalize on a series of evidence-based strategies for developing identity in science. In order to do this work, these programs seek to attend to different ways of knowing from different backgrounds by ensuring appropriate learning scaffolds that do not assume participant limits based on background. Moreover, participant contributions are not limited to data: participants are invited to bring previous knowledge into the work, which honors the cultural identity that participants bring into the project and allows participants to integrate identities rather than reject aspects of their cultural identity that might not "fit" in science. These strategies and others are highlighted in the following chapter on designing citizen science experiences to support science learning.

## Scientific Reasoning

Described in Chapter 4, engaging in scientific reasoning is a central part of doing science. However, it is a challenging outcome to pursue through citizen science and requires significant investment from both designers and participants. A small number of research and evaluation studies of citizen science projects have attempted to measure whether participants show gains in their understanding of the nature of science and their ability to engage in various aspects of scientific reasoning (see Strands 3 and 4 and the scientific practices described in Chapter 3). Reasoning and critical thinking are often difficult to measure reliably (National Research Council, 2011, 2014), and they may look different depending on the context of a specific project. As a result, measures of reasoning may vary across projects and may involve self-report (interview or survey), case studies, and observation methodologies (Bonney et al., 2009; Jordan et al., 2011).

Allowing participants an opportunity to understand the reasoning involved in making project decisions in different phases and aspects of a citizen science project has been shown to help them engage in more scientific thinking over the course of their participation. This can be as simple as regular or occasional updates from the project leads that discuss the scientific reasoning involved in project design and analysis, or as involved as a joint effort to design, implement, and evaluate new scientific approaches within a project. To give one example: the Cornell Laboratory of Ornithology analyzed unsolicited letters from more than 700 participants in a successful citizen science project focused on investigating seed preferences in ground feeders for common bird species to examine the degree to which participants (mostly older and well-educated) spontaneously indicated that they were engaging in scientific thinking related to the project (Trumbull et al., 2000). In this project, the experimental questions and research design were already given. Participants were provided with a research kit, including data forms, a full-color poster of common feeder birds, and step-by-step instructions to set up the experiment and gather and submit their tallies. They also received a subscription to a newsletter, which reported results from the project and included articles about how to analyze their own data if they chose to do so. While the data from participants' letters do not enable causal conclusions about whether people improved their scientific reasoning as a result of the project, they do provide evidence that, for some participants, the project provided occasions to engage in scientific thinking. Some letter writers provided detailed observations; others proposed their own hypotheses for the data they were observing. A few proposed more than one hypothesis or suggested other ways to test a hypothesis. The letters also revealed areas in which improvements could be made to help participants better understand scientific processes and reasoning. For example, multiple writers did not appreciate the power of a large nationwide sample or what role their own data collection played in the larger project. Some also did not appreciate the value of a consistent protocol across many different sites.

Going a step further, there is strong body of research on the learning outcomes from actively engaging in scientific reasoning activities, such as in hypothesis formulation and testing; research design; data modeling and interpretation; and the development, critique, and communication of evidence-based arguments. Opportunities to do this are available in some citizen science projects—typically those in which nonscientist participants have had significant collaborative roles and have participated in shared decision making in creating or implementing projects and activities (Bonney et al., 2009). For example, the Shermans Creek Conservation Association, started by a group of residents in south-central Pennsylvania in 1998, has run a long-term project with support from the Alliance for Aquatic Resources Monitoring (ALLARM, 2018) to monitor the health of the Shermans Creek Watershed. Volunteers have been trained by ALLARM to collect and analyze monthly samples and conduct seasonal assessments and have then used their data to make recommendations to target critical areas for restoration and protection, to engage in public education, and to empower community decision making related to land development and watershed management. While many participants are satisfied with participating primarily in data collection activities, some core organizers and volunteers have also been engaged in data analysis workshops aimed at teaching them to interpret project data and to evaluate the strength of evidence for drawing conclusions and framing recommendations. Working in conjunction with ALLARM, they have compiled detailed scientific reports covering multiple chemical and biological indicators and have developed and advocated for specific recommendations. In addition to cultivating strong data analysis skills, these more engaged participants developed a deeper understanding of scientific methodology through active participation in developing questions that could be successfully answered through scientific investigation, redesigning studies to improve their scientific quality, and matching data collection methods to the intended uses of data (Bonney et al., 2009; Wilderman, 2005).

The Virginia Master Naturalists is a citizen science program that provides significant supports to facilitate learning and the use of participatory modeling for environmental decision making (Virginia Master Naturalists, 2018). The volunteers participate in 40 hours of classroom and field work to become trained as Master Naturalists, and then participate in 8 hours of specialized training in citizen science. Their training is further enhanced by additional continuing education and annual recertification. They volunteer on a variety of environmental conservation projects involving citizen science, education, and stewardship of natural resources in Virginia. Using both online resources and facilitated in-person sessions, participants, scientists, and environmental managers are trained to do collaborative modeling using an online system known as Mental Modeler (Gray et al., 2013). This system allows collaborating teams to define issues; model and represent assumptions, existing information, and evidence; run scenarios to inform potential research or management options; and co-develop plans. Online tools allow teams to upload, view, and share data and also provide discussion forums and collaboration spaces. The Mental Modeler software supports the construction of models in the form of concept maps that specify variables and relationships among them, with associated evidence and confidence ratings. Concept maps are converted into a matrix structure that can be analyzed using matrix algebra calculations in which the relationships among variables are examined, classified, and assigned weights, and then used to run and compare scenarios. Once a team of Master Naturalist volunteers and professionals has collaboratively created a model, field data collection can be used to validate or reject aspects of a given model. Gray and colleagues (2013) provide case study evidence based on changes in concept maps over time that show how both individuals and collective groups engaged in new learning during the process of collaborative modeling. Further, the development of a shared conceptual model played a central role in the development of specific management plans and conservation action. In one case, a group focusing on the quality of woodpecker habitat ultimately developed and implemented an experimental design to evaluate different methods of controlling an invasive grass. In contrast to their early conceptual models, later models represented alternative hypotheses involving variables that either were not present originally or did not play a driving role in early models. Another group, which was focused on implementing best practices for agricultural water quality improvement, found in their modeling that cost was a central driving variable influencing the overall systems dynamics. As this emerged, this group's planning process led volunteers to seek out new funding sources.

Teaching people to evaluate evidence and understand the scientific process requires significant investments in terms of time, pedagogy, and instructional design in both formal and informal settings. Doing it in a way that does not privilege certain cultural values and marginalize others requires careful attention to sociocultural understandings of learning. It is essential for designers and implementers to be aware of some of the beliefs and patterns of reasoning that they may encounter in participants, and to treat those beliefs and patterns of reasoning with respect. The committee noted that key aspects of citizen science activities—namely their connection to scientific or community questions—provide potential inputs for learning and development of scientific reasoning. Active science problems or science-related community questions, by their very nature, are open-ended and ill-structured, and the practices and discourse processes of science focus squarely on generating reliable, relevant evidence and evaluating how it does or does not support explicit claims. For this reason, the committee sees distinct possibility in engaging in citizen science–inspired learning opportunities in order to achieve learning outcomes related to scientific reasoning.

## Summary

The examples listed above offer insight into how learning outcomes that might be more distal to citizen science are, in fact, possible to achieve through participation in citizen science projects with proper supports. Because structured learning settings such as K–12 classrooms and after-school programs may have access to specific resources (sustained meeting times, educators with experience supporting science learning, access to tools and resources, etc.), they may be poised to leverage citizen science in order to address some of these more challenging learning outcomes. In the following chapter, we discuss how project designers can make choices in project design and implementation that can specifically support science learning.

## SUMMARY

In summary, our investigation revealed that citizen science projects support a variety of learning outcomes. Some of these outcomes, such as developing motivation and learning new scientific skills, are relatively common within the activities and practices that are common across all citizen science projects. Others, such as encouraging the development of scientific reasoning, come only with significant supports and scaffolds that are less ubiquitous. The committee identified an affinity between citizen science practices and best practices for supporting learning. However, there are few investigations into the unique learning opportunities associated with citizen science, though the work around identity development in citizen science heads in this direction (as outlined in the paper contributed by Ballard). Similarly, there are few methods that have been consistently applied across a range of citizen science projects—indeed, there are relatively few common tools for analyzing learning within the community of people who study learning in citizen science. This is not surprising for a nascent field.

As a note, because citizen science invites nonscientists into science, it provides an opportunity to welcome and explore differing epistemologies and cultural traditions and how they enrich learning. This has the potential to shed light on the persistent underrepresentation and under-participation of many communities and their members in science, and these insights are likely to be useful well beyond citizen science. Further, this investigation of how epistemologies of science interact with other epistemologies may be particularly salient to learning outcomes related to the nature of science. We encourage the citizen science community to investigate how learning outcomes related to the nature of science are advanced by citizen science practices and participation. In fact, citizen science may provide a novel laboratory for education researchers to explore how people develop and refine their understanding of the nature of science.

In the following chapter, we will turn to in-depth descriptions of how the citizen science project design can support the learning outcomes highlighted above, as well as outline how the knowledge and experience of participants can be used to support desired learning outcomes. In order to do this work, we rely on our discussion of the common and divergent elements of citizen science described in Chapter 2 to frame an analysis of how project designers may leverage specific design choices in pursuit of particular learning outcomes. Using the cases highlighted above as concrete examples of the kinds of learning in citizen science, we are now poised to offer guidance to project designers, educators, and others interested in learning about how to support science learning.

## REFERENCES

Acadia Learning Project. (2018). Available: http://participatoryscience.org [May 2018].

Aikenhead, G.S., and Jegede, O.J. (1999). Cross-cultural science education: A cognitive explanation of a cultural phenomenon. *Journal of Research in Science Teaching, 36*(3), 269-287.

ALLARM (Alliance for Aquatic Resource Monitoring). (2018). Available: https://www.dickinson.edu/allarm [May 2018].

Alonzo, A.C., and Steedle, J.T. (2009). Developing and assessing a force and motion learning progression. *Science Education, 93*(3), 389-421.

American Indian Center. (2018). Available: https://www.aicchicago.org [May 2018].

Anderson, C.W., Sheldon, T.H., and Dubay, J. (1990). The effects of instruction on college nonmajors' conceptions of respiration and photosynthesis. *Journal of Research in Science Teaching, 27*(8), 761-776.

Bang, M., and Medin, D. (2010). Cultural processes in science education: Supporting the navigation of multiple epistemologies. *Science Education, 94*(6), 1008-1026.

Bonney, R., Ballard, H., Jordan, R., McCallie, E., Phillips, T., Shirk, J., and Wilderman, C.C. (2009). *Public Participation in Scientific Research: Defining the Field and Assessing Its Potential for Informal Science Education.* A CAISE Inquiry Group Report. Washington, DC: Center for Advancement of Informal Science Education.

Borun, M., Massey, C., and Lutter, T. (1993). Naive knowledge and the design of science museum exhibits. *Curator, 36*, 210-219.

Bowser, A., Hansen, D., He, Y., Boston, C., Reid, M., Gunnell, L., and Preece, J. (2013, October). Using gamification to inspire new citizen science volunteers. In *Proceedings of the First International Conference on Gameful Design, Research, and Applications* (pp. 18-25). New York: Association for Computing Machinery.

Catley, K., Lehrer, R., and Reiser, B. (2005). *Tracing a Prospective Learning Progression for Developing Understanding of Evolution.* Paper commissioned by the National Academies Committee on Test Design for K–12 Science Achievement.

Chi, M.T.H., Feltovich, P.J., and Glaser, R. (1981). Categorization and representation of physics problems by experts and novices. *Cognitive Science, 5,* 121-152.

Chi, M.T.H., Slotta, J.D., and de Leeuw N. (1994). From things to processes: A theory of conceptual change for learning science concepts. *Learning and Instruction 4,* 27-43.

Clark, D.B. (2006). Longitudinal conceptual change in students' understanding of thermal equilibrium: An examination of the process of conceptual restructuring. *Cognition and Instruction, 24*(6), 467-563.

COASST (Coastal Observation and Seabird Survey Team). (2018). C Available: https://depts. washington.edu/coasst [September 2018].

Cooper, S., Khatib, F., Treuille, A., Barbero, J., Lee, J., Beenen, M., Leaver-Fay, A, Baker, D., and Popovic, Z., and >57,000 Foldit players. (2010). Predicting protein structures with a multiplayer online game. *Nature, 466*(7307), 756-760.

Corcoran, T., Mosher, F.A., and Rogat, A. (May, 2009). *Learning Progressions in Science: An Evidence-Based Approach to Reform.* Consortium for Policy Research in Education, CPRE Research Report #RR-63.

Csikszentmihalyi, M., Rathunde, K., and Whalen S. (1993). *Talented Teenagers: The Roots of Success and Failure.* Cambridge, UK: Cambridge University Press.

Duncan, R.G., Rogat, A.D., and Yarden, A. (2009). A learning progression for deepening students' understandings of modern genetics across the 5th-10th grades. *JRST, 46*(6), 655-674.

Eveleigh, A., Jennett, C., Lynn, S., and Cox, A.L. (2013). "I want to be a Captain! I want to be a Captain!": Gamification in the Old Weather Citizen Science Project. In *Proceedings from the First International Conference on Gameful Design, Research, and Applications* (pp. 79-82). New York: Association for Computing Machinery.

EyesonAlz. (2018). Available: http://eyesonalz.com [May 2018].

Farland-Smith, D. (2012). Personal and social interactions between young girls and scientists: Examining critical aspects for identity construction. *Journal of Science Teacher Education, 23*(1), 1-18.

Foldit. (2018). Available: https://fold.it/portal [September 2018].

Gonzalez, P. A., Minkler, M., Garcia, A. P., Gordon, M., Garzón, C., Palaniappan, M., Prakash, S. and Beveridge, B. (2011). Community-based participatory research and policy advocacy to reduce diesel exposure in West Oakland, California. *American Journal of Public Health, 101*(S1), S166-S175.

Gray, S.A., Gray, S., Cox, L.J., and Henly-Shepard, S. (2013). Mental modeler: A fuzzy-logic cognitive mapping modeling tool for adaptive environmental management. In *Proceedings from the 46th Hawaii International Conference on System Sciences* (pp. 965-973). IEEE.

Greenhill, A., Holmes, K., Lintott, C., Simmons, B., Masters, K., Cox, J., and Graham, G. (2014). *Playing with Science: Gamised Aspects of Gamification Found on the Online Citizen Science Project-Zooniverse.* Paper presented at *GAMEON 2014.*

Gunckel, K.L., Covitt, B.A., Salinas, I., and Anderson, C.W. (2012). A learning progression for water in socio-ecological systems. *JRST, 49*(7), 843-868.

Iacovides, I., Jennett, C., Cornish-Trestrail, C., and Cox, A.L. (2013, April). Do games attract or sustain engagement in citizen science?: A study of volunteer motivations. In *CHI '13 Extended Abstracts on Human Factors in Computing Systems* (pp. 1101–1106). New York: Association for Computing Machinery.

iEvolve. (2018). Bowling Green State University. Available: http://www.bgsu.edu/nwo/current-grant-projects/ievolve.html [May 2018]

Jin, H., and Anderson, C.W. (2012). A learning progression for energy in socio-ecological systems. *JRST, 49*(9), 1149-1180.

Jones, M.G., Taylor, A., Minogue, J., Broadwell, B., Wiebe, E., and Carter, G. (2007). Understanding scale: Powers of ten. *Journal of Science Education and Technology 16*(2), 191-202.

Jordan, R.C., Gray, S.A., Howe, D.V., Brooks, W.R., and Ehrenfeld, J.G. (2011). Knowledge gain and behavioral change in citizen-science programs. *Conservation Biology, 25*(6), 1148-1154.

Khatib, F., Cooper, S., Tyka, M.D., Xu K., Makedon, I., Popovic, Z., Baker, D., and Foldit Players. (2011a). Algorithm discovery by protein folding game players. *Proceedings of the National Academy of Sciences of the United States of America, 108*(47), 18949-18953. doi: 10.1073/pnas.1115898108.

Khatib, F., DiMaio, F., Foldit Contenders Group, Foldit Void Crushers Group, Cooper, S., Kazmierczyk, M., Gilskil, M., Krzywda, S., Zabranska, H., Pichova, I., Thompson, J., Popovic, Jaskolski, M., and Baker, D. (2011b). Crystal structure of a monomeric retroviral protease solved by protein folding game players. *Nature Structural and Molecular Biology, 18*(10), 1175-1177. doi: http://doi.org/10.1038/nsmb.2119.

Libarkin, J.C., Kurdziel, J.P., and Anderson, S.W. (2007). College student conceptions of geological time and the disconnect between ordering and scale. *Journal of Geoscience Education, 55*(5), 413-422.

Lipstein, R., and Renninger, K.A. (2006). "Putting things into words": The development of 12-15-year-old students' interest for writing. In P. Boscolo and S. Hidi (Eds.), *Motivation and Writing: Research and School Practice* (pp. 113-140). New York: Elsevier.

McCloskey, M., Caramazza, A., and Green, B. (1980). Curvilinear motion in the absence of external forces: Naive beliefs about the motion of objects. *Science, 210*(4474), 1139-1141.

Mohan, L., Chen, J., and Anderson, C.W. (2009). Developing a multi-year learning progression for carbon cycling in socio-ecological systems. *Journal of Research in Science Teaching, 46*(6), 675-698.

Morris, M.W., Chiu, C.Y., and Liu, Z. (2015). Polycultural psychology. *Annual Review of Psychology, 66*, 631-659.

Munson, B.H. (1994). Ecological misconceptions. *Journal of Environmental Education, 25*(4), 30-34.

National Research Council. (2011). *Assessing 21st Century Skills: Summary of a Workshop.* Washington, DC: The National Academies Press.

National Research Council. (2012). *A Framework for K–12 Science Education: Practices, Crosscutting Concepts, and Core Ideas.* Washington, DC: The National Academies Press.

National Research Council. (2014). *Developing Assessments for the Next Generation Science Standards.* Committee on Developing Assessments of Science Proficiency in K–12. Washington, DC: The National Academies Press.

Parrish, J.K. (2013). Rigor, reliability, and scientific relevance: Citizen science lessons from COASST. In *American Geophysical Union Fall Meeting Abstracts.*

Project FeederWatch. (2018). Available: http://feederwatch.org [May 2018].

Rahm, J., and Ash, D. (2008). Learning environments at the margin: Case studies of disenfranchised youth doing science in an aquarium and an after-school program. *Learning Environments Research, 11*(1), 49-62.

Renninger, K.A., and Hidi, S. (2002). Student interest and achievement: Developmental issues raised by a case study. In A. Wigfield and J.S. Eccles (Eds.), *Development of Achievement Motivation* (pp. 173-195). San Diego, CA: Academic Press.

Rosenthal, L., and Levy, S.R. (2010). The colorblind, multicultural, and polycultural ideological approaches to improving intergroup attitudes and relations. *Social Issues and Policy Review, 4*(1), 215-246.

Rosenthal, L., and Levy, S.R. (2012). The relation between polyculturalism and intergroup attitudes among racially and ethnically diverse adults. *Cultural Diversity and Ethnic Minority Psychology, 18*(1), 1.

SciStarter. (2018). Available: https://scistarter.com [September 2018].

Smith, C.L., Wiser, M., Anderson, C.W., and Krajcik, J. (2006). Implications of research on children's learning for standards and assessment: A proposed learning progression for matter and the atomic-molecular theory. *Measurement: Interdisciplinary Research and Perspective, 4*(1-2), 1-98.

Stevens, S.Y., Delgado, C., and Krajcik, J.S. (2010). Developing a hypothetical multi-dimensional learning progression for the nature of matter. *Journal of Research in Science Teaching, 47*(6), 687-715.

Trumbull, D.J., Bonney, R., Bascom, D., and Cabral, A. (2000). Thinking scientifically during participation in a citizen-science project. *Science Education, 84*, 265-275.

Virginia Master Naturalists. (2018). Available: http://www.virginiamasternaturalist.org [May 2018].

Vital Signs Experience. (2018). Available: http://vitalsigns.gmri.org [May 2018].

Vosniadou, S., and Brewer, W.F. (1992). Mental model of the earth: A study of conceptual change in childhood. *Cognitive Psychology, 24*, 535-585.

Vosniadou, S., and Brewer, W.F. (1994). Mental models of the day/night cycle. *Cognitive Science, 18*, 123-183.

WOEIP. West Oakland Environmental Indicators Project. (2018). Available: http://www.woeip.org [May 2018].

Wildcam Gorongosa. (2018). Available: https://www.wildcamgorongosa.org [May 2018].

Wilderman, C.C. (2005). *Shermans Creek: A Portrait.* Harrisburg: Pennsylvania Department of Environmental Protection.

Wiser, M., Smith, C.L., and Doubler, S. (2012). Learning progressions as tools for curriculum development. In A.C. Alonzo and A.W. Gotwals (Eds.), *Learning Progressions in Science: Current Challenges and New Directions* (pp. 359-403). Rotterdam, The Netherlands: Sense.

Zoellick, B., Nelson, S.J., and Schauffler, M. (2012). Participatory science and education: bringing both views into focus. *Frontiers in Ecology and the Environment, 10*(6), 310-313.

# 6

# Designing for Learning

Prior chapters laid out the committee's perspective on learning, described general processes of learning as well as learning outcomes in science, and offered examples of science learning in citizen science contexts. This chapter will approach the question of how design can amplify opportunities for learning in citizen science. There are a few ideas that frame the committee's investigation into design, learning, and citizen science. First, design and design for learning are fields with evolving bodies of knowledge and practice that can be applied to citizen science. While there are very few explicit studies of the design process in citizen science, there is a wealth of scholarship more generally about design for learning that can be reasonably extrapolated to citizen science learning. Second, design for learning as a field has advanced, and researchers and practitioners now know more about how to enable learning for more learners than they did even 10 years ago. Third, as with many fields, design for learning has grown because of and in response to what researchers and practitioners have learned about the benefits of broad participation. Designing to engage the skills and contributions of diverse learners, especially learners whose insights may have been previously neglected or even rejected, maximizes learning for all learners.

Design for learning is also a practical set of evidence-based strategies for applying ideas and theories in connection to the environment, participants, context, and dealing with constraints while maximizing opportunities. Designing for learning is the application of learning theory to citizen science contexts, in both formal and informal settings, and for a variety of participants. In this way, this chapter can offer guidance to people who seek to maximize learning from citizen science, and especially to those who are designing the project. As we will see, however, an evolved design strategy that has proven very effective for maximizing learning opportunities intentionally blurs the boundary between project designer and project participant.

Design for learning is something that can happen at any point in a project's lifetime. For example, many citizen science projects are adapted to promote learning, and even citizen science projects designed for learning can be redesigned for new contexts. In fact, as we will also see later in the chapter, best practices in design suggest a process of iteration and constant refinement—design as an ongoing process.

Design for learning as a process implies intentionality. It is worth noting that design decisions are made whether or not they are consciously attended to: regardless of whether or not project designers are expressly intending to pursue a specific learning outcome, designers' decisions about how to implement projects have implications for what participants will experience. Sometimes citizen science projects are created with learning in mind, whereas for other projects learning is not an express goal. While learning can happen either way, it is more likely when the projects are designed (either created or adapted) with learning in mind.

Taking a design lens to citizen science means seeing program engagement as an opportunity to learn. Understanding how learning opportunities emerge in citizen science efforts requires making explicit the critical aspects of program design that can engage cognitive, affective, and social outcomes. In this chapter, the committee aims to suggest how learning opportunities can be realized in citizen science efforts, especially those in which creating opportunities to learn was not the primary design intent. To do so requires a necessary focus on the inherent variability of these efforts. From the previous chapters, we can understand that:

- There is a wide range of organizers and of potential participants.
- The needs of both the organizers and the intended participants will differ.
- The opportunity to make meaningful contributions to science and communities (i.e., the authenticity of citizen science) creates unique learning opportunities.
- Planning for meeting the needs of the intended participants is vital.
- Attending to learning advances broader citizen science project goals.
- Designing for diversity maximizes learning opportunities for all participants. Conversely, not designing a program for diverse audiences means that the program is designed for the default audience, which usually matches the demographics of the designer or dominant group.

In our review of the design and planning literature (see Appendix A) we identified nine considerations for designing to achieve learning objectives. Based on the citizen science projects we surveyed, we can say that projects that attended to these considerations were able to capitalize on the learning opportunities associated with citizen science and maximize learning outcomes for all participants. Further, based on theories of learning and the state-of-the art theory of design, we can say that projects that attend to these considerations will maximize learning for all participants. To be clear, the committee is not making new recommendations here; instead we are summarizing guidance found in the research literature of design for learning and mapping that guidance onto citizen science with illustrative examples. The recommendations themselves are general, but when they are implemented in the context of citizen science, we believe they have a novel utility. The committee did not find evidence for design strategies that are unique to citizen science, though we would encourage that line of research. Instead we found evidence for how well-known, time-tested, and fairly ubiquitous design recommendations can be applied effectively to citizen science. The guiding considerations are

1. Know the Audience
2. Adopt an Asset-Based Perspective
3. Intentionally Design for Diversity
4. Engage Stakeholders in Design
5. Capitalize on Unique Learning Opportunities Associated with Citizen Science
6. Support Multiple Kinds of Participant Engagement
7. Encourage Social Interaction
8. Build Learning Supports into the Project
9. Evaluate and Refine

## 1. KNOW THE AUDIENCE

For any project being designed for learning, the literature on designing makes clear that it is essential to have some frame of understanding of the intended audience. To effectively communicate and educate, an individual, such as a project manager or the scientist designing the citizen science project, begins with an implicit or explicit definition regarding what audience they are designing for (Slater, 1996). In designing for learning, defining the audience as explicitly and accurately as possible is an important step.

The challenge and goal of knowing the audience is knowing and growing an audience of participants/volunteers that is not homogeneous. It is important to design messages and programming based on the underlying needs and preferences that drive individuals to engage in the natural exchange of benefits between program planner/educator/program lead and the desired audience (Garver, Divine, and Spralls, 2009). Program planning decisions need to come from a clear understanding of the audiences' wants and needs (Grier and Bryant, 2005). One perspective on this interchange comes from exchange theory, which suggests that people have resources, such as time. Individuals exchange these resources for perceived program benefits, such as learning from the tasks and protocols in a citizen science project (Lefebvre and Flora, 1988).

Segmentation studies can provide an insight into understanding those who volunteer in citizen science projects. To retain volunteers, it is useful to first understand why they volunteer and then why they continue to volunteer or not (Asah, Lenentine, and Blahna, 2014). As described in Chapter 5, there are several examples of citizen science projects that attempt to capitalize on motivation and interest. For example, volunteers in an urban landscape restoration project listed various sources of motivation, which include helping the environment, getting outdoors, emotional well-being, community, socializing, meaningful actions, values, learning, career, health, personal growth, protection, and user of the landscape (Asah, Lenetine, and Blahna, 2014).

The DEVISE scale on motivation to participate in citizen science measures motivations that range from interest and enjoyment to factors such as worry or guilt (Phillips et al., in press). Motivations can be interpreted from the very simplistic and superficial "why" question to a very complex psychological framework or structure. For example, in a community health context, motivations included a need to be useful/productive, a need for affiliation, a need to help others, a need for status, a need to make oneself more marketable, and a strong personal concern for a cause (Garver, Divine, and Spralls, 2009). By understanding why people participate, designers can find overlap across participants' goals for participation as well as projects' scientific goals.

## 2. ADOPT AN ASSET-BASED PERSPECTIVE

When considering the audience, it is important to approach the audience with an asset-based frame of reference. In previous chapters, we discuss how people learn more when learning is connected to their previous experiences and draws on all their cultural and intellectual capacity—and that simply is harder to do if the project designers think only in terms of deficits or gaps. Thinking in terms of what individuals need to know but do not know and designing for community disadvantages invites deficit framing. It can be tempting to think in terms of naïve conceptions that distort new information and experiences, but sociocultural learning suggests that simply dismissing the conceptions that learners bring as wrong or naïve can hinder learning.

Instead, design practice and learning theory suggest welcoming the views and conceptions that participants may bring into the project, and offering participants the chance to connect their experience in the project to existing knowledge and experience, as well as support engagement. People come with prior knowledge and experience, and it increases the power of any experience to see how the present learning builds on what the participant already knows (Knowles, 1970, 1984). It is particularly important to make sure these connections are available and respected for participants whose knowledge systems or traditions have been treated dismissively in the past—for example, Indigenous knowledge systems.

A good way to ensure that projects offer the opportunity to connect with participants' existing knowledge is for project designers to invite people who hold knowledge into the design of the project. If a project is already designed, it can be helpful for designers to invite participants into the design of learning experiences that support their goals for the project. For projects that do not have face-to-face engagement, written questions can serve as a means of allowing the individual to reflect on prior experience and knowledge and share these reflections with others. Allowing or creating space—either in person or online—for sharing culturally, community, or individually held perspectives helps people integrate prior knowledge and perceptions with project learning. Learning progressions (see Chapter 4 of this report), which are empirically based maps of how people can develop understanding over time, can be useful frameworks for anticipating and building on the conceptual models people may have as they enter projects.

As an example, many participants in the Community Collaborative, Rain, Hail, and Snow Network (CoCoRaHS) join the project because of their strong interest in the topic of weather (CoCoRaHS, 2018). When asked what sources they used for learning during participation, greater than 60 percent relied on pre-existing knowledge (Phillips, 2017). Support for sharing pre-existing knowledge with other participants can lead to role expansion or mentorship opportunities for individuals, which also can deepen learning.

## 3. INTENTIONALLY DESIGN FOR DIVERSITY

Research suggests that in the absence of explicit consideration of diversity, design will default to meeting the needs and expectations of members of dominant or majority groups (e.g., Henderson, 1996). This can be true even if the design team includes members of nondominant groups. Even ideas such as universal design that are meant to promote inclusivity in design (discussed in this section, below) can be applied in ways that reinforce narrow aspects of identity and perpetuate marginalization (Edyburn, 2010). This is visible in consumer product design, urban planning and architecture, and, most importantly to this report, education (Valencia, 2012).

Designing for diversity, across all learning environments, means avoiding deficit framings, which are especially likely to be applied to members of historically underserved and underrepresented communities. In simple terms, designers should avoid ascribing negative characteristics to any identity. Proactively, designers should design with participants so that participants can engage multiple, intersecting identities that change over time, as well as invite input from multiple, sometimes intersecting, identities (Settles, 2004). Designers should consider issues of power and recognize and design to minimize differences in power (Elmesky and Tobin, 2005). Designing for diversity means designing projects that allow and value contributions and connections for multiple experiences, knowledge, and even epistemological frameworks (Bang and Medin, 2010). It means avoiding assumptions or making choices about what participants will or will not be capable of (Burgstahler, 2009).

There is a small body of research exploring how to design for diversity in citizen science, which mostly borrows strategies that have proven effective in other education settings. This literature points to projects that focus on key concerns or priorities of underserved and underrepresented communities, participatory program design, applying principles of Community-Based Participatory Research or community science, place-based projects, designing for accessibility across multiple languages, considering structural barriers to participation (e.g., transportation, language), and linking projects to culturally relevant reference points (Pandya, 2012).

As suggested by the limited research focusing on broadening participation in citizen science, there are effective and proven practices to promote diversity and equity in science education and career development that can be adapted for citizen science. For example, in research on interventions to support students of color in science, it has been shown that careful mentoring (Haring, 1999; Pfund et al., 2016), strong supportive social networks (Stolle-McAllister, 2011), visible affirmation of the importance of diversity from institutional leaders (Best and Thomas, 2004; Tsui, 2007), and positive experience of research (Russell, Hancock, and McCollough, 2007) are practices that support continued participation of learners from underrepresented groups. Experience with research is an inherent part of citizen science, and project leads can intentionally foster a positive experience. Likewise, the other practices can also easily be incorporated: Project leads can talk about the contribution diverse perspectives make toward project outcomes, social networks can be nurtured, and mentoring can be built into participant role.

A useful frame for designers is the notion of universal design for learning (Rose, 2000), which points out that disability is not a quality of an individual, but the result of curricula too inflexible to provide pathways for all learners. The same idea can be applied to citizen science: Designers can develop multiple pathways for engagement and especially design around factors that could be barriers to engagement. For instance, if project materials are only English, that will be a barrier for people who do not speak English, but one which translation can readily overcome. GLOBE and eBird have developed supports in several languages (eBird, 2018; GLOBE, 2018). As another example, projects that assume access to natural settings might be inaccessible for people who do not have ready access to parks, but partnering with an urban garden or botanical center can remove that barrier, as through the partnership between Project Budburst and the Chicago Botanic Garden (Meymaris et al., 2008; Project Budburst, 2018).

Project design often makes assumptions about the people who will participate in projects, and our committee recommends that designers interrogate those assumptions, and especially question whether the extent to which those assumptions are informed by systemic and structural inequities or personal biases. As we stated in earlier sections of this report, *all* participants require support and scaffolding to participate in projects, and *all* designers make choices about what scaffolds and supports to provide. These choices are necessarily informed by the context in which they are made, but when designers are explicit about why, how, and for whom they are designing, they are better poised to address the needs of all learners.

All of these considerations point to the fundamental question of who is designing for whom, and points toward the next recommendation as a way to uncover the design assumptions and decisions—sometimes unconscious—that limit access. The next design consideration looks at how the concerns listed above can often be addressed by including a diverse cross-section of stakeholders in the co-design process *and* ensuring that they have voice and agency in design decisions.

## 4. ENGAGE STAKEHOLDERS IN DESIGN

Design thinking has evolved toward an emphasis on design that is more user centered (Norman, 2013) and learner centered (Soloway, Guzdial, and Hay, 1994). Current design thinking emphasizes making the needs and aspirations of users paramount, and suggests a process of rapid prototyping to arrive at useful and usable services. An audience is easier to understand from within, which means the idea of knowing your audience is a strong additional argument for engaging stakeholders in the design process. When done well, design with stakeholders should foreground an asset-based model and attend to diversity, as co-design is about mining diverse expertise and perspectives for a better product for all.

The Thriving Earth Exchange (TEX) worked with local community organizations to co-design a project to collect indoor air quality data in Colorado (Thriving Earth Exchange, 2018). The partnership involved the community during every phase of the project, starting with understanding what the local priorities were and providing workshops to determine how to address air, soil, and water pollution. Additionally, these conversations introduced scientists to community-based participatory research methods.

## 5. CAPITALIZE ON UNIQUE LEARNING OPPORTUNITIES ASSOCIATED WITH CITIZEN SCIENCE

In the following sections, we consider how the specific learning opportunities associated with citizen science—mentioned in Chapter 3 of this report—can provide specific, desirable leverage points for project designers looking to support science learning. In each, we discuss how this unique feature of citizen science, when harnessed appropriately, can make citizen science a particularly useful learning context.

### Develop Data Knowledge

As discussed in Chapters 3 and 4, the centrality of data—both collecting it and working with it—in citizen science means that it provides a unique opportunity to introduce participants to developing data knowledge. Again, this outcome does not happen without intention. Like other scientific reasoning, learning about data requires a combination of content background or disciplinary grounding, and facilitation in developing, testing, and refining data-based concepts. This facilitation can take the form of software tools, prompts, curriculum, explicit instruction, etc. For instance, one form of facilitation can involve building, or accelerating, data visualization literacy. Shared data visualizations can be constructed from simple x/y visuals by overlaying additional information while holding constant a data point provided by participants and adds to the relevancy of the exercise.

eBird documents the presence, absence, and abundance of bird species using checklist data submitted by volunteers from around the world (eBird, 2018). eBird provides a simple Web-based interface to view project results via interactive queries of the database. The interface enables visualization of data in the form of maps, graphs, and bar charts. Moreover, the data are provided in raw form so they can be downloaded, analyzed, and used by anyone for numerous purposes including baseline monitoring, natural resource management, education and outreach, and policy formulation (Sullivan et al., 2014).

## Highlight the Authenticity of Participants' Experiences Through Real-World Contexts

One of the key features that is common across many citizen science projects is the authenticity of citizen science, or the fact that individual participation contributes to something bigger, such as research, conservation, etc. As discussed in Chapter 4, this is a learning opportunity that is intimately tied to a learning outcome. It can motivate other strands of learning, and can be leveraged to amplify participants' identities as contributors to science or to support the application of science to a community issues. Knowing their participation is leading to important, usable data reinforces the value of participation for citizen scientists.

Highlighting the authenticity of participation can be as simple as facilitating frequent feedback from scientists who use the collected data, or as complex as using data to advocate for new policies. Feedback can take many forms including written documentation shared with participants about how scientists have used the data in the past; regular updates about potential future uses of the data; lists of publications; online databases for broader use; education about using results in ways that support civic decision making; and discussions about how project results can be used to inform policy.

Nearly all citizen science projects that gather and use data can leverage the authenticity of participants' activity. The Galaxy Zoo project provides regular and timely feedback regarding data contribution milestones and an extensive up-to-date list of publications that use the data (Galaxy Zoo, 2018). Furthering their learning and role expansion in the science process, certain "super users" who were integral to particular discoveries or manuscript development have been included as authors on peer-reviewed Galaxy Zoo publications.

## Design for Community Science Literacy

Community science literacy (as discussed earlier) is distributed science knowledge and the ability to use that knowledge, in connection with a broad suite of community knowledge and capabilities, to leverage science for its community goals. Citizen science projects that explicitly offer different roles and make clear how those roles contribute to the common goal can encourage community science literacy. Some projects, such as community-based participatory research projects, obviously benefit from thinking about community science literacy. But other types of projects can also think of ways in which the whole is greater than the sum of its parts. For example, community-based participatory citizen science projects bring together people with a broadly distributed knowledge of the community, the issue being addressed, and the systems in which the project will unfold. This collective sharing allows all participants to be both learners and educators by providing an opportunity for all voices to bring their knowledge to the discussion to look for the best solution for the community.

Silver City Watershed Keepers of New Mexico emphasize the role that citizen scientists can play in monitoring watersheds and collecting water quality data, taking personal responsibility to be an informed citizen, and sharing information to build community knowledge (Silver City Watershed Keepers, 2018). Based on the knowledge they gather, they also provide "rural mining communities with the skills and capacities they need to make their neighborhoods/watersheds better places to live and work."

## 6. SUPPORT MULTIPLE KINDS OF PARTICIPANT ENGAGEMENT

In citizen science projects, there are dabblers and divers, both within and across projects (Eveleigh et al., 2014). It is well studied and understood that repeated engagement enhances learning of facts and concepts. For many citizen science projects, a basic way of considering participant engagement, over time, is that regularity in participation matters. More frequent regular participation in short activities (e.g., data collection and reporting) has better potential for enhancing learning than less regular participation. For instance, projects that require daily observations, even if the observations are relatively easy and take a short amount of time are good for learning the process, knowledge, and concepts associated with those observations. Projects can encourage this mode of learning by providing pathways, in the form of levels of engagement that change participants' engagement over time.

Project FeederWatch has been operating for more than 30 years using the same protocol where participants watch their bird feeders every 2 weeks for 2 consecutive days throughout the winter months (Project FeederWatch, 2018). The structured engagement allows for repeated practice to hone skills of identification and improve confidence. In turn, this results in increased participant retention and higher quality, long-term data.

Repeated engagement can also take place across projects, and stronger science and conservation outcomes occur when volunteers participate in multiple, varied projects, as shown in an analysis of participants in the Audubon's 116th Christmas Bird Count (Cooper et al., 2016). All of the 3,000 people who were surveyed report participation in at least one other birding citizen science project, and over one-third also participate in nonbirding projects. Approximately 15–20 percent of respondents said this participation influenced their donation of conservation funds, voting for habitat conservation, and creation of wildlife habitat at home. Those who did multiple types of projects were more likely to contribute more to science outcomes and grassroots conservation actions than those who only did bird projects.

Collectively encouraging participants to do multiple projects may also make the process of recruiting, supporting, and retaining participants, as well as undertaking scholarly studies of participation, more effective and efficient. To foster participation in multiple projects across topics and activities and to surface and support synergies that might occur as individuals engage with multiple projects, SciStarter 2.0 offers citizen scientists tools to find and join multiple projects, manage and display their citizen science activities, record their progress in projects, network, and consent to have their online participation studied across citizen science projects; and offers project organizers tools to connect with people who are interested in or experienced with similar projects as well as access to analytics to understand the movement of and interests of their own participants (SciStarter, 2018).

## 7. ENCOURAGE SOCIAL INTERACTION

Learning is a sociocultural activity, so anything that encourages interaction provides the opportunity for learning. There are many different approaches to what is seen as "social." Activities as diverse as online fora for participants, data collection in teams, in-person meetings, and having people verify others' classifications all can be designed to provide opportunities for interaction that can enhance learning.

We know some participants in citizen science projects desire and/or benefit from engaging in science as a social activity. Even individual data collection projects can be structured to communicate to individual citizen scientists that they are part of a larger endeavor that has social implications.

It is important in designing for social interactions that promote learning to consider the comfort for all participants. Projects that support learning offer participants a place of "comfort," trust in the environment, and social engagement around learning (Kop, Fournier, and Sui Fai Mak, 2011). Kop and colleagues suggest that within these conditions, it is possible to create a pedagogy that supports people in their learning, through the active creation of resources and learning places by participants and educators/facilitators. Such a pedagogy would be based on building connections, collaborations, and the exchange of resources between people, the building of a community of learners, and harnessing of information flows on networks.

The Hudson River American Eel Research Project mobilizes community members of all ages to count, weigh, and release juvenile American eels along the tributaries of the Hudson River (Hudson River American Eel Research Project, 2018). In addition to learning through the data collection experience, and through training and project materials, participants report that in-person interactions are a major source of learning (Phillips, 2017). Learning is likely heightened by the diverse and intergenerational nature of these social interactions, often involving inner-city high school students and local retirees. The project also boasts an end-of-year "Eelebration" where data from each of the sites are presented to all the volunteers in a jovial and fun setting.

## 8.  BUILD LEARNING SUPPORTS INTO THE PROJECT

Knowing what both designers and participants want to learn and then creating supports for that learning is important. People will learn without supports, but they will learn faster with supports (Rogoff, 1995). Once you have decided on learning goals, build supports that help people achieve these learning goals. Think of those supports in terms of tools people can use, interactions they can have with each other, and guidance they can get from project leaders.

Some of the supports the committee has seen that work effectively include tutorials, mentoring new participants by more advanced participants, curriculum, newsletters, personalized communications, in-person and online training, and interactive multimedia tools such as quizzes and peer-to-peer communication forums. This consideration also relates to making the purpose of the learning visible. For example, curriculum-based projects such as BirdSleuth (2018) and GLOBE (2018) provide robust classroom activities and lesson plans aligned with the Next Generation Science Standards. Other projects such as BeeSpotter (2018) and Nature's Notebook (2018) provide comprehensive training materials, such as identification keys, presentations, lecture notes, and quizzes.

Because the field is young, there is relatively little research on the kinds of supports that are inherent in or well-matched to citizen science. However, as summarized in the previous three chapters, there is a large and robust body of education research on learning outcomes and how to work with stakeholders to achieve those outcomes. Some high-level strategies that can help guide the design of learning supports are described below.

### Give Participants Opportunities to Communicate and Apply What They Learn

Communication often prompts reflection about a participant's learning, which can reveal gaps, guide future learning, and aid in long-term retention. Application allows participants to extend their knowledge to new domains, which is, itself, a kind of learning, and helps with retention. Some ways to do this could include project-related discussions, an asynchronous online discussion, or a reflective prompt for the individual to consider. Other approaches include using results in civic processes or inviting participants to help describe project findings and results in both scientific and nonscientific fora. The opportunities to communicate are closely related to the notion of authenticity in citizen activity discussed above.

The Alliance for Aquatic Resource Monitoring (ALLARM), originally developed to help communities deal with acid rain deposition, provides training and technical support for mitigating point source pollution in local watersheds (ALLARM, 2018). ALLARM was designed to engage individuals in all aspects of project design and to specifically empower them to participate in community efforts that led to solutions. Currently, ALLARM provides a decision tree for guiding action. Through letters to the editor, discussions with government representatives, and presentations at community events, participants used their newly acquired knowledge to describe the acid deposition problem.

### Give Participants Many Examples and Frequent Feedback

Where enhanced perceptual learning is a goal of participation, project designers can support this objectifying by offering participants a chance to interact with many examples of the kind of data that participants will be collecting, classifying, or analyzing, coupled with feedback about that interaction. Galaxy Zoo is a good example of a project that provides many examples for participants alongside frequent feedback. In Galaxy Zoo participants learn to classify by making and comparing their classifications against those of others. Thinking of creative ways to provide feedback directly or indirectly might lead some citizen science projects to richer designs and more committed participants. For projects that tend to attract one-time engagement, building feedback into the experience may increase individuals' satisfaction, which can help lead to interest in additional engagement in citizen science.

### Link the Project's Scientific Goals with Its Learning Goals

Projects will have an easier time reaching their nonlearning-related goals if the participants are motivated, have agency, identify with the project, and have relevant domain knowledge and perceptual knowledge. For many participants, learning is a benefit to participation; for many project owners, participant learning may be critical for their science. Either way, for the learning to have meaning to the project, the goals for learning must connect to the desired outcomes for the project (Bennett, 1978). The mission of the Monarch Larva Monitoring Project (MLMP) for example, is to "better understand the distribution and abundance of breeding monarchs and to use that knowledge to inform and inspire monarch conservation" (Monarch Larva Monitoring Project, 2018). By linking science and conservation goals directly to the design of the project, MLMP participants not only learn a great deal about monarchs, they are also motivated to actively enhance habitats for monarchs, which in turn supports the overall project goals.

The West Oakland Environmental Indicators Project is a resident-led, community-based environmental justice organization, which operates the Community Leadership Academy (West Oakland Environmental Indicators Project, 2018). The Academy is a formal training program that offers 12 hours of leadership training on topics specific to the development of the Port of Oakland including the impact of the freight transportation industry on local development, the health impacts of diesel exhaust and air pollution, technological solutions to air pollution, how the air quality regulation works, and how to advocate successfully for social justice and community health. This is a clear example of relating learning to overall project goals.

## Connect Science Process to Science Content

Research makes it clear that learning to engage in scientific practices—such as constructing and testing scientific arguments and evaluating scientific evidence—is facilitated by simultaneously learning disciplinary concepts and facts, and vice-versa. In fact, it is often easier for people to learn processes of science by applying the process directly to a specific problem, rather than as an abstract exercise. However, many projects wrongly assume that an emphasis on the content will result in learning about the process. For this reason, projects that explicitly design for both content and process are more likely to advance learning. Projects can do this by being explicit about the nature of science (such as the aims of and claims made with data), providing models of reasoning from the participants' work, and encouraging participants to propose and discuss their own claims and perhaps compare their claims against those of the scientist. Projects that are explicit in this way can contribute to scientists' learning, as they provide other perspectives. The protocol for COASST was developed to specifically train participants to evaluate scientific evidence (in this case, seabird carcasses) to accurately identify the species (COASST, 2018). COASST also provides feedback on the accuracy of each data point to participants, thereby enhancing both content knowledge and the development of science process skills. In a pre-post evaluation of COASST, Haywood (2014) showed an increase in volunteers' ability to correctly weigh evidence to determine whether sufficient information existed for accurate species identification.

## Emphasize the Constructed Nature of Project Knowledge

Letting people interact with open-ended problems is a good way to accelerate this learning progression. Citizen science projects are sometimes emergent, exploratory, or descriptive. When appropriate, it can be valuable to design the program so that participants can engage in data analysis, have access to the tools necessary to discuss the evidence, and be part of, or at least follow along with, the evolving understanding of scientific learning through project data. Projects that provide the most opportunities to engage participants in co-constructing knowledge typically involve participants in using and sharing project results to affect change, helping to determine the intended uses of data, and collaborating on the design of the project. Projects emphasizing a collective effort to develop understanding, with opportunities for participants to propose, critique, and refine ideas with their peers, are best at this strand of learning.

## 9. EVALUATE AND REFINE

Good design for learning is an iterative process, and it is necessary to design evaluation, reflection, and revision into the design process. Again, there are relatively few tools for evaluation and iteration that are specific to citizen science or that work across all citizen science projects, so the committee urges the citizen science community to borrow, adapt, refine, and share. Remember that good evaluation is always answering the question: How do I improve *this* effort? Participants involved in an evaluation program can provide evaluative thinking. This often strengthens the evaluation much more than the evaluation activity itself (Patton, 1997). The values that are part of the culture of evaluation are demonstrated through evaluative thinking and include clarity; specificity and focusing; being systematic and making assumptions explicit; operationalizing program concepts, ideas, and goals; distinguishing inputs and processes from outcomes; valuing empirical evidence; and separating statements of fact from interpretation and judgements (Patton, 2002).

## SUMMARY

The fundamental message of this chapter is that citizen science projects can be designed in ways that enhance learning for all participants. The evolution of design shows that more involvement of diverse stakeholders, especially when they are welcomed for the contributions they can bring to the project, improves project outcomes. This is true for all outcomes, including the learning outcomes explored in previous chapters. Further, there are actionable strategies that can be used to promote learning in the

context of citizen science and take advantage of the unique learning opportunities associated with citizen science. If the committee had to sum it up
in sentence, albeit a long one, we would suggest that iterative, cooperative
engagement in design and implementation, with a diversity of stakeholders who are respected for the knowledge they bring to the design process,
results in more learning for all participants, and that this learning can support other project goals.

# REFERENCES

ALLARM (Alliance for Aquatic Resource Monitoring). (2018). Available: https://www.dick-
inson.edu/allarm [May 2018].
Asah, S.T., Lenentine, M.M., and Blahna, D.J. (2014). Benefits of urban landscape eco-volun-
teerism: Mixed methods segmentation analysis and implications for volunteer retention.
*Landscape and Urban Planning, 123*, 108-113.
Bang, M., and Medin, D. (2010). Cultural processes in science education: Supporting the
navigation of multiple epistemologies. *Science Education, 94*(6), 1008-1026.
BeeSpotter. (2018). Available: https://beespotter.org [September 2018].
Bennett, S.N. (1978). Recent research on teaching: A dream, a belief, and a model. *British
Journal of Educational Psychology, 48*(2), 127-147.
Best, D.L., and Thomas, J.J. (2004). Cultural diversity and cross-cultural perspectives. In A.H.
Eagly, A.E. Beall, and R.J. Sternberg (Eds.), *The Psychology of Gender* (pp. 296-327).
New York: Guilford Press.
BirdSleuth. (2018). *Cornell Lab of Ornithology.* Available: http://www.birdsleuth.org [Sep-
tember 2018].
Burgstahler, S. (2009). *Universal Design of Instruction (UDI): Definition, Principles, Guide-
lines, and Examples.* Seattle, WA: DO-IT. Available: https://www.washington.edu/doit/
sites/default/files/atoms/files/UD_Instruction_05_26_15.pdf [October 2018].
COASST (Coastal Observation and Seabird Survey Team). (2018). Available: https://depts.
washington.edu/coasst [September 2018].
CoCoRaHS (Community Collaborative Rain, Hail, and Snow Network). (2018). Available:
https://www.cocorahs.org [September 2018].
Cooper C., Larson, L., Shipley, N., Dayer, A., Dale, K., LeBaron, G., and Takekawa, J. (2016).
*Divers and Dabblers: Which Types of Birdwatchers Are Most Valuable to Citizen Science
Research and Grassroots Conservation?* Paper presented at the 2016 American Ornithology Society Conference.
eBird. (2018). *The Cornell Lab of Ornithology.* Available: https://ebird.org/home [September
2018].
Edyburn, D.L. (2010). Would you recognize universal design for learning if you saw it? Ten
propositions for new directions for the second decade of UDL. *Learning Disability
Quarterly, 33*(1), 33-41.
Elmesky, R., and Tobin, K. (2005). Expanding our understandings of urban science education
by expanding the roles of students as researchers. *Journal of Research in Science Teaching, 42*(7), 807-828.
Eveleigh, A., Jennett, C., Blandford, A., Brohan, P., and Cox, A.L. (2014, April). Designing
for dabblers and deterring drop-outs in citizen science. In *Proceedings of the SIGCHI
Conference on Human Factors in Computing Systems* (pp. 2985-2994). New York: As-
sociation for Computing Machinery.
Galaxy Zoo. (2018). Available: https://www.zooniverse.org/publications [May 2018].

Garver, M.S., Divine, R.L., and Spralls, S.A. (2009). Segmentation analysis of the volunteering preferences of university students. *Journal of Nonprofit and Public Sector Marketing, 21*(1), 1-2e.

GLOBE (Global Learning and Observations to Benefit the Environment Program). (2018). Available: https://observer.globe.gov [September 2018].

Grier, S., and Bryant, C.A. (2005). Social marketing in public health. *Annual Review of Public Health, 26,* 319-339.

Haring, M.J. (1999). The case for a conceptual base for minority mentoring programs. *Peabody Journal of Education, 74*(2), 5-14.

Haywood, B.K. (2014). *Birds and Beaches: The Affective Geographies and Sense of Place of Participants in the COASST Citizen Science Program.* (Doctoral dissertation). University of South Carolina, Columbia. Available: http://scholarcommons.sc.edu/etd/2748 [September 2018].

Henderson, L. (1996). Instructional design of interactive multimedia: A cultural critique. *Educational Technology Research and Development, 44*(4), 85-104.

Hudson River American Eel Research Project. (2018). *New York Department of Environmental Conservation.* Available: https://www.dec.ny.gov/lands/49580.html [September 2018]

Knowles, M.S. (1970). *The Modern Practice of Adult Education: Andragogy versus Pedagogy.* Oxford, UK: Association Press.

Knowles, M.S. (1984). *Andragogy in Action: Applying Modern Principles of Adult Education.* San Francisco, CA: Jossey Bass.

Kop, R., Fournier, H., and Mak, J.S.F. (2011). A pedagogy of abundance or a pedagogy to support human beings? Participant support on massive open online courses. *The International Review of Research in Open and Distributed Learning, 12*(7), 74-93.

Lefebvre, R.C., and Flora, J.A. (1988). Social marketing and public health intervention. *Health Education Quarterly, 15*(3), 299-315.

Meymaris, K., Henderson, S., Alaback, P., and Havens, K. (2008, December). Project Budburst: Citizen science for all seasons. In *American Geophysical Union Fall Meeting Abstracts.*

Monarch Larva Monitoring Project. (2018). Available: https://monarchlab.org/mlmp [September 2018].

Nature's Notebook. (2018). Available: https://www.usanpn.org/natures_notebook [September 2018].

Norman, D. (2013). *The Design of Everyday Things: Revised and Expanded Edition.* New York: Basic Books.

Pandya, R.E. (2012). A framework for engaging diverse communities in citizen science in the US. *Frontiers in Ecology and the Environment, 10*(6), 314-317.

Patton, M.Q. (1997). Toward distinguishing empowerment evaluation and placing it in a larger context. *Evaluation Practice, 18*(1), 147-163.

Patton, M.Q. (2002). A vision of evaluation that strengthens democracy. *Evaluation, 8*(1), 125-139.

Pfund, C., Byars-Winston, A., Branchaw, J., Hurtado, S., and Eagan, K. (2016). Defining attributes and metrics of effective research mentoring relationships. *AIDS and Behavior, 20*(2), 238-248.

Phillips, C.B. (2017). *Engagement and Learning in Environmentally Based Citizen Science: A Mixed Methods Comparative Case Study.* (Doctoral dissertation). Cornell University, Ithaca, NY.

Phillips, T.B., Porticella, N., Constas, M., and Bonney, R.E. (In press). A framework for articulating and measuring individual learning outcomes from citizen science. *Citizen Science: Theory and Practice, 3*(2), 3. doi: http://doi.org/10.5334/cstp.126.

Project Budburst. (2018). Available: http://www.budburst.org/ [September 2018].

Project Feederwatch. (2018). Available: https://feederwatch.org/ [September 2018].

Rogoff, B. (1995). Observing sociocultural activity on three planes: Participatory appropriation, guided participation, and apprenticeship. In J.V. Wertsch, P. del Rio, and A. Alvarez (Eds.), *Sociocultural Studies of Mind* (pp. 139-164). Cambridge, UK: Cambridge University Press. Reprinted (2008) in K. Hall and P. Murphy (Eds.), *Pedagogy and Practice: Culture and Identities*. London: Sage.

Rose, D. (2000). Universal design for learning. *Journal of Special Education Technology*, *15*(3), 45-49.

Russell, S.H., Hancock, M.P., and McCullough, J. (2007). Benefits of undergraduate research experiences. *Science*, *316*(5824), 548-549.

SciStarter. (2018). Available: https://scistarter.com [September 2018].

Settles, I.H. (2004). When multiple identities interfere: The role of identity centrality. *Personality and Social Psychology Bulletin*, *30*(4), 487-500.

Silver City Watershed Keepers. (2018). Available: http://silvercitywatershedkeepers.org/index.html [September 2018].

Slater, T.F. (1996). Portfolio assessment strategies for grading first-year university physics students in the USA. *Physics Education*, *31*(5), 329.

Soloway, E., Guzdial, M., and Hay, K.E. (1994). Learner-centered design: The challenge for HCI in the 21st century. *Interactions*, *1*(2), 36-48.

Stolle-McAllister, K. (2011). The case for summer bridge: Building social and cultural capital for talented black STEM students. *Science Educator*, *20*(2), 12-22.

Sullivan, B.L., Aycrigg, J.L., Barry, J., Bonney, R.E., Bruns, N.E., Dhondt, A.A., Farnsworth, A., Fitzpatrick, J.W., Fredericks, T., Gerbracht, J., Gomes, C., Iliff, M.J., Lagoze, C., La Sorte, F.A., Merrifield, M., Reynolds, M., Rodewald, A.D., Rosenberg, K.V., Trautmann, N.M., Winkler, D.W., Wong, W-K., Yu, J.L., and Kelling, S. (2014). The eBird enterprise: An integrated approach to development and application of citizen science. *Biological Conservation*, *169*, 31-40.

Thriving Earth Exchange. (2018). Available: https://thrivingearthexchange.org [September 2018].

Tsui, A.S. (2007). From homogenization to pluralism: International management research in the academy and beyond. *Academy of Management Journal*, *50*(6), 1353-1364.

Valencia, R.R. (Ed.). (2012). *The Evolution of Deficit Thinking: Educational Thought and Practice*. London: Falmer.

WOEIP (West Oakland Environmental Indicators Project). (2018). Available: http://www.woeip.org [May 2018].

# 7

# Conclusions and Recommendations

## CONCLUSIONS

### Characterizing Citizen Science

One of the goals of this report is to share the committee's synthesis of what is known about how practitioners can support science learning through participation in citizen science. In this chapter, we summarize the committee's findings throughout the report, offer brief summaries of our major messages, and give some recommendations for how to further the work of supporting science learning through citizen science for both practitioners and researchers. Finally, we offer a formal conclusion.

In engaging in that work, the committee found it necessary to clarify terms and unpack challenging concepts. First, we needed to calibrate different understandings of what constitutes citizen science. We recognized that our different understandings arose, in part, from the multiple histories that have contributed to citizen science. In particular, the committee noticed three converging histories for citizen science: one rooted in established science, characterized by scientists reaching out to nonscientists for their help advancing science. Another history is rooted in community groups reaching out to scientists to bring science to bear on a community priority. Finally, youth educators in both formal and informal settings represent a third community that has contributed to developing relationships between citizen science and science learning and has been active in pointing the way toward new ways of integrating them. These different histories are not mutually exclusive or complete, but they do illuminate the range of approaches, motivations, and participation that are part of citizen science. The committee believes that this diversity is a strength and opportunity of citizen science, and rather than constrain citizen science with a singular definition, we found it useful to describe how it is distinct from more traditional science inquiry.

> **CONCLUSION 1: Citizen science projects investigate a range of phenomena using scientific practices across varied social, cultural, and geographical contexts and activities. Citizen science allows people with diverse motivations and intentions to participate in science.**

The committee identified several traits common to many citizen science projects. Though projects do not necessarily have to possess these traits in order to count as citizen science, these traits are often characteristic of citizen science activities. The traits identified by the committee show that, generally, citizen science projects actively engage participants, engage participants with data, use a systematic approach to producing reliable knowledge, help advance science, and communicate results. Participants in citizen science generally chose to be involved and benefit from participation.

There is ample evidence that diversity[1] enhances scientific discovery and impact. Diversity is a source of new scientific questions, practices, insights, and evidence, all of which enhance discovery and innovation. Broader participation in science can help ensure that the priorities and needs of all communities, not just majority communities, are reflected in the research agenda of science. As an activity that explicitly broadens participation in science by welcoming people who are not and do not intend to be practicing scientists, citizen science has the potential to bring more and different people into the fold of science, and can be a mechanism by which marginalized groups can influence scientific agendas and guide science in directions that reflect their priorities.

> **CONCLUSION 2: Because citizen science broadens the scope of who can contribute to science, it can be a pathway for introducing new processes, observations, data, and epistemologies to science.**

As the committee will discuss in the recommendations, the fact that citizen science could introduce new ideas into science does not mean it will. Moreover, the fact that citizen science allows opportunities for more diversity does not mean designers and other stakeholders will use that

---

[1]The committee defines diversity in Chapter 1 of this report to mean "the differences among individuals, including demographic differences such as sex, race, ethnicity, sexual orientation, socioeconomic status, ability, and country of origin, among others."

opportunity effectively. Taking advantage of these opportunities requires conscious attention to issues of power, willingness to examine practices for implicit and explicit bias, and skill in engaging diverse perspectives. All of this, evidence suggests, is facilitated by engaging in a process of collaborative project design.

### Participation in Citizen Science

In attempting to address its statement of task, the committee recognized that it was important to first understand who engages in citizen science. That is, before it is possible to plan for learning through participation in citizen science, it is critical to know who participates, what the modes of participation look like, and what kinds of learning outcomes are reasonable to expect through participation. Our efforts to identify who participates in citizen science were frustrated by incomplete data. Though the data that do exist points to certain trends in participation, the committee was surprised to find that popular notions of who participates in citizen science are often based on limited data.

Only a small number of projects collect and make available data about participants, and there are significant differences in how different projects characterize their participants. Both of these make it challenging to draw overarching conclusions about who participates in citizen science. The committee observed that where the data do exist, they are likely to over-represent large-scale projects with sufficient technological and financial support to have a Web presence, as well as those projects that are connected to educational researchers at universities. We learned about several projects with a community-driven history that did not report their participation in peer-reviewed literature, suggesting that these projects (and their more diverse participants) may be undercounted. Youth who participate in citizen science may also be undercounted, potentially because many people who use citizen science projects as part of formal and informal education activities do not publish as often. For these reasons and others detailed in this report, the committee finds that this limited participant data is likely to underrepresent critical populations, such as communities of color, youth participants, and people from lower socioeconomic statuses.

**CONCLUSION 3: There is limited systematic, cumulative information about who participates in citizen science. Community and youth projects are underrepresented in the available data, suggesting that existing data is biased toward white middle- and upper-class populations.**

Though limitations in the availability of data may fail to recognize certain kinds of participants or modes of participation, the committee did observe some trends in the data that do exist. In Chapter 2 of this report, the committee delves into some emergent trends in the kinds of projects that report participation data. The committee reflects on these trends throughout the report and offers additional relevant recommendations to the field below.

## Learning Through Citizen Science

In examining learning in citizen science projects, the committee was struck by the way that attending to learning could advance other goals that are often part of citizen science. For example, we saw evidence that helping participants develop and practice the skills associated with data collection improved the quality of data collected, which is good both for science and the communities who base subsequent action on that data.

> **CONCLUSION 4: Participants' learning through citizen science has benefits not only for participants and scientists but also for communities and science.**

One of the committee's primary tasks was to distinguish between the aspirations for citizen science to support science learning and the actual documented evidence of science learning through participation. For instance, the committee heard reports that citizen science engaged students who did not participate in other science activities, but we did not find widespread evidence that citizen science reached all reluctant learners. We found that enthusiasm about citizen science's potential occasionally clouds what is actually known about what kinds of learning occur in citizen science. While there is some evidence that participation in citizen science projects can enhance science learning, more studies are needed that examine processes of learning and document specific learning outcomes in a wider variety of contexts including more diverse learners. Such studies would buttress these early findings and provide more robust guidance that could be used to maximize learning outcomes for all learners.

> **CONCLUSION 5: There is evidence that citizen science projects can contribute to specific learning outcomes in particular contexts and for some learners.**

Based on emerging evidence from available research and the carefully articulated observations of practitioners, the committee was convinced that multiple kinds of learning through citizen science are achievable with intentional planning. The committee considered what learning outcomes were accessible in citizen science through the framework offered in the

National Research Council study *Learning Science in Informal Environments* (National Research Council, 2009). These six strands of science learning helped the committee to delineate what kinds of outcomes might be reasonably expected and offer insight into what conditions are necessary to bring about specific kinds of learning.

> **CONCLUSION 6:** Citizen science supports learning outcomes related to scientific practices, content, identity, agency, data, and reasoning. Whether these outcomes are realized depends on the provision of learning supports and on intentional design.
>
> > **CONCLUSION 6a:** Citizen science can be readily mobilized to help participants learn scientific practices and content directly related to the specific activities in the project.
> > **CONCLUSION 6b:** With careful planning, intentional design, and learning supports, citizen science can
> >
> > - amplify participants' identity/ies as individuals who contribute to science and support their self-efficacy in science;
> > - provide an opportunity for participants to learn about data, data analysis, and interpretation of data; and
> > - provide a venue for participants to learn about the nature of science and scientific reasoning.

Supporting learning in citizen science requires recognition of the various ways that people enter into and travel through a citizen science experience. Participants bring personal motivations and interests into citizen science projects, which can support and enhance science learning and may change over time. Knowing about and responding to this shifting array of motivations and interests can help project designers and implementers advance learning goals. For example, knowing how a participant might begin his or her work as an interested volunteer who collects data according to a well-established protocol and then move on to help guide the project can help project implementers and designers to enable pathways like these and to enhance learning along these pathways.

Research shows that more learning occurs when learners' knowledge and previous experiences are welcomed into learning environments, and learners are given opportunities to connect previous experience and knowledge to new concepts or ideas. Research also suggests that when learners' prior knowledge and experiences are neglected, marginalized, or treated as wrong, it slows science learning, undermines interest in science, and diminishes agency to use science. Evidence reveals that this happens more often to individuals from communities of color, lower income communities, and Indigenous communities. The committee emphasizes the value in using citizen science to engage with participants' lived experience, cultural knowledge, and rich epistemologies in a way that underscores rather than rebukes connections to science.

Learners' identities influence learning outcomes. Here, identities need to be understood in terms not only of identity within the scientific enterprise, but also their larger cultural identity and how that intersects with science. A historic and comprehensive understanding of how the scientific community has treated traditionally marginalized groups or cultures allows for projects to explicitly address longstanding and ongoing tensions and facilitate individual learning.

> **CONCLUSION 7: Science learning outcomes are strongly related to the motivations, interests, and identities of learners. Citizen science projects that welcome and respond to participants' motivations and interests are more likely to maximize participant learning.**

Science learning has been extensively studied in many contexts, and for many learners. Certain principles discovered about science learning are especially relevant to citizen science.

> **CONCLUSION 8: Research on learning science in other contexts provides insight into some fundamental principles that can advance science learning through citizen science. These principles include the following:**
>
> • **Prior knowledge and experience shape what and how participants learn.**
> • **When participants' prior knowledge and experience are treated respectfully in the learning process, learning is advanced.**
> • **Motivation, interest, and identity play a central role in learning, create learning opportunities, and are learning outcomes themselves.**
> • **Most science learning outcomes will only be achieved with structured supports. These supports can come from specific tasks, tools, and facilitation.**

The committee recognizes that within the institution of science, social structures exist to continually privilege some demographic groups in ways that mirror society at large. If issues of power and privilege are not explicitly investigated and managed in ways that minimize inequity, citizen science projects are likely to default to the same kinds of power structures already at work. For instance, a project can amplify existing inequity by preferentially engaging people with previous scientific experience. On the other hand, explicitly building projects to welcome, include, and advance learners and their contributions from a wide variety of backgrounds creates a richer learning environment for all learners.

**CONCLUSION 9: Being aware of issues of power, privilege, and inequality, and explicitly addressing them in citizen science projects can help enable learning for all participants.**

## Community Learning

In addition to learning outcomes for individuals, the committee found that citizen science can contribute to learning outcomes at the community level. Indeed, some projects can be designed with community outcomes, including science literacy, as the primary goal. In this context, the committee found the notion of community science literacy—a community's ability to leverage collectively held but individually distributed expertise—particularly useful (National Academies of Sciences, Engineering, and Medicine, 2016). The committee acknowledges that science literacy and science learning are not synonymous but notes that community science literacy can be bolstered when some constituent individual learning outcomes (such as content area expertise, or facility with the use and misuse of scientific methodologies) are grown and strengthened. Though evidence in this arena is limited, the committee found some case study evidence that community participation in citizen science can contribute to a community's science literacy when some specific learning outcomes are realized. As with learning by individuals, we found that the potential for citizen science to contribute to community science literacy is not realized automatically but requires attention in design and implementation.

**CONCLUSION 10: Community participation in citizen science activities can support the development of community science literacy.**

In creating opportunities for communities that have historically been marginalized to develop scientific projects that pursue their goals and enhance their community science literacy, citizen science has the potential to shift traditional scientific notions of whose questions are considered worthy of scientific investigation, what kinds of data and methods are considered scientific, and who gets to lead and participate in scientific inquiry. The committee recognizes that while participation in citizen science has the potential to enact these shifts, they are unlikely to occur without acknowledging past inequities and finding and changing current practices that either ignore or perpetuate inequity. Bringing a historic and comprehensive understanding of how traditionally marginalized groups have been treated by the scientific community allows for project design that explicitly addresses longstanding (and ongoing) tensions.

> **CONCLUSION 11:** Citizen science can create opportunities for communities, especially communities who have been marginalized, neglected, or even exploited by scientists, to collaborate with scientists and the science community.

## Design for Learning

Design is the process of turning ideas and intent into action. Being intentional in design is a critical component in achieving science learning through citizen science. To intentionally design in the ways the committee has talked about in this report requires a level of commitment and resources that may differ from historical approaches to developing citizen science projects. There are, however, free resources to do this, and the committee has attempted to identify such resources in this report where appropriate.

> **CONCLUSION 12:** Specific learning goals can be achieved with intentional design. Without intentional design, it can be hard to anticipate what learning outcomes will be achieved.

Modern theories of design describe it as an ongoing process of learning, prototyping, gathering feedback, and refining. State-of-the-art design includes engaging stakeholders[2] in all aspects of the design process. In science, this understanding of design can be seen in participatory methods for science such as coproduction, participatory research, and boundary-spanning organizations. Applied to science learning, and science learning in citizen science, modern design theory makes it clear that design for learning outcomes, and therefore learning outcomes themselves, is enhanced by designing with learners and other participants in an iterative process.

> **CONCLUSION 13:** Research on program design shows that designing with input from stakeholders and building iteratively is an effective strategy for supporting learning. This is true for designing for science learning from citizen science.

---

[2]For the purposes of this report, the committee considers "stakeholders" to be individuals concerned with the immediate design and implementation of a citizen science project. These entities include project designers, project facilitators, participants, and relevant community actors.

The committee finds no evidence that designing for learning in this way undermines the larger scientific goals of a project; rather, we see that designing in this way advances learning in ways that may even enrich the project outcomes and project experience for all stakeholders. In summary, citizen science projects that are designed *with* participants rather than *for* participants are better poised to actually bring about desired learning in the context of citizen science participation. This collaborative approach, while always recommended, is especially helpful for uncovering and addressing some of the factors that undermine traditionally underserved and under-represented groups and individuals. By working to enable learning and participation for a wider range of learners, participatory design enhances learning opportunities for all learners.

Some contexts may be more appropriate for certain kinds of learning outcomes and, accordingly, context (and all the considerations therein) should be carefully addressed in project design. The committee discussed the role of learning environment in project design and found that while there are benefits to recommend citizen science activities to formal learning environments, it is critical that the educators engage with citizen science with the appropriate level of support to achieve specific outcomes.

**CONCLUSION 14: Formal learning environments have more structured and intentional learning outcomes. Citizen science can provide useful activities for formal learning environments; however, educators may need to incorporate additional supports to achieve more challenging learning outcomes.**

In summary, there is clear evidence that citizen science presents opportunities for individuals to learn science, and that individual science learning can help advance a broader set of project goals and a community's ability to leverage science for their benefit. Learning outcomes around science content and process require some supports for learning, while learning outcomes related to scientific reasoning, identity, and data require even more explicit support. All learning outcomes are more likely with intentional design, and design is better when done with a broad range of stakeholders.

Identity, interest, and motivation are especially rich areas of inquiry. Citizen science can contribute to identity as someone who participates in science, and that is both a learning outcome and something that enables other learning outcomes. Identity is also connected to a larger cultural and social context, and that larger cultural and social context is an especially important consideration for communities and members of communities that have had their identity undermined, marginalized, or neglected. Citizen science, by virtue of expanding the scope of science, has the potential to mediate these tensions if it is willing to take up that challenge. If it does, it can pioneer practices and approaches that could be used in science writ large.

## RECOMMENDATIONS AND RESEARCH AGENDA

### Enabling Learning

The committee was asked to develop a set of evidence-based principles to guide the design of citizen science projects. In this chapter, the committee offers general principles that are relevant across citizen science and should be applied to the design and implementation of all projects. Many of these principles derive from research and best practices in science education more generally. We present these overarching principles as recommendations. They are offered to all designers of citizen science projects, with the understanding—discussed throughout—that designers include a wide and representative range of stakeholders and that effective design extends well into implementation.

These overarching recommendations for enabling learning from citizen science are supplemented by a set of evidence-based suggestions that can be used by designers (again, broadly construed) to advance learning in specific citizen science projects. These suggestions, or guidelines, are developed in detail in Chapter 6.

In thinking about learning in citizen science, our committee was confronted early and often with the reality that citizen science is embedded in a larger set of cultural practices and that these practices can be less than equitable. Assumptions about who is eligible and prepared to participate in science activities, what kind of knowledge counts as science, and even who is entitled to ask or answer scientific questions are influenced, not always positively, by attitudes and practices in society at large. To put it another way, science, especially citizen science, is a sociocultural activity. Along with the positive learning opportunities that come with social and cultural interaction, comes the possibility of inheriting and propagating biases that inhibit learning. And these biases do not just inhibit learning for members of the groups that are targeted by the biases; by limiting the breadth of people and ideas, they inhibit learning for everyone.

In order to ensure that participation in citizen science does not unquestioningly accept biases and inadvertently propagate existing and historical inequities that undermine learning, the committee positioned its first recommendation around understanding issues of power and intentionally designing to promote equity. The history of design and sociocultural theories of learning both make it clear that if citizen science stakeholders do not explicitly question implicit biases and inequitable distributions of power, and work to minimize their impact, they are likely to design projects that cater to a narrow range of learners. Most often, the narrow range consists of members of dominant social groups, defined above. Conversely, explicitly considering inequity, finding ways to minimize barriers for all learners, and designing to welcome and respect members and ideas from nondominant groups can result in more diverse, equitable participation, which improves project outcomes for all stakeholders. It also offers insight into how science as a whole can move toward more equitable outcomes and broader participation.

In order to engage in this work, the committee recommends that designers, researchers, participants, and other stakeholders in citizen science examine existing inequities that can impede participation in all facets of citizen science, and design pathways around those inequities. This work entails welcoming diverse ideas, methods, and epistemologies, particularly from communities whose contributions have been neglected or minimized, in the design and implementation of citizen science projects.

> **RECOMMENDATION 1: Given the potential of citizen science to engage traditionally underrepresented and underserved individuals and communities, the committee recommends that designers, researchers, participants, and other stakeholders in citizen science carefully consider and address issues of equity and power throughout all phases of project design and implementation.**

In examining existing citizen science projects, the committee found a number of projects that could take better advantage of the state-of-the art understanding about science learning. Often, these projects were designed and led by scientists with deep expertise in the discipline of the project, but less experience in education, educational design, or education research. Conversely, projects that involved education researchers, educators, and people with expertise in education presented more evidence of learning. By the same token, these kinds of partnerships can also help advance research about learning from citizen science.

> **RECOMMENDATION 2: In order to maximize learning outcomes through participation in citizen science, the committee recommends that citizen science projects leverage partnerships among scientists, education researchers, and other individuals with expertise in education and designing for learning.**

The committee cannot underscore the next point enough: Success in learning outcomes through citizen science is enhanced by intentionally designing for learning.

RECOMMENDATION 3: In order to advance learning, project designers and practitioners should intentionally design for learning by defining intended learning outcomes, identifying a participant audience,
integrating learning outcomes into project goals, and using evidence-
based strategies to reach those outcomes.

Design theory makes it clear that strong collaborations among multiple stakeholders helps to broaden participation and support learning.
Strong collaborations approach citizen science design as a partnership
where all stakeholders are active participants with valuable insights and
contributions. Further, strong collaborations avoid positioning participants
as "targets" of citizen science activities who must be managed by others
who seek to help them overcome a lack of knowledge, but focus instead
on understanding participants needs, expectations, and areas of expertise.

In practice, this looks like engaging with potential stakeholders early
and often in the process of designing a citizen science project or adapting
an existing citizen science project to promote learning. This can be done by
engaging in discussions with a broad range of stakeholders (including scientists, education researchers, educators, learners, and members of learners'
communities) about learning goals and how they can support individual or
community goals. In those discussions, project leads should make a con-
certed effort to talk with individuals from a diverse range of communities
to learn about their participation—what it might look like, what might get
in the way, and what might produce more value for them to participate.
If there are difficulties—for example, a community with limited access to
the project—exploring how to overcome those barriers is preferable to not
continuing to work with that community. A leadership team that includes
scientists and potential participants can facilitate these conversations. From
these discussions, it can be helpful to build a prototype, and use that prototype to anchor subsequent discussions. Strong collaborations grow from
these discussions and the iterative work afterward, and they are aided by
being explicit about the collaboration and developing a common and clear
understanding around roles, decision making, data collections and sharing,
and ownership of intellectual property.

RECOMMENDATION 4: In designing or adapting projects to support
learning, designers should use proven practices of design, including
iteration and stakeholder engagement in design.

### Building the Field

As an emerging field, citizen science has opportunities to advance
in itself, contribute to what we know about how people learn science,

and broaden participation in science. The next several recommendations explore how to maximize that potential; they are recommendations for building the field of citizen science.

The committee was also asked to lay out a research agenda that can fill gaps in the current understanding of how citizen science can support science learning and enhance science education, and those recommendations are outlined below.

Existing research can begin to point stakeholders toward understanding the mechanisms at work when attempting to design citizen science to support science learning. Given the somewhat nascent nature of the field of citizen science as its own research domain, however, more research on the long-term strategies for how to support science learning is necessary in order to clarify and develop evidence-based practices and understand common elements and variations across a variety of sociocultural and practical contexts. The committee wishes to point out that design-based research may be especially fruitful here: Not only will future research inform the design of citizen science projects but also design-based research in citizen science could also offer significant contributions to developing and refining theories about learning in citizen science. In particular, design-based research is well suited to characterize the challenges and opportunities presented by the range of contexts in which citizen science learning takes place.

More rigorous research, more documentation of effective practice, and more attention to equity will grow the foundation of practice that can be used to advance learning outcomes in citizen science.

RECOMMENDATION 5: The committee recommends that the educational research community perform regular analyses of the available evidence on learning in citizen science in order to identify and disseminate effective strategies.

Research is essential to continued advancement in citizen science, and formal, peer-reviewed research remains a gold standard for understanding how learning happens in citizen science and leveraging citizen science to advance our understanding of how people learn in many contexts. This report is a starting point for future analyses that go into more depth on key parts of science learning or consider new results made available after this report.

There are three important factors to consider. First, citizen science extends beyond academia, and this means that evidence for successful practices that advance learning can be found outside of published peer-reviewed journals. In the process of preparing this report, the committee learned from conversations with a variety of stakeholders, blogs, and other online communications about citizen science, posters and informal presentations,

and unpublished papers. In disseminating strategies that are useful for supporting learning, the citizen science research community should continue to
learn from a wide variety of communication formats and not confine itself
to the peer-reviewed literature.

Second, research should include attention to practice and link theory to
application. The committee heard from practitioners and researchers alike
about the challenges of translating emerging research on learning to actual
practice in citizen science. Citizen science, as a nascent field, does not have
codified divisions between educational researchers and practitioners. For
instance, practitioners and researchers involved in citizen science attend the
same conference and are members of the same professional society. This
interaction between research and practice is unique, and the committee sees
it as an opportunity to investigate how research-to-practice can work well.
More importantly, we see the interplay of researchers and practitioners as
one facet of productive collaborative design and urge the citizen science
community to continue to welcome and respect contributions from both
theory and practice. Examining the interplay of research and practice in
citizen science could point to strategies for linking research and practice
that can be used beyond citizen science.

Finally, the committee underlines the importance of paying attention to
diversity in all of these meta-analyses, including ensuring broad participation in the design and implementation of the research.

Citizen science has the opportunity to develop research methodologies
that allow more intercomparison across and among projects, as well as
practical tools to help build capacity among practitioners seeking to support science learning. Pursuing these new lines of inquiry can help add value
to the existing research, make future research more productive, and provide
support for effective project implementation.

> **RECOMMENDATION 6:** The committee recommends that relevant
> researchers perform longitudinal studies of participation and changes
> in individuals' and communities' scientific knowledge, skills, attitudes,
> and behaviors, both within individual projects and across projects.

The committee acknowledges that the field could strongly benefit from
the creation, testing, and improvement of accessible tools for practitioners
to use to support science learning through citizen science. Though the committee holds that effective collaboration remains the primary way to design
for specific learning outcomes in specific learning contexts, the committee
also recognizes that not all stakeholders will always have access to the best
collaborators. As a result, the committee notes that it would be particularly
useful if practitioners were able to rely on proven design tools to help iso-
late desired learning outcomes and backward map program participation to

support achievement in learning. When developing these tools, researchers need to find ways to account for the unique assets and insights that different individuals bring to their experience with citizen science, especially for individuals who come from historically underrepresented communities.

**RECOMMENDATION 7: The committee recommends the citizen science community collaborate to identify, enhance, and develop shared tools and platforms that they can use to support science learning across a large number of citizen science projects.**

This report represents our attempt to synthesize the best available research on citizen science and science learning. Future work should build on the evidence drawn out in this report and continue to realize the potential of citizen science.

## REFERENCES

National Academies of Sciences, Engineering, and Medicine. (2016). *Science Literacy: Concepts, Contexts, and Consequences*. Washington, DC: The National Academies Press.
National Research Council. (2009). *Learning Science in Informal Environments: People, Places, and Pursuits*. Washington, DC: The National Academies Press.

# Appendix A

# Demographic Analyses of Citizen Science

Pandya (2012) points out that participation in citizen science, at least in the United States, does not reflect the demographics of the population, and that this schism hurts both citizen science and unrepresented groups. There is a generalized assumption that participants in citizen science are generally white, older/retired females with above average education. However, there are no analyses across the citizen science community exploring this assertion. To address that gap in service of this report, we cite three different analyses of participation data. The first is a simple analysis of reported participant data on online citizen science aggregator platform SciStarter 2.0 (SciStarter, 2018), the second is a published analyses of participant data, and the third is an original meta-analysis of published literature on citizen science projects reporting participant data.

## SCISTARTER 2.0

SciStarter is a Web platform for individuals looking to "find, join, and contribute to science." The platform offers access to more than 2,700 searchable citizen science projects and events, as well as helping interested parties access tools that facilitate project participation (SciStarter, 2018). As of September 2018, SciStarter 2.0 has offered a profile feature, allowing individuals to record demographics and other attributes to a profile. Once a profile has been completed, information about the individual can be attached to projects listed on SciStarter as a "bookmark," which indicates potential interest in the project, or because the individual elects to join the project. The committee reviewed sex and age information about individuals electing to fill out a profile on SciStarter (N = 653) as a function of the type of project (hands-on versus online), based on SciStarter profile data.

Of the 653 SciStarter profiles completed by the end of 2017, the majority of individuals were female (64%) and in the 35–44 age range (female median = 41; male = 47). Individuals with profiles have the option to join projects through SciStarter and/or bookmark them, allowing some determination of preference as a function of project type. Females represented the vast majority of bookmarkers (80%), and appeared to bookmark both online and hands-on projects equally. Other statistics were slightly more revealing: whereas females comprised 68 percent of SciStarter users joining hands-on projects, this value dropped to 57 percent for online projects.

## Dimensions of Biodiversity Meta-Analysis

Theobald and colleagues (2015) and Burgess and colleagues (2017) surveyed biodiversity citizen science projects as part of a large, multi-university project funded by the Dimensions of Biodiversity Program within the Division of Environmental Biology at the National Science Foundation (hereafter the Dimensions meta-analysis). In these studies, biodiversity was defined as explicit inclusion of the presence and/or abundance of identified taxonomic, genetic, or functional groups, and citizen science was defined as projects engaging volunteers not otherwise paid or receiving college credit for their participation, and collecting and/or processing quantifiable information related to an issue or question. Of the original 388 projects harvested from a comprehensive Internet search for English-version project Websites, contact information for extant projects was available for 329. Surveys sent to this set resulted in 125 responses. Questions included information on the demographics of participants, including sex and qualitative exclusive categorization (all, most, some, few, or none) of age, education, and race/ethnicity. Although the vast majority of projects were centered in the United States, the demographic analysis included projects from a range of countries; therefore, race/ethnicity categories were simultaneously general and specific to U.S. census categories (e.g., black or African American). Age and education data were visualized in Figure 4 (Burgess et al., 2017); sex and race/ethnicity data have not appeared elsewhere.[1]

Of the 125 projects where managers/directors responded to the survey, a subset (44–69%) were able to provide some amount of demographic information, most often age-education and least often race/ethnicity (see Table A-1). This sampling of hands-on, outdoors, ecologically focused citizen science projects indicates that participants are principally white, well-educated adults with no gender bias. Almost all project managers

---

[1]See Theobald et al. (2015) and Burgess et al. (2017) for complete methods.

**TABLE A-1** Percentage of the Responding Population Indicating the Abundance of a Particular Demographic Class of Project Participants (e.g., retirees)

| Sample | Demographic Category | All | Most | Some | Few | None |
|---|---|---|---|---|---|---|
| 83 | Retirees | 1.2 | 37.3 | 41.0 | 15.7 | 4.8 |
| | Adult Nonscientists | | | | | |
| 86 | w/ a college degree | 2.3 | 48.8 | 39.5 | 9.3 | 0.0 |
| 84 | w/out a college degree | 0.0 | 11.9 | 54.8 | 25.0 | 8.3 |
| | Students | | | | | |
| 82 | College | 0.0 | 3.7 | 54.9 | 35.4 | 6.1 |
| 83 | High School | 3.6 | 14.5 | 34.9 | 36.1 | 10.8 |
| 79 | Middle School | 1.3 | 6.3 | 32.9 | 38.0 | 21.5 |
| 77 | Primary School | 1.3 | 5.2 | 16.9 | 41.6 | 35.1 |
| 53 | Caucasian, Non-Hispanic | 7.5 | 81.1 | 9.4 | 0.0 | 1.9 |
| 49 | Hispanic | 0.0 | 6.1 | 22.4 | 51.0 | 20.4 |
| 44 | Asian | 2.3 | 2.3 | 27.3 | 50.0 | 18.2 |
| 46 | Black, African American | 0.0 | 0.0 | 15.2 | 54.3 | 30.4 |
| 46 | Indigenous, Native American | 0.0 | 0.0 | 10.9 | 43.5 | 45.7 |
| 41 | Hawaiian Native or Pacific Islander | 0.0 | 0.0 | 0.0 | 31.7 | 68.3 |
| 62 | Male | 1.6 | 21.0 | 77.4 | 0.0 | 0.0 |
| 61 | Female | 0.0 | 27.9 | 70.5 | 1.6 | 0.0 |

NOTE: Majority response categories are highlighted in bold, and where all responses less than 3 percentage points apart are highlighted. Sample indicates number of project managers responding.
SOURCE: Data from Theobald et al. (2015) and Burgess et al. (2017).

who reported race/ethnicity demographics indicated that "all" or "most" of their participants were white (88.6%), while only 6.1 percent indicated this same level of participation for Hispanics, with slightly lower levels (4.6%) for Asians, including Asian Americans. No projects reported overwhelming participation among blacks or African Americans, indigenous peoples including Native Americans, or Hawaiian/Pacific Islanders. Projects with a higher than average participation of one or more minority groups were either outside of the United States (e.g., Migrant Watch and Citizen Sparrow are two bird-focused citizen science projects in India, with a majority of Asian participants), or geographically local and linked to a site and/or taxon with high cultural importance (e.g., the Camas Citizen Science Monitoring Program, centered on the Nez Perce National Historical Park's Weippe Prairie Site, is a project of the National Park Service in which high school students monitor camas flowering and incorporate aspects of the cultural and ecological values of this native prairie plant). These projects may have been tied directly to local schools; the Bosque Ecosystem Monitoring Program is a collaboration between the Bosque School and the University of New Mexico to engage students and volunteers in riparian forest–*bosque*–monitoring along the middle Rio Grande).

Youth were clearly not the focus of projects reporting demographics. Adult nonscientists with a college degree made up just over one-half (51.2%) of the combined "all" and "most" categories, versus only 11.9 percent for adult nonscientists without a degree. Finally, while most student categories had relatively low representation at the higher participation levels, 18.1 percent of high school students fell into the combined "all" "most" category, or almost five times the rate of college student participation.

There were no clear trends in participation of females versus males. Although females were slightly overrepresented in the combined "all" or "most" category (27.9% vs. 22.6%), only males were cited as having total representation in some projects (1.6%).

## Literature Search and Meta-Analysis

Using Web of Science (2018), we performed searches of the topic fields (title, keywords, abstract) for literature from the year 2000 to present, language = English and peer-reviewed articles only, using combinations of the search terms:

1.  crowd sourc* or crowd-sourc* or crowd-sourc*
2.  online or on-line or online
3.  citizen science or public participation in scien*
4.  assessment or evaluation

5. demographic
6. survey or interview

We augmented this set with articles not previously captured from all issues of the journal *Citizen Science: Theory and Practice*, as well as volumes dedicated to citizen science of the journals *Conservation Biology* (30:3), *Biological Conservation* (208:SI), and *Maine Policy Review, 26*(2). To this set we added the following:

1. *Online Citizen Science Projects: An Exploration of Motivation, Contribution and Participation*, a dissertation awarded by The Open University, focused on three citizen science projects (Curtis, 2015)
2. *Engagement and Learning in Environmentally-based Citizen Science: A Mixed Methods Comparative Case Study*, a dissertation awarded by Cornell University, focused on participant learning in six citizen science projects (Phillips, 2017)
3. Eleven primary research chapters from the book *Citizen Science for Coastal and Marine Conservation* (Cigliano and Ballard, 2017)
4. Eleven primary research chapters from the book *Citizen Inquiry: Synthesizing Science and Inquiry Learning* (Herodotou, Sharples, and Scanlon, 2018)

Our initial source count, including duplications and nonrelevant sources (defined as those without a focus on citizen science) was 735. Excluding duplications and nonrelevant sources to include a corpus of primary research articles, case studies, and meta-analyses pertaining to citizen science resulted in 303 sources. Of these, 32 included numerically or graphically extractable information on at least one of the following demographics, such that the data could be included in subsequent central tendency (mean, median, range, variation) measure. Because several sources were meta-analyses, the final "project" count (including composite samples of unnamed project volunteers, N = 7) was 68.

Extracted data included any of the following, and no source provided all fields:

1. Gender (recorded as % female)
2. Age (recorded as any of the following: mean or median, standard deviation, range, or % distribution)
3. Retirees (recorded as % of total)
4. Race/Ethnicity (recorded as % distribution across all reported categories)

5. Education (recorded as % completing college, and % with a graduate degree)
6. Income (recorded as % within all reported categories)
7. Previous participation in a citizen science or relevant (e.g., conservation, restoration, community, etc.) project based on the context of the surveyed population (recorded as % of total)

Metadata included the following:

1. Citation
2. Project/program name or description of research audience in the case of multiproject research (e.g., individuals involved in conservation or environmental projects in Colorado)
3. Whether the project/program involved out-of-doors activities (Y/N)
4. Project location
5. Whether the project/program involved only computer-based (e.g., crowdsourcing) work (Y/N)
6. The research vehicle used to collect the information (e.g., survey, interview)
7. The sample size (e.g., number of participants for which information were available)
8. Whether the information was part of a meta-analysis, defined as research on a suite of projects/programs versus targeting a single project (Y/N). In the case of meta-analyses, if data were reported at the project level, individual data lines were created

Because age information was variously reported as mean, median, range, and/or percent distribution across age classes (e.g., 55% 18–29), we created a central tendency super-category as follows. If mean and median were reported, we used the mean. Because studies reporting both resulted in only a small difference, we included median age if that was the only central tendency measure reported. For studies reporting percent distribution across age classes, we created a median value by multiplying each proportion by the median of the class (e.g., 23 is the median value of the age class 18–29) and then summing across all classes. For lowest and highest classes, which were often reported as open-ended (e.g., 28% 60+), we assumed a minimum age of 18 (unless otherwise specified) and a maximum age of 75.

Our publication meta-analysis resulted in 32 sources detailing 68 projects broadly representative of citizen science from entirely online gaming projects (e.g., Foldit) through to long-term environmental data collection projects (e.g., COASST). Literature included multiproject case studies (e.g., Curtis, 2015; Phillips, 2017), studies specific to some aspect of the demographics of participation (e.g., Cooper and Smith, 2010), studies focused on a range of participants involved in similar activities (e.g., volunteers in outdoor conservation projects; Bruyere and Rappe 2007), and an array of publications evaluating a project, or reporting on project findings. However, this sample represents only 10 percent of the articles examined, and only 3.7 percent of the hands-on (N = 1,014) plus online (N = 297) projects listed on SciStarter, suggesting that the results should be interpreted with caution.

Most studies described projects where participants were outdoors doing hands-on work (N = 39; 80%); and projects situated wholly (N = 25) or partially (N = 13) in the United States (N = 38 in total; 74%). A minority of projects were entirely online (N = 11; 22%), and the majority of these (N = 8 of 11) garnered a worldwide participant audience, albeit mostly from developed countries. Almost all studies gathered data via survey (N = 36 projects) although one meta-analysis used participant lists maintained by individual projects to assess gender (N = 11 projects). Respondent sample sizes ranged widely (mean = 1,281; range 12-13, 649) with a total person count of 65, 336.

There were striking patterns in the reported participant demographics, which generally described a slightly male-biased, overwhelmingly white, and well-educated population with somewhat of a tendency to have previously participated in other projects (see Table A-2).

Women were only slightly underrepresented across all studies (42%) although gender statistics were biased by the type of project. For online

**TABLE A-2** Demographics of Surveyed or Interviewed Participants in 48 Citizen Science Projects and/or Meta-Populations

|  | Gender (% F) | Age (years) | Race/ Ethnicity (% white) | Education (% college degree) | Previous Experience |
|---|---|---|---|---|---|
| Sample Size | 43 | 22 | 9 | 23 | 11 |
| Grand Mean | 42% | 44 | 94% | 73% | 56% |
| Standard Deviation |  | 14 |  |  |  |
| Grand Minimum | 2% | 21 | 87% | 52% | 25% |
| Grand Maximum | 80% | 62 | 100% | 96% | 81% |
| Absolute Minimum |  | 3 |  |  |  |
| Absolute Maximum |  | 100 |  |  |  |

NOTE: Sample is number of projects. Minima and maxima are divided into grand statistics (assessed over all project average or median values) and absolute statistics (assessed at the participant level over all range-reporting projects).

**TABLE A-3** Amalgamated Gender Demographics of Bird-Oriented Organizations Inviting Public Involvement, Organized by the Degree of Expected Participation and Type(s) of Interaction

| Project Category | Description | Total Count | % Female |
|---|---|---|---|
| Supportive | Paid membership | 1,095,346 | 54 |
| Participatory | Submit bird observations to a database | 83,112 | 45 |
| Competitive | Evaluate the quantity/quality of birds reported on lists | 6,933 | 2 |
| Authoritative | Acknowledged as experienced or expert in bird-related activities; may lead such activities and/or train others | 256 | 10 |

NOTE: Data are from 21 U.S. and UK birding organizations where gender was assessed from membership lists.
SOURCE: Adapted from Cooper and Smith (2010).

projects, average female participation dropped to 27 percent (range 2–67%; N = 11). For outdoors projects, female participation was higher (43%, N = 32). However, Phillips (2017), one of the sources used in this meta-analysis, found that even within outdoors projects gender skew toward male was apparent in physical versus biological science projects (e.g., CoCoRHaS, a citizen science project focused on collecting daily precipitation data was 80% male). Across the four projects in this meta-analysis classified as outdoors and entirely physical science, female participation was 37 percent. Cooper and Smith (2010), one of the sources used in this meta-analysis, point out the extreme bias of gender in outdoor environmental projects focused on birds as a function of the structure and expected role of the participants (see Table A-3). Although women were more often likely to be members in organizations focused on birds and bird protection, they were increasingly less likely to participate as the expected role moved through participatory (analogous to hands-on citizen science) to projects where a degree of competition or acknowledged expertise and authority was required.

Participant age (N = 22 projects) was extremely broad across our literature meta-analysis, an indication of the life-long, life-wide, life-deep learning inherent in citizen science. Average age tended toward middle age; however, the central tendency range across all projects was large (21–62) and the absolute range over all projects was essentially birth to death (3–100). The reported number of retirees was also extremely broad (range 5–75%; N = 8). Online projects were only slightly younger in average age (grand mean = 43; N = 6) relative to those performed outdoors (grand mean = 45; N = 17), although the former had a greatly curtailed range (of project means: 37–51) suggesting that online, crowdsourcing projects may have limited appeal to all age classes. A serious caveat to participant age findings is that demographic information was only available for projects focused on adults and/or the entire participant population. We were not able to find published demographics for a single youth-focused project, perhaps due to the combination of age-gating (i.e., a third-grade project would, by definition focus on students primarily ages 7–9) and privacy requirements (i.e., Family Educational Rights and Privacy Act [FERPA]).

By far the most extreme trends were in race and education. Of the nine projects reporting race and/or ethnicity, only one reported statistics on non-white participants, an indication of the overwhelming trend of white participation (94%). Although the Casler, Bickel, and Hackett (2013) study is not citizen science per se, shifts in the race/ethnography patterns in populations recruited to their study as a function of recruitment vehicle are informative: social media postings resulted in 93 perent white study participants whereas Amazon MTurk recruitment resulted in only 37 percent of this demographic, with the gap replaced by Asian Americans (40%), Hispanics (6%), and African Americans (6%).

Education trends were similarly extreme, with a large proportion of the surveyed population (and here it should be noted that all studies focused on nonyouth projects) completing a college degree (73%) and a substantial proportion also completing a graduate or professional degree (mean 34%; range 20–52%; N = 10). Income statistics were rare (N = 6) and not comparatively reported, making specific generalizable conclusions difficult. Of the four U.S. projects with any income information, all reported median incomes above $50,000. Compared to the 2016 median household income of ~$59,000 (U.S. Census Bureau, 2017), this figure does not necessarily indicate wealth, although it certainly suggests a minority of those in the bottom half of the U.S. income strata participate in citizen science activities.

## REFERENCES

Bruyere, B., and Rappe, S. (2007). Identifying the motivations of environmental volunteers. *Journal of Environmental Planning and Management*, 50(4), 503-516.

Burgess, H.K., DeBey, L.B., Froehlich, H.E., Schmidt, N., Theobald, E.J., Ettinger, A.K., Hille Ris Lambers, J., Tewksebury, J., and Parrish, J.K. (2017). The science of citizen science: Exploring barriers to use as a primary research tool. *Biological Conservation*, 208, 113-120.

Casler, K., Bickel, L., and Hackett, E. (2013). Separate but equal? A comparison of participants and data gathered via Amazon's MTurk, social media, and face-to-face behavioral testing. *Computers in Human Behavior*, 29(6), 2156-2160.

Cigliano, J.A., and Ballard, H.L. (Eds.). (2017). *Citizen Science for Coastal and Marine Conservation*. New York: Routledge.

Cooper, C.B., and Smith, J.A. (2010). Gender patterns in bird-related recreation in the USA and UK. *Ecology and Society, 15*(4), 4.

Curtis, V. (2015). *Online Citizen Science Projects: An Exploration of Motivation, Contribution and Participation* (Doctoral dissertation). The Open University.

Herodotou, C., Aristeidou, M., Sharples, M., and Scanlon, E. (2018). Designing citizen science tools for learning: Lessons learnt from the iterative development of nQuire. *Research and Practice in Technology Enhanced Learning, 13*(1), 4.

Pandya, R.E. (2012). A framework for engaging diverse communities in citizen science in the U.S. *Frontiers in Ecology and the Environment, 10*(6), 314-317.

Phillips, C.B. (2017). *Engagement and Learning in Environmentally Based Citizen Science: A Mixed Methods Comparative Case Study* (Doctoral dissertation). Cornell University, Ithaca, NY.

SciStarter. (2018). Available: https://scistarter.com [September 2018].

Theobald, E.J., Ettinger, A.K., Burgess, H.K., DeBey, L.B., Schmidt, N.R., Froehlich, H.E., Wagner, C., Hille Ris Lambers, J., Tewksebury, J., Harsch, M.A., and Parrish, J.K. (2015). Global change and local solutions: Tapping the unrealized potential of citizen science for biodiversity research. *Biological Conservation, 181*, 236-244.

U.S. Census Bureau. (2017). *Report on Household Income: 2016. (ACSBR/16-02).* Available: https://www.census.gov/content/dam/Census/library/publications/2017/acs/acsbr16-02.pdf [September 2018].

Web of Science. (2018). Available: https://webofknowledge.com/ [September 2018].

# Appendix B

# The Evolution of Learning for Design

The committee found the planning literature and the learner-centered design literature to be valuable resources in understanding the evolution of citizen science as an enterprise that supports learning. These resources were consistent in their characterization of the history of design. Both literatures are aligned in organizing the evolution of human-centered design into two broad eras. In its early evolution, prior to 1970, human-centered design was in its infancy. Users and learners were largely seen as pliable, moldable to fit the needs of program designers. By and large, the citizen science projects of the time were aligned with this ethos. Growing out of decision theory and decision science, the Program Planning Model (PPM) offered by Delbecq and Van de Ven (1971) was one such instantiation of this view of design. It had the goal of providing an orderly process for structuring decision-making at different phases of planning. The PPM included five phases with each phase requiring a different combination of stakeholders including (1) problem exploration, (2) knowledge exploration, (3) priority development, (4) program development, and (5) evaluation. Influenced by Taylorism, designers believed that participants could be "planned" for, with little in the way of input from participants. For example, in 1981, Boyle surveyed program development models and found that most models used three specific phases in program planning: (1) program planning, (2) program design and implementation, and (3) program evaluation and accountability. While the broad brush of linearity fails to capture all the programs of the time, it is true that this era produced many classically contributory projects that did not foreground the needs of learners. Early citizen science experiences were sharply focused on participants collecting data and providing data to scientists (Bonney et al., 2009). As long as the aspirations of designers were limited to constrained roles for participant-learners, linear and relatively noninteractive approaches to design adequately supported individual learners. The attendant learning design challenges, are what scholars like Nelson and Stolterman (2003) would call *tame*. Tame, here, suggests that, among other things, the problems are straightforward and the solution, while perhaps requiring many steps, is known at the start of the exercise.

When citizen science programs take up ambitious learning goals, the attendant design bar is raised. Following Nelson and Stolterman's nomenclature, these newer aspirations place citizen science learning challenges firmly in the realm of *wicked* problems. Wicked problems—unlike tame problems that can be clearly and exhaustively formulated from the start— are complex, multicausal, and cannot be fully understood from the beginning. The components contributing to the wicked problem in citizen science are the balance between data quality, data quantity, and the varied learning outcomes; the complex ways the desired balance can be achieved; the diversity in the learning contexts; and the potential tension among the outcomes and the means of achieving them.

With the increased attention to the wicked aspects of citizen science, there has been a growing recognition that citizen science programs can lead to rich, educational experiences. Many in the field have recognized that there is a tremendous opportunity to support rich learning on the part of participants (Ballard, Dixon, and Harris, 2017; Bonney et al., 2009; Masters et al., 2016). Learning that extends beyond tame aspirations is more likely to be addressed in intentional structures that are designed for the programs. We know that learning can be supported in formal, non-formal, informal, incidental, and everyday structures (Heimlich and Reid, 2016) within citizen science programs. To realize complex learning opportunities in cognitive, affective, and social realms, citizen science programs need more powerful approaches to design.

In the second era of human-centered design, designers recognized that while learners are indeed malleable, they are not infinitely pliable. Context matters when trying to construct a designed artifact that is both useful and usable. This context includes the participants' own prior experiences. Past learning experiences will shape future learning. The social setting matters as well. What supports learning for well-off people might not work for those who are economically changed. Local politics matters to belief, and beliefs matter to learning. Modern design practices have evolved to see these, and other aspects of the human experience, and to register their import to the construction of designed artifacts that allow for complex learning.

In the late 1990s and early 2000s the field of learning design made a pivot in the conception of human services and adult learning with the movement toward asset-based community development (e.g., Bohach, 1997; Bradshaw, 2007; Greene and Haines, 2009; Kretzmann, McKnight, and Puntenney, 2005; Lerner, 2003; Mathie and Cunningham, 2003; Snow and DicKard, 2001). The major shift in this approach to service construction was seen in more collaboratively produced planning; this approach became known as consultant-based models. The idea of the consultant model is that the change agent works within the community to facilitate community engagement in its own planning process. Most community development models include steps such as understanding the context for planning, developing links with the public, facilitating an inventory of needs and assets (Rennekamp, 1999), fostering engagement of community actors, involving locals to resist or support a cause or issue, helping community residents understand what is happening and recognize choices (e.g., Friere, 1970), and working collectively to address common interests (e.g., Brundage and MacKeracher, 1980). In our review, it appears that most recent citizen science projects are using either a linear or consultant model in designing to achieve their scientific goals. These projects grow from what the study needs, and then build the program to ensure the output of scientific data. Community-based participatory research is also a consultant model but grows from the community-development models driven by the needs in the community with the study being designed to address the data needed to answer the community's question(s). This shift has demanded a new approach to design that is more user centered (Norman, 2013) and learner centered (Soloway, Guzdial, and Hay 1994). The body of design knowledge puts pressure on service construction to make the needs of users a priority. This shift toward user-centered design marked the abandonment of what might be described as a waterfall model of design in favor of iterative and rapid prototyping to arrive at useful and usable services.

## REFERENCES

Ballard, H.L., Dixon, C.G.H., and Harris, E.M. (2017). Youth-focused citizen science: Examining the role of environmental science learning and agency for conservation. *Biological Conservation, 208,* 65-75.

Bohach, A. (1997). Fundamental principles of asset-based community development. *Journal of Volunteer Administration, 15*(4), 22-29.

Bonney, R., Cooper, C.B., Dickinson, J., Kelling, S., Phillips, T., Rosenberg, K.V., and Shirk, J. (2009). Citizen science: A developing tool for expanding science knowledge and scientific literacy. *BioScience, 59*(11), 977-984.

Boyle, P.G. (1981). *Planning Better Programs.* New York: McGraw-Hill.

Bradshaw, T.K. (2007). Theories of poverty and anti-poverty programs in community development. *Community Development, 38*(1), 7-25.

Brundage, D.H., and MacKeracher, D. (1980). *Adult Learning Principles and Their Application to Program Planning.* Toronto, ON: Ministry of Education.

Delbecq, A.L., and Van de Ven, A.H. (1971). A group process model for problem identification and program planning. *The Journal of Applied Behavioral Science*, 7(4), 466-492.

Friere, P. (1970). *Pedagogy of the Oppressed*. New York: Continuum.

Haines, A. (2009). Asset-based community development. In R. Phillips and R.H. Pittman, *An Introduction to Community Development* (pp. 38-48). New York, NY: Routledge.

Kretzmann, J.P., McKnight, J., and Puntenney, D. (2005). *Discovering Community Power: A Guide to Mobilizing Local Assets and Your Organization's Capacity*. Evanston, IL: Asset-Based Community Development Institute, School of Education and Social Policy, Northwestern University.

Lerner, R.M. (2003). Development assets and asset-building communities: A view of the issues. In R.M. Lerner and P. Benson (Eds.), *Developmental Assets and Asset-Building Communities* (pp. 3-18). Boston, MA: Springer.

Masters, K., Oh, E.Y., Cox, J., Simmons, B., Lintott, C., Graham, G., Greenhill, A., and Holmes, K. (2016). Science learning via participation in online citizen science. *Journal of Science Communication, Special Issue: Citizen Science, Part II*, 15(3), A07-133. doi: https://doi.org/10.22323/2.15030207.

Mathie, A., and Cunningham, G. (2003). From clients to citizens: Asset-based community development as a strategy for community-driven development. *Development in Practice*, 13(5), 474-486.

Nelson, H.G., and Stolterman, E. (2003). *The Design Way: Intentional Change in an Unpredictable World: Foundations and Fundamentals of Design Competence*. Cambridge, MA: MIT Press.

Norman, D. (2013). *The Design of Everyday Things: Revised and Expanded Edition*. New York: Basic Books.

Rennekamp, R.A. (1999). *Planning for Performance: Developing Programs That Produce Results*. Lexington: University of Kentucky Cooperative Extension Service.

Snow, L.K., and DicKard, S. (2001). *The Organization of Hope: A Workbook for Rural Asset-based Community Development: A Community Building Workbook*. Evanston, IL: Asset-Based Community Development Institute, Institute for Policy Research, Northwestern University.

Soloway, E., Guzdial, M., and Hay, K.E. (1994). Learner-centered design: The challenge for HCI in the 21st century. *Interactions*, 1(2), 36-48.

# Appendix C

# Characteristics of Science Learning in Citizen Science Projects: An Ad Hoc Review

In order to better understand the characteristics of citizen science projects as they relate to learning, the committee conducted an ad hoc review of 28 typical citizen science projects. This review was critical to the committee's subsequent discussion of project design: So that we may be useful to the field in offering assistance related to how to leverage design for learning, we wanted to first ensure that we fully understood the existing landscape of what projects are currently doing to support learning. This review is in no way intended to be exhaustive nor does it suggest that atypical approaches do not make meaningful contributions to learning, but it does represent the committee's best efforts to uncover how learning is both characterized and actualized according to the current literature.

To be considered a "typical" project for the purposes of this review, one or more committee members nominated it as such, as outlined by the common traits and variations in projects described in Chapter 2 of this report. Some of the characteristics that individual committee members used in defining a typical citizen science project included but are not limited to: the project had mutually dependent tasks that the participants and the scientists needed to do to achieve the scientific pursuit; the participants were part of the science team; and participants learned as part of their involvement. To be included in the sample, a project must have either a Website or detailed online information about the project. The projects included here are of varying size, scope, and focus.

Though multiple taxonomies classifying citizen science projects have emerged in the literature (as outlined throughout this report) the committee declined to apply any of these classifications because no single taxonomy encompassed the universe of citizen science projects as envisioned by the committee. The committee instead decided to discuss projects in terms of significant characteristics (described in the text of this report) and the various considerations of these characteristics. As with the committee's decision not to apply a standardized definition to the field of citizen science, so too did we elect to include programs in this review based on the constellation of their relevant traits and characteristics. Though our initial solicitation for projects included "typical," "atypical," and "close-but-not" citizen science, this ad hoc review focuses solely on projects the committee ultimately deemed typical. For each project, the committee analyzed quotations from the project that described the project itself, the learning goals of the project, claims for learning achieved, evidence of learning achieved, and learning aids provided by the project.

## GOALS FOR PARTICIPANTS

Almost all of the citizen science projects had an explicitly stated goal or claim around the benefits of the project. Almost all of the projects claimed that participation would contribute to science, and that participation in projects was fun. A minority of projects aimed or claimed to contribute to stewardship of the natural world. A few projects aimed or claimed to lead to connecting with nature, developing a sense of place, physical exercise, social interaction, opportunities to educate others, a calming effect, or an empowering effect.

The most commonly cited learning goal was a statement around learning science concepts. A minority of projects had statements of learning goals or learning claims around: learning science skills, learning about science and society, and learning the scientific process. The majority of the projects, even those without explicit learning goals or claims, still offered some form of product to aid learning. The most common learning support were social media accounts. Many projects also offered background readings, FAQs, blogs, videos, newsletters, participation guides, training programs, news stories, online data exploration, and presentations. A notable minority offered educators' guides, tutorials, activity plans, lesson plans, publications, discussion boards, identification keys, and alignments with science standards. Only a few projects offered data reports, photo galleries, webinars, interactive online resources, listservs, and materials in foreign languages.

## SUPPORTS FOR LEARNING

Of the projects that aim or claim to increase knowledge of science concepts, most sought to aid learning with informational products about basic and applied science concepts directly relevant to the project. For this subset of projects, all had online background information and many offered newsletters, social media, and other forms of communication with participants. These products were largely informative and passive; by engaging with the material, motivated participants could learn new scientific concepts. However, these informational products do not appear to be structured with a certain pedagogy or theory of learning in mind. Only a small minority of these projects offered lesson or activity plans that were explicitly designed for educational purposes. One exception to this observation is the trainings or participation guides, which often included information on science concepts and were offered by most of the projects. This ad hoc review did not examine the structure of the trainings and guides; however, given the purpose of these materials, it is possible that these materials were intentionally composed around pedagogy or theories of learning.

## EVIDENCE OF LEARNING

Within this broad claim that participating in citizen science projects can lead to increased knowledge, the aim of learning science concepts has the most supporting evidence of any other aim or claim. One study found evidence of learning science concepts in multiple case studies. Pre- and posttests showed an increased understanding of bird biology in one project and increased knowledge of invasive plants in another (Brossard et al., 2005; Jordan et al., 2011). Anecdotally, one project Website included testimonials from project participants, several of whom noted that training materials and participating in the project helped them learn to identify different bird species.

Of the projects that aim or claim to increase science skills, this benefit was limited to the skills needed to conduct the project. All of these projects involve the participants in data collection. Most of the projects in this subset are also projects that desire or require a long-term commitment and repeated data collection. Most involve participants in data recording and most do not have a process for verifying the validity of every individual data point. Thus, for these projects it is important that participants can reliably collect and record accurate data. To achieve this, most of the projects in this subset offer in-person training or extensive online tutorials and participant guidebooks.

There is no obvious relationship between projects that aim or claim to lead to learning about the scientific process, those that use the term citizen scientist, those that involve participants in higher level scientific skills such as analysis and project design, and those that offer learning aids specifically tailored to learning about the scientific process. This suggests that there may not be substantive design intentionality around learning about the scientific process. Most projects seem to assume that simply engaging in the scientific process is an adequate means of learning about the scientific process. However, one study that examined this found that most participants did not improve their understanding of the scientific process as a result of being involved in a citizen science project.

In comparison to other projects, those that do not have any goals or make any claims about learning tend to be more extractive. Projects in this vein recruit participants to collect or classify information that the project organizers cannot collect or classify themselves. These projects offer few benefits in exchange for the service provided by participants other than the opportunity to contribute to science. This subset of projects has fewer products that support learning. In addition, most of these projects do not require repeated or long-term commitment to participating in the project. Also, most of these projects tend to involve the participants interacting with information via a computer; they usually do not require that the participant collect information or engage the natural world. The projects that do involve data collection and engaging the natural world but do not have learning aims or claims typically involve participants submitting information about a natural event that they (and not scientists) were uniquely positioned to observe.

## REFERENCES

Brossard, D., Lewenstein, B., and Bonney, R. (2005). Scientific knowledge and attitude change: The impact of a citizen science project. *International Journal of Science Education*, 27(9), 1099-1121.

Jordan, R.C., Gray, S.A., Howe, D.V., Brooks, W.R., and Ehrenfeld, J.G. (2011). Knowledge gain and behavioral change in citizen-science programs. *Conservation Biology*, 25(6), 1148-1154.

# Appendix D

# Biographical Sketches of
# Committee Members and Staff

**RAJUL (RAJ) PANDYA** (*Chair*) is the director of the American Geophysical Union's (AGU) Thriving Earth Exchange. The Thriving Earth Exchange helps volunteer scientists and community leaders work together to use science to advance community priorities related to sustainability, resilience, disaster risk reduction, and environmental justice. Dr. Pandya serves on the boards for Public Lab and the Anthropocene Alliance and is a member of the Independent Advisory Committee on Applied Climate Assessment. He helped launch the Resilience Dialogues, a public-private partnership that uses facilitated online dialogues to advance community resilience. Before working at AGU, Dr. Pandya led education, engagement, and diversity programs associated with the National Center for Atmospheric Research, led an international research and development project that used weather data to better manage meningitis in Africa, and held a faculty position at West Chester State University. For the National Academies, Dr. Pandya served on the Committee on the Review of the National Oceanic and Atmospheric Administration's Education Program. Dr. Pandya is a founding member of the executive board of the Citizen Science Association, which is currently the only membership organization dedicated to the dissemination of scholarship related to designing and implementing citizen science. He holds a Ph.D. in atmospheric science from the University of Washington.

**MEGAN BANG** is a professor in the School of Education and Social Policy at Northwestern University and senior vice president of the Spencer Foundation. She previously held multiple faculty positions in the education department at the University of Washington-Seattle. Dr. Bang's research aims to improve educational opportunities for disadvantaged children, families and communities, specifically through STEM education and the education of indigenous peoples. She is involved in three primary strands of work: the study of learning and development in everyday contexts, community-based design research that creates science learning environments based on indigenous systems of knowledge, and the study of child and teacher learning in novel environments. Dr. Bang holds numerous awards from the American Education Research Association, as well as having won the Spencer Foundation Dissertation Fellowship and Outstanding Advising Award from the University of Washington. She was also Cognitive Science Graduate Fellow for Interdisciplinary Research Projects at Northwestern University. She earned a Ph.D. in learning sciences and a certificate in cognitive science from Northwestern University.

**DARLENE CAVALIER** is a professor at Arizona State University's Center for Engagement and Training, part of the School for the Future of Innovation in Society. Ms. Cavalier is the founder of SciStarter, an online platform for identifying, supporting, and participating in citizen science opportunities. She is also the founder of Science Cheerleader, an organization of more than 300 current and former professional cheerleaders pursuing STEM careers, and a cofounder of ECAST: Expert and Citizen Assessment of Science and Technology, a network of universities, science centers, and think tanks that produces public deliberations to enhance science policy making. She is a founding board member of the Citizen Science Association, an advisor at National Geographic's Citizen Explorer Labs, and a member of the Environmental Protection Agency's National Advisory Council for Environmental Policy and Technology. She is the author of *The Science of Cheerleading* and coeditor of *The Rightful Place of Science: Citizen Science* published by Arizona State University. Ms. Cavalier holds a master's degree in liberal arts with a concentration on science history and policy from the University of Pennsylvania.

**JESSICA COVINGTON** is a senior program assistant with the Board on Science Education and is currently supporting the America's Lab Report Update and Citizen Science projects. Before joining the DBASSE team, she was the administrative assistant to an architectural and interior design firm in Metro Center called VOA Associates, which is now known as Stantec Consulting. In 2015, she received her B.S. in psychology and is currently pursuing a B.S. in accounting with an expected graduation date in 2018.

**KENNE DIBNER** (*Study Director*) is a program officer with the Board on Science Education. She served as the study director for the National Academies consensus study *Science Literacy: Concepts, Contexts, and*

*Consequences,* as well as the deputy director for *Indicators for Monitoring Undergraduate STEM Education.* Prior to this position, Dr. Dibner worked as a research associate at Policy Studies Associates, Inc., where she conducted evaluations of education policies and programs for government agencies, foundations, and school districts, including an evaluation of a partnership with the U.S. Department of Education, the National Park Service, and the Bureau of Indian Education to provide citizen science programming to tribal youth. She has also served as a research consultant with the Center on Education Policy and served as a legal intern for the U.S. House of Representatives' Committee on Education and the Workforce. She has a B.A in English literature from Skidmore College and a Ph.D. in education policy from Michigan State University.

**DANIEL EDELSON** is the executive director of BSCS, a national center for research and development in science education. Dr. Edelson possesses significant experience as a curriculum and educational software developer, educational researcher, and advocate for science and social studies education. Prior to his work at BSCS, Dr. Edelson served as vice president for education at the National Geographic Society and executive director of the National Geographic Education Foundation, as well as a professor at Northwestern University, where he had a joint appointment in education and computer science. As a curriculum and software developer, Dr. Edelson is the lead author of a high school environmental science course and an author of units in two comprehensive middle school science programs. He has written extensively on the importance of geoscience, geography, and environmental science education, and he has published numerous research papers on motivation, instructional design, educational technology and teacher professional development. Dr. Edelson received a Ph.D. in computer science from Northwestern University.

**LETICIA GARCILAZO GREEN** is a senior program assistant for the Board on Science Education. Since joining the staff in 2014, she has supported numerous studies focusing on issues related to criminal justice, science education, and climate change. Prior to joining the National Academies, she worked as a legal assistant with a law firm that specialized in security clearances and white-collar crime in Washington, DC. She earned a B.S. in psychology and a B.A. in sociology with a concentration in criminology from Louisiana State University, and an M.A. in forensic psychology from The George Washington University.

**LOUIS GOMEZ** is the MacArthur Chair in Digital Media and Learning at Univeristy of California, Los Angeles' (UCLA's) Graduate School of Education & Information Studies. Before joining the UCLA faculty, he was the

Helen S. Faison professor of urban education and senior scientist at the Learning Research and Development Center at the University of Pittsburgh. Dr. Gomez is also currently serving as a senior fellow at the Carnegie Foundation for the Advancement of Teaching in Palo Alto, California. His scholarship focuses on understanding how to support organizational change in schools and other institutions. Dr. Gomez has been dedicated to collaborative research and development with urban communities to bring the current state-of-the-art instruction and support for community formation to traditionally underserved schools. Most recently, Professor Gomez has turned his attention to problem-solving research and development. He received a B.A. in psychology from the State University of New York at Stony Brook and a Ph.D. in cognitive psychology from the University of California, Berkeley.

**JOE E. HEIMLICH** is codirector for the Center of Science and Industry's (COSI) Lifelong Learning Group, and director of research for COSI. His research and evaluation work focuses on projects related to informal learning and capacity building for zoos, nature centers, parks, gardens, science centers, and other museums. He is also an academy professor emeritus with the Ohio State University where he was an extension specialist in museums and organizational capacity building and held appointments in the School of Environment and Natural Resources, the Environmental Science Graduate Program, and the College of Education and Human Ecology. Dr. Heimlich received his Ph.D. in educational psychology from the Ohio State University.

**LEKELIA "KIKI" JENKINS** is an associate professor at Arizona State University in the School for the Future of Innovation. Dr. Jenkins has worked as an environmental consultant for the Natural Resource Defense Council, while also actively participating in the burgeoning field of Studies in Expertise and Experience. Dr. Jenkins was awarded a Ford Foundation Diversity Postdoctoral Fellowship and the David H. Smith Conservation Research Fellowship, which is granted to rising conservation scientists who have the potential to change the face of conservation through entrepreneurial approaches. She became an assistant professor at the School of Marine and Environmental Affairs at the University of Washington and during this time was awarded an Alfred P. Sloan Research Fellowship in Ocean Sciences. Dr. Jenkins has published extensively on adult science learning through fisheries learning exchanges (FLEs), in which representatives from different fisher communities collaborate to build capacity and share knowledge. FLEs are regarded as useful for developing and sharing fisheries solutions (which are often conservation technologies) and empowering fisher leaders. Dr. Jenkins received her Ph.D. in marine conservation from Duke University.

**BRUCE V. LEWENSTEIN** is professor of science communication and chair of the Department of Science and Technology Studies at Cornell University. He is active in international pursuits that contribute to education and research on public communication of science and technology, and has published frequently on evaluation and other aspects of citizen science. Trained as a historian of science, he works across the field of public communication of science and technology, including informal science education and communication training for scientists. Dr. Lewenstein is a faculty-elected member of the Cornell University Board of Trustees and serves on the board of directors of Embarcadero Media, Palo Alto, California, which produces community newspapers and related digital media. For the National Academies, Dr. Lewenstein cochaired the Committee on Learning Science in Informal Environments and was a member of the Committee on Communicating Chemistry in Informal Settings, as well as the Roundtable on Public Interfaces of Life Sciences. He earned his Ph.D. and M.A. in history and sociology of science from the University of Pennsylvania.

**CHRISTINE MASSEY** is a research psychologist in the Department of Psychology at the University of California, Los Angeles. Her major areas of concentration include cognitive development and learning in mathematics and science. She was previously the director of research and education and head of a research lab at the Institute for Research in Cognitive Science at the University of Pennsylvania, where she worked to link recent theory and research in cognitive science to education efforts in public schools, cultural institutions, and higher education. She has led a number of major collaborative research and development projects that combine research investigating students' learning and conceptual development in science and mathematics with the development and evaluation of new curriculum materials, adaptive learning technology, and educational programs for students and teachers—from preschool through graduate school and across both formal and informal education. For the National Academies, Dr. Massey served as a member of the Committee on Defining Deeper Learning and 21st Century Skills. Dr. Massey earned her M.A. and Ph.D. in psychology from the University of Pennsylvania.

**JOHN C. MATHER** is a senior astrophysicist and is the senior project scientist for the James Webb Space Telescope at NASA's Goddard Space Flight Center in Greenbelt, Maryland. His research centers on infrared astronomy and cosmology. As a National Research Council postdoctoral fellow at NASA's Goddard Institute for Space Studies (New York City), he led the proposal efforts for the Cosmic Background Explorer, and joined the Goddard Space Flight Center to be the study scientist, project scientist, and the principal investigator for the Far IR Absolute Spectrophotometer

(FIRAS) on COBE. Dr. Mather is the recipient of numerous awards, including the Nobel Prize in Physics (2006) with George Smoot, for the COBE work, and the NASA Distinguished Service Medal (2007). He is a member of many professional societies including the American Academy of Arts and Sciences. Dr. Mather currently serves on the National Academies' Board on Science Education and served on the committee that developed the Framework for K–12 Science Education. He also served on the National Academies' Review Committee for the Koshland Science Museum, as well as the Board on Physics and Astronomy and the Task Group on Gravity Probe B, in addition to a number of other committees and National Academies activities. He received his Ph.D. in physics from the University of California, Berkeley.

**JULIA K. PARRISH** is the Lowell A. and Frankie L. Wakefield professor of ocean fishery sciences at the University of Washington, where she also serves as associate dean for academic affairs in the College of the Environment. She also directs the Coastal Observation and Seabird Survey Team (COASST), a citizen science project with more than 1,000 coastal residents monitoring beach-cast marine birds, and marine debris, as indicators of nearshore ecosystem health. Dr. Parrish is a marine biologist, a conservation biologist, and a specialist in citizen science. She is an elected fellow of the Ecological Society of America and of the American Ornithological Union. In 1998, she was honored as a NOAA Year of the Oceans Environmental Hero by Vice President Al Gore for the development of the COASST project; and in 2013 was recognized by the White House Office of Science Technology Policy (OSTP) as a Champion of Change for her citizen science work with COASST. In 2015, COASST was cited by the OSTP and the National Science Foundation as an exemplary example of rigorous citizen science. Dr. Parrish received her Ph.D. in zoology from Duke University.

**TINA PHILLIPS** is the assistant director of the Citizen Science Program at the Cornell Lab of Ornithology where she conducts social science research and evaluation across numerous citizen science projects both within and outside the Lab. Her research interests center on understanding and documenting the educational, social, and conservation impacts of citizen science globally. Dr. Phillips spearheaded DEVISE, a National Science Foundation-funded project aimed at building capacity for project design and evaluation of learning outcomes from citizen science. Her current research examines the relationship between engagement in citizen science and outcomes related to skills, efficacy, behavior, and science identity. She has authored or coauthored several articles and chapters on citizen science and science education and was one of the authors of a landmark Center for the Advancement of Informal Science Education report: *Public Participation in Scientific*

*Research: Defining the Field and Assessing Its Potential for Informal Science Education.* Dr. Phillips is currently serving as a board member of the Citizen Science Association and is an advisor on several citizen science initiatives around the world. She holds a B.S. in biology from Stony Brook University and a Masters and Ph.D. in education from Cornell University.

**HEIDI SCHWEINGRUBER** (*Board Director*) is the director of the Board on Science Education at the National Academies. She has served as study director or costudy director for a wide range of studies, including those on revising national standards for K–12 science education, learning and teaching science in grades K–8, and mathematics learning in early childhood. She also coauthored two award-winning books for practitioners that translate findings of National Academies' reports for a broader audience, on using research in K–8 science classrooms, and on information science education. Prior to joining the National Academies, she worked as a senior research associate at the Institute of Education Sciences in the U.S. Department of Education. She also previously served on the faculty of Rice University and as the director of research for the Rice University School Mathematics Project, an outreach program in K–12 mathematics education. She has a Ph.D. in psychology (developmental) and anthropology and a certificate in culture and cognition, both from the University of Michigan.